Hungarian

An Essential Grammar

This is a concise, user-friendly guide to the most important structures of this fascinating language.

All students of Hungarian, whether beginners or at intermediate and advanced levels, will welcome its clarity of presentation and jargon-free explanations. It is ideal for those studying independently or following a taught course.

Topics include:

- Verbal prefixes
- Aspect and tense
- Word-formation mechanisms
- Linking vowels
- The case system and its uses
- Word order

Appendices include the formation of irregular verbs, complete noun declensions and irregular noun patterns.

With numerous language examples bringing grammar to life, this truly essential reference work will prove invaluable to all students looking to master the patterns and irregularities of modern Hungarian.

Carol Rounds lectures in Hungarian at Columbia University, New York.

Routledge Essential Grammars

Essential Grammars are available for the following languages:

Chinese
Danish
Dutch
Finnish
Modern Hebrew
Norwegian
Polish
Portuguese
Swedish
Urdu
English

Other titles of related interest published by Routledge:

Colloquial Hungarian
By Jerry Payne

Hungarian: Descriptive Grammar
By István Kenesei, Robert M Vago and Anna Fenyvesi

Hungarian

An Essential Grammar

 **Carol Rounds**

London and New York

First published 2001
by Routledge
11 New Fetter Lane, London EC4P 4EE

Simultaneously published in the USA and Canada
by Routledge
29 West 35th Street, New York, NY 10001

Routledge is an imprint of the Taylor & Francis Group

© 2001 Carol Rounds

Designed and Typeset in Sabon and Gill
by Florence Production Ltd, Stoodleigh, Devon

Printed and bound in Great Britain
by TJ International, Padstow, Cornwall

British Library Cataloguing in Publication Data
A catalogue record for this book is available from the British Library.

Library of Congress Cataloging-in-Publication Data
Rounds Carol, 1959–
    Hungarian: an essential grammar / Carol Rounds.
        p. cm.
    Includes index.
    1. Hungarian language—Grammar.   I. Title.
    PH2105 .R68 2001
    494`.51182421–dc21   2001016014

ISBN 0–415–22611–2 (hbk)
ISBN 0–415–22612–0 (pbk)

Contents

Preface

This book is designed for all students of Hungarian – but perhaps especially for those who have been told it is too hard to learn. College students, business men and women, people of Hungarian heritage or spouses of Hungarians can use this book as an anchor in their quest to master the intricacies of Hungarian.

The Hungarian language is complex, wonderfully expressive and like no other language you know. This book guides you through the patterns of building words, phrases and sentences with clear explanations and paradigms. What at first seems complex to the Hungarian student becomes a regular and predictable – and therefore a *learnable* – pattern used to inspire your own Hungarian expression. Have fun with it!

Acknowledgements

I would like to thank the people who have helped greatly in writing this book. I must begin by expressing my appreciation and great respect for my first Hungarian teacher, Daniel Abondolo, who taught me to look most systematically at this language and thereby help make it learnable; I also thank him for his helpful comments on the manuscript. I owe an enormous debt of gratitude to Erika Sólyom for her painstaking reading of the Hungarian examples and suggestions for improvement. I also thank Sophie Oliver at Routledge for her help and patience in seeing the project through. Finally, my greatest thanks are offered to my husband, John Schiemann, for his meticulous editorial comments, and numerous re-readings of the manuscript during the months of its preparation.

Abbreviations

abl.	ablative
acc.	accusative
adess.	adessive
all.	allative
caus.-fin.	causal-final
dat.	dative
delat.	delative
def.	definite
distr.	distributive
elat.	elative
ess.-for.	essive-formal
illat.	illative
indef.	indefinite
iness.	inessive
instr.	instrumental
intrans.	intransitive
lit.	literal(ly)
nom.	nominative
part.	participle
pl.	plural
pl1	first person plural
pl2	second person plural
pl3	third person plural
poss.	possessive
pres.	present
relat.	relative
s1	first person singular
s2	second person singular
s3	third person singular
sg.	singular

sociat.	sociative
sublat.	sublative
superess.	superessive
sy	somebody
term.	terminative
transl.	translative

PART I

Alphabet, pronunciation and vowel harmony

Chapter 1
Alphabet

Hungarian uses the Roman alphabet in addition to some diacritics placed over some vowels. The accent mark(s) above the vowels indicate that the vowel is 'long' – see the pronunciation section to follow. Some consonants are digraphs, i.e., they consist of two letters; one consonant (**dzs**) is a trigraph. Although they are written with more than one letter, digraphs (and the trigraph) are each individual letters of the alphabet.

a á b c cs d dz dzs e é f g gy h i í j k l ly m n

ny o ó ö ő p (q) r s sz t ty u ú ü ű v (w) (x) (y) z zs

Unless found in the spellings of foreign words, the letters *q*, *w* and *x* are not used; the letter *y* is found only in old spellings (pronounced as the letter *i*) and in digraphs.

Chapter 2

Pronunciation

2.1 Consonants

2.1.1

Many of the consonants in Hungarian are pronounced as in English. All consonants are pronounced – there are no silent letters. The following are the consonants pronounced differently from those in English.

c	as in ca*ts*	**cukor** 'sugar' **ecet** 'vinegar'
cs	as in *church*	**bocsánat** 'excuse me' **csal** 'deceive'
g	(always hard) as in go	**igen** 'yes' **gaz** 'weed'
j	as in yes	**jó** 'good' **fáj** 'hurt'
r	trill the tongue on the top of the mouth	**kérem** 'please' **ró** 'carve'
s	as in *she*	**este** 'evening' **sárga** 'yellow'
sz	as in *sat*	**szervusz** 'hi' **asztal** 'table'
zs	as in a*z*ure	**garázs** 'garage' **zseb** 'pocket'

2.1.2 *The palatal series*

The following four consonants are palatalized, i.e., they are pronounced with the tongue gliding off the top of the palate.

gy similar to a *dy* sound as in *during*	**magyar** 'Hungarian' **gyár** 'factory'

ly as in *yes* (thus the same   **személy** 'person' **lyuk** 'hole'
     as the Hungarian letter **j**)

ny as in ca*ny*on   **kenyér** 'bread' **nyár** 'summer'

ty similar to a *ty* sound   **kártya** 'card' **tyúk** 'hen'
     as in *stu*dio

2.2 Consonant length

All consonants can be long or short. Long consonants are written as
double consonants and are pronounced approximately twice as long as
short ones. Great care should be paid to differences in length; it can
change the meaning of a word, e.g.,

szeretem I love him/her   vs.   **szerettem** I loved him/her

Length of digraphs is indicated by doubling the first consonant of the
digraph. For example, a long **sz** is written **ssz**: **vissza** 'back'; long **ny** is
written **nny**: **lánnyal** 'with a girl', etc.

2.2.1 Lengthening of consonants before j

The consonants **d, gy, t, ty, n, ny** are pronounced long when preceding
the letter **j** (though this is not represented in the orthography):

ad + ja	→ **adja**	[addja]	s/he gives it
hagy + ja	→ **hagyja**	[haddja]	s/he leaves it
mutat + ja	→ **mutatja**	[mutattja]	s/he shows it
báty + ja	→ **bátyja**	[báttja]	his/her brother
kíván + juk	→ **kívánjuk**	[kívánnjuk]	we wish it
any + ja	→ **anyja**	[annja]	his/her mother

2.3 Voicing and devoicing of consonants

Consonants can be classified as voiced and unvoiced. The following are
the voiced and unvoiced consonants of Hungarian:

Unvoiced	p t k f sz s c cs ty h
Voiced	b d g v z zs dz dzs gy j ly m n ny l r

2.3.1 | Voicing of unvoiced consonants

Unvoiced consonants (except **h**) become voiced when preceding voiced consonants (except **j, ly, m, n, ny, l, r, v**). Some examples:

Unvoiced		Voiced	Examples	
p	→	b	**népdal** [nébdal]	folk song
t	→	d	**kertben** [kerdben]	in the garden
k	→	g	**lakbér** [lagbér]	rent
s	→	zs	**kisgyerek** [kizsgyerek]	(small) child
c	→	dz	**ketrecbe** [ketredzbe]	into the cage
cs	→	dzs	**bográcsgulyás** [bográdzsgulyás]	kettle goulash
sz	→	z	**részben** [rézben]	in part
f	→	v	**kuglófban** [kuglóvban]	in (a) cake

2.3.2 | Devoicing of voiced consonants

Voiced consonants (except **j, ly, m, n, ny, l, r**) are devoiced when preceding unvoiced consonants. Some examples:

Voiced		Unvoiced	Examples	
b	→	p	**zsebkendő** [zsepkendő]	handkerchief
d	→	t	**tudtok** [tuttok]	you (pl.) know
g	→	k	**megszeret** [mekszeret]	(start to) like/love
v	→	f	**nyelvtan** [nyelftan]	grammar
z	→	sz	**dolgoztok** [dolgosztok]	you (pl.) work
zs	→	s	**varázspálca** [varáspálca]	magic wand

dz	→ c	**edztek** [ectek]	you (pl.) train
dzs	→ cs	**bridzstől** [bricstől]	from bridge
gy	→ ty	**nagyterem** [natyterem]	main hall

2.4 Assimilation of sibilants

Hissing sibilants (**sz, z**) when preceding hushing sibilants (**s, zs**) become hushing sibilants (the above voicing and devoicing rules also apply if applicable).

Hissing	Hushing	Becomes	Examples	
sz	+ s	ss (long s)	**egészség**	[egésség] health
z	+ s	ss	**igazság**	[igasság] truth
sz	+ zs	zzs (long zs)	**horgászzsinór**	[horgázzsinór] fishing line
z	+ zs		**tíz zsinór**	[tízzsinór] ten lines

2.5 Vowels

Vowels can also be either long or short. Length in the vowels is marked by long marks over the vowel and long vowels are pronounced approximately twice as long as short ones. For two sets of vowel pairs, a ~ á and e ~ é there is a difference not only in length but of quality in the vowel as well. For all other vowel pairs the difference between them is primarily of length.

Hungarian has no diphthongs, i.e., each vowel is pronounced separately.

a	**aw** as in 'awl'	**nap** day
á	**aa** as in 'baa'	**ár** price
e	a sound between the **a** in 'bat' and the **e** in 'bet'	**reggel** morning
é	**ay** as in 'say', but without the y-sound (diphthong) at the end	**kérem** please

i	e as in 'he'	**mi**	what
í	a longer version of the above, as the **ee** in 'green'	**tíz**	ten
o	**oh** as in 'note'	**kívánok**	I wish
ó	a longer version of the above	**jó**	good
ö	purse your lips as though to say **oh** but say **eh**	**köszönöm**	thank you
ő	a longer version of the above	**hétfő**	Monday
u	**oo** as in 'food'	**tud**	know
ú	a longer version of the above	**út**	road
ü	purse your lips as though to say **oo** but say **ee**	**üveg**	bottle
ű	a longer version of the above	**egyszerű**	simple

2.6 Stress

The first syllable of every word is stressed.

Unless otherwise emphasized, the articles **a**, **az**, **egy**, and the particle **is** receive no stress. Thus in the following phrase, the only stressed element is the first syllable of **kutya**:

    \
a kutya is   the dog too

2.7 Intonation

2.7.1

Hungarian declarative sentences have a primarily descending intonation:

Szép idő van.   The weather is beautiful.

2.7.2

A question containing a question word has a higher rise on the question word:

Milyen idő van?   What is the weather like?

2.7.3

A yes–no question has a rise–fall intonation where a high rise in intonation is found on the penultimate syllable of the sentence, a sharp fall is on the last syllable.

Szép idő van?   Is the weather nice?

(Note here that intonation may be the only way to differentiate between declarative and interrogative sentences.)

In yes–no questions with fewer than three syllables, the rise in intonation takes place on the final syllable followed by an immediate drop:

Ez az?   Is this it?

Kedves?   Is she nice?

Chapter 3
Vowel harmony

Hungarian vowels are classified according to front vs. back assonance and rounded vs. unrounded. These terms come from describing the tongue position in the mouth and the roundedness of the lips, respectively. The following is the vowel inventory of Hungarian:

Back vowels: **a, á, o, ó, u, ú**

Front unrounded vowels: **e, é, i, í**

Front rounded vowels: **ö, ő, ü, ű**

Vowel harmony rules in Hungarian require that front or back assonance in the vowels of a stem be maintained throughout the entire word, thus for the most part – except for recent loan words – Hungarian words have either only back vowels in them or only front vowels.

3.1 Suffixing and back vs. front vowels

Because vowel assonance is maintained throughout the whole word, most suffixes have front and back vowel variants, e.g., the dative case **-nak** (back vowel) and **-nek** (front vowel). Thus, if a stem contains back vowels, it affixes back vowel suffixes; should the word contain only front vowels it can affix only front vowel suffixes.

3.2 Suffixing and rounded vs. unrounded vowels

When words contain only front vowels, a second distinction in vowel type may be necessary: the rounded/unrounded distinction in the *last* vowel requires a second stage in vowel harmony rules: if the stem's *last* vowel is front and rounded it takes a suffix with a front rounded vowel.

If the stem's *last* vowel is front and unrounded, it takes a front unrounded suffix. Although suffixes for most words have front/back vowel variants only a few endings have rounded/unrounded variants (examples include the allative case, -hoz/-hez/-höz, or the plural suffix, -ok/-ek/-ök).

3.3   Neutral vowels

Finally, the front unrounded vowels, i, í, e and é, may occur in stems containing either front or back vowels. As such they are considered neutral with respect to vowel harmony rules; a word containing back vowels and neutral vowels is considered a back vowel word. If *only* neutral vowels occur in a stem, however, the stem is considered to be of front vowel assonance and will require front vowel suffixes.[1]

3.4   Application of the rules of vowel harmony

To show how vowel harmony works, we will use the plural suffix, which has both front/back vowel harmony and the rounded/unrounded distinction. The plural ending is either -ok (back), -ek (front and unrounded), or -ök (front and rounded).

Stem		Description of stem	Plural
asztal	table	only back vowels	**asztalok**
gyerek	child	only neutral (front) vowels, last vowel unrounded	**gyerekek**
füzet	notebook	only front vowels, last vowel unrounded	**füzetek**
ismerős	acquaintance	only front vowels, last vowel rounded	**ismerősök**
papír	paper	back vowel with neutral vowel	**papírok**

---

[1] This is particularly true for nouns although there are numerous exceptions; most verbs, however, that contain *only* the vowel i or í have back vowel assonance. Compare: **szív** 'heart' is a noun with front vowel assonance and **szív** 'inhale' is a verb with back vowel assonance.

PART II

Parts of speech

Chapter 4

Verbs

The Hungarian conjugation includes the past and present indicative, the subjunctive (also used for the imperative) and conditional moods. There is no inflectional passive mood or future tense; the passive is expressed by means of other constructions with no agency, the future is expressed by the use of coverbs and/or the auxiliary verb **fog**.

Conjugation of verbs includes the suffixing of tense or mood and personal endings. The personal endings indicate the subject and may indicate the presence of a direct object (see section 4.2). With few exceptions, the rules of vowel harmony extend through the conjugations.

This chapter first illustrates the verb stem types of Hungarian followed by the conjugations and usage of the tenses and moods. The formation and usage of the non-finite forms (participles and the infinitive) as well as the highly productive verbal suffixes of modality (potential, causative, and frequentative) follow. For more on verbal derivational suffixes, see chapter 12 on word formation.

Verbal prefixes, henceforth referred to as coverbs, cause a particular problem for students of Hungarian; the end of this chapter contains extensive descriptions of the common uses of the most frequently used coverbs. Although some reference is made in this chapter to the order of verbs and coverbs in the sections on usage, refer to chapter 16 for a more complete explanation of Hungarian word order.

4.1 Verb stems

In general, Hungarian verb stems are identical with the third person singular present tense indefinite form. This is the citation form found in good dictionaries.

The shape of the verb stem determines in part the shape of the suffix which attaches to it. For most verbs, the verb stem remains the same throughout the conjugations. Some important exceptions are discussed in this section.

4.1.1 | -ik verbs

A very large group of verbs end in -ik in the third person singular present tense indefinite conjugation (and as such, appear as the citation form). The verb stem for -ik verbs is found by removing the -ik ending; the verbs then conjugate on the -ik-less stem. For example, the verb **utazik** 'travel' has the stem **utaz-** to which the verbal endings attach, e.g., **utazni** 'to travel (infinitive)'.

In addition to the stem change, -ik verbs also display a regular alternation in the personal endings of some conjugations. In the present tense, the ending **-om/-em/-öm** may be used for the first person singular indefinite conjugation instead of the regular ending (**-ok/-ek/-ök**).[1] A similar alternation is found in the first person singular in the subjunctive and conditional paradigms as well, though in these conjugations the regular endings have all but replaced the now archaic -ik endings.

regular ending ~ *-ik ending*

Present tense:	**utazom**	~ **utazok**	I travel
Subjunctive:	**utazzam**	~ **utazzak**	that I travel
Conditional:	**utaznám**	~ **utaznék**	I would travel

In the subjunctive and conditional conjugations there is also a separate ending for -ik verbs in the indefinite conjugation for third person singular: -ék. This ending is also considered a more archaic form, and is rarely used in speech.

-ik ending ~ *regular ending*

Subjunctive:	**utazzék**	~ **utazzon**	that he/she play piano
Conditional:	**utaznék**	~ **utazna**	he/she would play piano

---

[1] Much variation is found in the use of the first person endings of -ik verbs; this is dependent not only on the idiolect of the speaker, but the verb as well – some verbs are prone to take the -ik verb endings, some to take the regular. However, the **-om/ -em/ -öm** endings are always correct, if not always colloquial.

4.1.2 | *Fleeting vowel stems*

In this large class of verb stems the last vowel is omitted when vowel-initial suffixes are added, yielding a stem-final consonant cluster. Although you cannot tell by its shape whether a verb is a fleeting vowel stem, a pattern emerges with familiarity. In all cases[2] the vowel which elides is o/e/ö; at least one of the consonants in the resulting cluster is always j, l, ly, r, n, ny, m, z, or zs.

The vowel is omitted only when the suffix attached begins with a vowel, thus there are no tri-consonantal clusters. Vowel-initial suffixes are found in the present and past tense conjugations as well as with present and past participles, and the noun-forming suffixes -at/-et and -ás/-és. The presence of a vowel-initial suffix does not always trigger vowel elision and, in fact, the absence of a consistent trigger is what makes this group of stems so irregular. Only the present participle -ó/-ő will consistently trigger the omission of the fleeting vowel.

mosolyog ~ mosolyg-

mosolyognak they smile   **mosolyogtam** I smiled
mosolyogni to smile

mosolygok I smile   **mosolygott** he/she smiled
mosolygó smiling (pres. part.)

érez ~ érz-

éreztem I felt (it)   **érezzük** we feel it   **érezni** to feel

érzem I feel it   **érzitek** you (pl.) feel it   **érzés** feeling

üdvözöl ~ üdvözl-

üdvözölsz you (sg.) greet   **üdvözöltek** they greeted (us)
üdvözölni to greet

üdvözlöm I greet him/her   **üdvözlik** they greet him/her
üdvözlet greeting

---

[2] With the one exception of **őriz** 'guard'.

| 4.1.3 | v-stems |

This is a small class of verbs whose third person singular form ends in a vowel, but requires a v-stem before suffixes beginning with a vowel.

The v-stem verbs are: **fő** cook **nő** grow **ró** carve

lő shoot **nyű** wear out **sző** weave

With the exception of **nyű**, the final vowel is shortened before the v: **ró:** **rov-** 'carve'. The present tense paradigm illustrates the pattern of v-stem verbs:

sző ~ szöv	indefinite	definite	ró ~ rov	indefinite	definite
én	szövök	szövöm		rovok	rovom
te	szősz	szövöd		rósz	rovod
ő	sző	szövi		ró	rója
mi	szövünk	szőjük		rovunk	rójuk
ti	szőtök	szövitek		rótok	rójátok
ők	szőnek	szövik		rónak	róják

The following are the verb stems for the past, subjunctive and conditional as well as the non-finite verb forms for this class. (Note the deviation from the stem for the definite subjunctive **te** form.)

past tense stem	subjunctive stem	s2def	conditional stem	present participle	infinitive	adverbial participle
főtt-	főj-	—	fő-	fövő	főni	főve
lőtt-	lőj-	lődd	lő-	lövő	lőni	lőve
nőtt-	nőj-	nődd	nő-	növő	nőni	nőve
nyűtt-	nyűj-	nyűdd	nyű-	nyűvő	nyűni	nyűve
rótt-	rój-	ródd	ró-	rovó	róni	róva
szőtt-	szőj-	sződd	sző-	szövő	szőni	szőve

| **4.1.4** | -szik *stems* |

Another class of verbs ends in -szik in the citation form. If a vowel precedes the -szik ending the verb conjugates normally. (Two exceptions are **esküszik** 'swear' and **alkuszik** 'bargain', to be discussed below.) If, however, a consonant precedes the -szik ending, the -sz of this ending alternates with other consonants throughout the verbal paradigm.[3] The -szik verbs can be divided into four main groups, depending on which consonants -sz- alternates with.

(a) **sz ~ d ~ v**: This group include some very common verbs. There is considerable variation within this group; note in the following table the stem variants for the potential, causative and adverbial participles. The verbs **alszik** 'sleep' and **fekszik** 'lie' use the short form for the past tense, the rest of the verbs in this group use the long form.

The sz ~ d ~ v alternation is also found with five frequentative verbs having the present tense forms ending in -kodik/-kedik alternating with -szik. The present tense conjugation may occur in either stem variant; the other verb forms conform to the pattern established in the table for **cselek-szik ~ cselekedik**.

cselekszik ~ cselekedik	do, act
dicsekszik ~ dicsekedik	boast
gyanakszik ~ gyanakodik	suspect
növekszik ~ növekedik	grow, increase
törekszik ~ törekedik	strive, try

(b) **sz ~ d**: This alternation is found in a number of verbs including:

dulakszik ~ dulakodik	grapple, wrestle
furakszik ~ furakodik	push through
gazdagszik ~ gazdagodik	become rich
gyarapszik ~ gyarapodik	increase

---

[3] Exceptions are **hallatszik** 'be heard', **játszik** 'play', **látszik** 'appear', and **tetszik** 'be pleasing' which do not have variable stems and conjugate regularly. The verb **alapszik** 'found', 'establish' is found only in the present tense and conjugates regularly. All other verb forms of **alapszik** require the synonymous verb (root) **alapul**.

lerészegszik ~ lerészegedik	become drunk
megelégszik ~ megelégedik	be satisfied
meghidegszik ~ meghidegedik	grow cold
melegszik ~ melegedik	become warm
megbetegszik ~ megbetegedik	become ill
mosakszik ~ mosakodik	wash oneself
öregszik ~ öregedik	become old, age
tanakszik ~ tanakodik	reflect, consider (**tanakszik** variant is rare)
telepszik ~ telepedik	settle
tolakszik ~ tolakodik	push oneself through, impose
ülepszik ~ ülepedik	settle, deposit
vastagszik ~ vastagodik	grow thick
verekszik ~ verekedik	fight
veszekszik ~ veszekedik	argue, fight
vetekszik ~ vetekedik	rival, vie

(c) sz ~ z: This alternation is found in only three verbs:

emlékszik ~ emlékezik	remember
gyülekszik ~ gyülekezik	assemble, gather
szándékszik ~ szándékozik	intend

(d) sz ~ z ~ v: This alternation is found only with the verb igyekszik ~ igyekezik 'strive'.

-szik verbs and stem variants

Consonant alternation	Present tense stem	Past tense, subjunctive, conditional, infinitival stem	Present part., past part.	Potential causative	Adverbial part.
	alsz- sleep	alud-	alvó aludt	al(ud)hat al(ud)tat	al(ud)va
	feksz-	feküd-	fekvő feküdt	fek(üd)het fek(üd)tet	fek(üd)ve
sz ~ d ~ v	lie				
	esküsz- swear	esküd-	esküvő esküdött	esküdhet esküdtet ~ esket	esküdve
	haragsz- be angry	haragud-	haragvó haragudott	haragudhat haragudtat	haragudva
	nyugsz- be calm	nyugod-	nyugvó nyugodott	nyug(od)hat nyugtat	nyugodva
	alkusz- bargain	alkud-	alkuvó alkudott	alkudhat alkudtat	alkudva
	cseleksz- cseleked- do, act	cseleked-	cselekvő cselekedett	cselekedhet cselekedtet	cselekedve
sz ~ d	öregsz- öreged- grow old	öreged-	öregedő öregedett	öregedhet ———	öregedve
	veszeksz- veszeked- argue	veszeked-	veszekedő veszekedett	veszekedhet veszekedtet	veszekedve
	mosaksz- mosakod- wash	mosakod-	mosakodó mosakodott	mosakodhat mosakodtat	mosakodva
sz ~ z	emléksz- emlékez- remember	emlékez-	emlékező emlékezett	emlékezhet emlékeztet	emlékezve
sz ~ z ~ v	igyeksz- strive	igyekez-	igyekvő igyekezett	igyekezhet igyekeztet	igyekezve

| 4.1.5 | *The group of seven:* lesz, tesz, vesz, hisz, visz, eszik, iszik |

This finite class of verbs exhibits a present tense -sz-stem which alternates with other consonants throughout the paradigms as illustrated in the following table. The personal endings for the tenses and moods attach regularly to the verb stems indicated by a dash; forms with no dash are complete second person singular forms; other exceptions are indicated. Full paradigms of these verbs are given in appendix 1.

The group of seven

	Present tense stem	Past tense stem	Subjunctive stem[4]	Conditional stem	Infinitive
lesz will be; become	**lesz-**	**lett-**	**legy-** **légy**	**len-**	**lenni**
tesz put; do	**tesz-**	**tett-**	**tegy-** **tégy** **tedd**	**ten-**	**tenni**
vesz take; buy	**vesz-**	**vett-**	**vegy-** **végy** **vedd**	**ven-**	**venni**
visz take, carry	**visz-**	**vitt-**	**vigy-** **vidd**	**vin-**	**vinni**
hisz believe	**hisz-**	**hitt-**	**higgy-** **hidd**	**hin-**	**hinni**
iszik drink	**isz-**	**itt-** **ivott**[5]	**igy-** **idd**	**in-**	**inni**
eszik eat	**esz-**	**ett-** **evett**[5]	**egy-** **edd**	**en-**	**enni**

[4] There is a good deal of variation (in vowel length and stem shape) throughout the subjunctive paradigm for these verbs. See the full paradigm in appendix 1.
[5] The third person singular indefinite past tense of these verbs is formed from a

4.1.6 | The verbs van 'be', jön 'go', and megy 'come'

These three verbs are irregular in all moods and tenses. The past tense and conditional are formed regularly from the stems indicated in the table. The present tense and subjunctive forms exhibit some variation in the stems; for full paradigms see appendix 1.

	Present tense stem(s)	Past tense stem	Subjunctive stem	Conditional stem	Infinitive
van	**vagy-**	**volt-**	**legy-**	**vol-**	**lenni**
be	**van(-)**		**légy**	**len-**	
jön	varied	**jött-**	**jöjj-**	**jön-**	**jönni**
come			**gyere**		
			gyertek		
			gyerünk		
megy	**megy-**	**ment-**	**menj-**	**men-**	**menni**
go	**men-**				

4.2 Definite and indefinite conjugations

For each mood and tense, Hungarian verbs have two conjugations. The **definite conjugation** is used if the sentence contains a definite direct object. The **indefinite conjugation** is used at all other times. Thus, in the translation of the sentences 'I see a house' and 'I see the house' the verb **lát** is conjugated differently because of the presence or absence of a definite direct object.

Látok egy házat.   I see a house.

Látom a házat.   I see the house.

v-stem and is given here in full. The rest of the past tense conjugates regularly from the **itt-** and **ett-** stems.

4.2.1 | Determining the definiteness of an object

Several factors go into determining whether a direct object is to be considered definite. If a direct object does not conform to one of the points below, or if there is no direct object in the sentence at all, the indefinite conjugation of the verb is used. A direct object is considered definite if:

(a) it is preceded by the definite article **a** or **az**.

Látom a házat.   I see the house.

(b) it is a demonstrative pronoun (**az** or **ez**, **azok** or **ezek**) or is modified by a demonstrative pronoun.[6]

Látom ezt/azt.   I see this/that.

Látom ezt/azt a házat.   I see this/that house.

The demonstrative pronouns are also frequently used cataphorically[7] and as such they may be overt or implied. In either instance, they are still considered definite.

(Azt) látom, hogy esik az eső.   I see that it is raining.

(c) it has a possessive suffix.

Látom a házadat.   I see your house.

Látom a házát.   I see his/her house.

Since a possessed noun is almost always preceded by a definite article, this may also be considered a sub-class of (a). Although the definite article may be omitted in possessive constructions, any direct object with a possessive suffix is still considered definite. Note, also, that possessive and reflexive pronouns contain possessive suffixes and they are also considered definite.

Látom magam(at).   I see myself.

Mutasd meg a tiedet!   Show me yours!

---

[6] A contextually frequent, though semantically singular, exception to this is found when the direct object **azt** has the meaning 'that kind of', 'such a'; in this case, the indefinite conjugation is used:

Azt kérek.
I would like that kind.

[7] See section 7.9 for discussion of cataphoric pronouns.

(d) it is a proper noun.

Látom Zsuzsát/Budapestet. I see Zsuzsa/Budapest.

(e) it is a third person pronoun (overt or implied).

Látom (őt).	I see him/her.
Látom (őket).	I see them.
Látom (magát).	I see you (singular, polite).
Látom (magukat).	I see you (plural, polite).
Látom (önt).	I see you (singular, very polite).
Látom (önöket).	I see you (plural, very polite).

The third person direct object pronoun need not be overtly expressed and therefore the sentence **Látom** can mean 'I see him/her/them/you' (formal forms, sg. and pl.) – only context will provide the correct meaning. (It is common in speech, however, to overtly express the third person plural pronoun **őket** 'them' even when the context is otherwise clear.)

(f) it is the reciprocal pronoun, **egymás**.

Látják egymást.   They see each other.

(g) it is a modifier ending in -ik, or is preceded by a modifier ending in -ik (e.g. **melyik, hányadik**).

Melyiket kéred?	Which one would you like?
Melyik könyvet kéred?	Which book would you like?

4.2.2   -lak/-lek

There is one more personal form in all moods and tenses we shall include here in the definite conjugations (though not because the object is inherently definite). A unique verb conjugational form (**-lak/-lek**) exists for verbs when the subject is **én** and direct object is a second person pronoun (**téged, titeket, benneteket**). With any subject other than **én**, however, second person objects occur with indefinite conjugations.

Látlak (téged).   I see you (singular, familiar).

Látlak (benneteket/titeket).   I see you (plural, familiar).

4.3 Conjugation and usage

4.3.1 Present tense: conjugation

The present tense (unlike the past and the other moods) has no marker of its own on the verb; personal endings are added directly to the stem.

4.3.1.1 Indefinite conjugation

As illustrated in the following table, the personal endings for the present tense indefinite conjugation have either two or three vowel choices dependent on vowel harmony. Verb stems ending in two vowels or a long vowel plus -t require a linking vowel before the endings that begin with a consonant. Finally, for verb stems ending in the sibilants s, sz, z, dz, the personal ending for te is -ol/-el/-öl instead of the -sz found for non-sibilant stems.

Present tense indefinite – personal endings			
		Front vowel	
Singular	Back vowel	unrounded	rounded
1st person **én**	-ok	-ek	-ök
-ik verbs (optional)	-om	-em	-öm
2nd person **te**		-sz	
after two consonants or long vowel + **t**	-asz	-esz	
after **s, sz, z, dz**	-ol	-el	-öl
3rd person **ő, maga, ön**		——	
-ik verbs		-ik	
Plural			
1st person **mi**	-unk	-ünk	
2nd person **ti**	-tok	-tek	-tök
after two consonants or long vowel + **t**	-otok	-etek	-ötök
3rd person **ők, maguk, önök**	-nak	-nek	
after two consonants or long vowel + **t**	-anak	-enek	

Due to their different shapes, the following verbs trigger different endings; the relevant triggers are indicated in brackets; their conjugations follow.

wait	**vár**	[back vowel]
ask for	**kér**	[front unrounded vowel]
translate	**fordít**	[back vowel ending in long vowel + **t**]
cook	**főz**	[front rounded vowel ending in a sibilant]
play	**játszik**	[back vowel **-ik** verb with a stem ending in two consonants; the stem-final consonant is a sibilant]

Present tense indefinite conjugations

	vár	kér	fordít	főz	játszik
én	**várok**	**kérek**	**fordítok**	**főzök**	**játszok** **(~ játszom)**
te	**vársz**	**kérsz**	**fordítasz**	**főzöl**	**játszol**
ő	**vár**	**kér**	**fordít**	**főz**	**játszik**
mi	**várunk**	**kérünk**	**fordítunk**	**főzünk**	**játszunk**
ti	**vártok**	**kértek**	**fordítotok**	**főztök**	**játszotok**
ők	**várnak**	**kérnek**	**fordítanak**	**főznek**	**játszanak**

4.3.1.2 | Present tense definite conjugation

In addition to observing vowel harmony rules, the personal endings of the present tense definite conjugation are subject to another phonological rule: the -**j**- of the **j**-initial endings (-**ja**, -**juk**/-**jük**, -**játok**, -**ják**) regularly assimilates to the final consonant of verb stems ending in a sibilant (**s**, **sz**, **z**, **dz**). Recall from chapter 1 that when digraphs (**sz**, **dz**, etc.) are long, i.e., doubled, they are written by doubling only the first letter of the digraph: **sz** + **sz** → **ssz**.

olvas + ja	→	**olvassa**	s/he reads (it)
vesz + jük	→	**vesszük**	we take (it)
hoz + játok	→	**hozzátok**	you (pl.) bring (it)
edz + jük	→	**eddzük**	we train him/her

Present tense definite – personal endings

Singular	Back vowel	Front vowel	
		unrounded	rounded
1st person **én**	-om	-em	-öm
2nd person **te**	-od	-ed	-öd
3rd person **ő, maga, ön**	-ja	-i	
Plural			
1st person **mi**	-juk	-jük	
2nd person **ti**	-játok	-itek	
3rd person **ők, maguk, önök**	-ják	-ik	
1st person singular subject with 2nd person object	-lak	-lek	
after two consonants or long vowel + **t**	-alak	-elek	

The following verbs trigger different endings; the relevant triggers are indicated in brackets; their conjugations follow.

give **ad** [back vowel]

read **olvas** [back vowel, ends in sibilant]

play **játszik** [back vowel, ends in sibilant, -**ik** verb]

ask for **kér** [front unrounded vowel]

cook **főz** [front rounded vowel, ends in sibilant]

Present tense definite conjugations

	ad	olvas	játszik	kér	főz
én	adom	olvasom	játszom	kérem	főzöm
te	adod	olvasod	játszod	kéred	főzöd
ő	adja	olvassa	játssza	kéri	főzi
mi	adjuk	olvassuk	játsszuk	kérjük	főzzük
ti	adjátok	olvassátok	játsszátok	kéritek	főzitek
ők	adják	olvassák	játsszák	kérik	főzik

The form for verbs with the subject **én** 'I' and direct object **téged, titeket,
benneteket** 'you' (familiar, sg. or pl.):

vár	wait	**várlak**	I wait for you
szeret	love	**szeretlek**	I love you
tart	hold	**tartalak**	I hold you
ért	understand	**értelek**	I understand you

4.3.2 | *Present tense: usage*

4.3.2.1

The present tense can be used to indicate both present and habitual
actions.

Sétálunk a parkban.   We are walking in the park.

Mari nagy cégnél dolgozik.   Mari works for a large firm.

Minden nap bemegyek a   I go into the city every day.
városba.

4.3.2.2

The present tense may also be used to indicate future actions. In many
instances coverbs and/or time expressions indicating a future date are

used with the present tense of the verb to express the future. (See section **4.6.3** on aspect and coverbs for more on the use of aspect to indicate future.)

Holnap egész nap dolgozom.	I will be working all day tomorrow.
Jövő héten lemegyek a Balatonra.	Next week I'm going to the Balaton.
Később írom meg házi feladatomat.	I'll do my homework later.

4.3.2.3

The present tense is often used in colloquial Hungarian when relating a story that happened in the past. This is found in very colloquial English as well.

Bemegyek **a boltba, és kit** *látok?* **Egyik amerikai bará-tomat, aki rögtön** *elkezdi* **mesélni, hogy mi** *történik* **vele, amióta nem láttuk egymást.**
I go into the store, and who do *I see?* An American friend, who immediately *begins* to tell me what *has been going on* with him since we last met.

4.3.2.4

Reported speech: In English reported speech tolerates both the past and present tense, for example, 'You said that you *were/are (still) reading.*' In Hungarian, on the other hand, reported speech is expressed in the tense in which it was originally stated.

Lajos mondta, hogy Szegeden *akar* **lakni.**
Lajos said that he *wants/wanted* to live in Szeged. (At the time of his statement he used the present tense.)

Lajos mondta, hogy három évvel ezelőtt Szegeden *akart* **lakni.**
Lajos said that three years ago he *wanted* to live in Szeged. (At the time of his statement, he used the past tense.)

4.3.2.5

The present tense is used in time expressions meaning 'since', 'for a period of time' if the action continues into the present.

Január óta dolgozom a könyvtárban.
I have been working in the library since January.

Mióta tanulsz magyarul?
How long have you been studying Hungarian?

4.3.3 | *Past tense: conjugation*

The past tense marker appears between the verb stem and the personal endings. It has two shapes: (1) the long form, -**ott**/-**ett**/-**ött** (where the vowel alternation is dependent on vowel harmony rules) and (2) the short form, -**t**. The shape of the verb stem determines whether it will take the long or short form. Three classes of verb stems are pertinent:

Class A verbs always require the long form -**ott**/-**ett**/-**ött** and are defined as follows:

1 verbs ending in a long vowel + **t**
2 verbs ending in two consonants
3 monosyllabic verbs ending in a short vowel + **t**. Only eight verbs in the language have such a shape:

fut	run
hat	have an effect
jut	get, come to
köt	tie
nyit	open
süt	bake
üt	strike
vet	cast

Class B verbs always require the short form **t** and are defined as follows:

1 verbs ending in (single) **j, l, ly, n, ny,** or **r**.
2 many bisyllabic verbs ending in -**ad** or -**ed**.

Class C verbs require the long form in the third person singular indefinite conjugation and the short form for all other persons. Class C is (negatively) defined as containing all verbs not of class A or class B.

31

Exceptions:

(a) Some verbs that look as though they belong to Class A but conjugate as Class C include **lát** 'see', **küld** 'send', **mond** 'say', **kezd** 'begin', **függ** 'hang', 'depend', **fedd** 'reprove'.

(b) Verbs that look as though they belong to Class A but conjugate as Class B are **áll** 'stand', **száll** 'fly', **varr** 'sew', **forr** 'boil'.

(c) The verb **fürdik** 'bathe' conjugates as either Class A or C: **fürödtem ~ fürdöttem** 'I bathed', only the long form is used in the third person singular: **fürdött** 'she/he bathed'.

| 4.3.3.1 | Past tense indefinite

After the correct past tense marker has been determined, the personal endings are attached with no further changes to the stem.

Past tense indefinite – personal endings		
Singular	Back vowel	Front vowel
1st person **én**	-am	-em
2nd person **te**	-ál	-él
3rd person **ő, maga, ön**	——	
Plural		
1st person **mi**	-unk	-ünk
2nd person **ti**	-atok	-etek
3rd person **ők, maguk, önök**	-ak	-ek

The following verbs trigger different endings; the relevant triggers are indicated in brackets; their conjugations follow.

bake	**süt**	[Class A, front rounded vowel]
remain	**marad**	[Class B, back vowel]
love	**szeret**	[Class C, front unrounded vowel]
olvas	**read**	[Class C, back vowel]

Past tense indefinite conjugations

	süt	marad	szeret	olvas
én	sütöttem	maradtam	szerettem	olvastam
te	sütöttél	maradtál	szerettél	olvastál
ő	sütött	maradt	szeretett	olvasott
mi	sütöttünk	maradtunk	szerettünk	olvastunk
ti	sütöttetek	maradtatok	szerettetek	olvastatok
ők	sütöttek	maradtak	szerettek	olvastak

4.3.3.2 | Past tense definite

Past tense definite – personal endings

Singular	Back vowel	Front vowel
1st person **én**	**-am**	**-em**
2nd person **te**	**-ad**	**-ed**
3rd person **ő, maga, ön**	**-a**	**-e**
Plural		
1st person **mi**	**-uk**	**-ük**
2nd person **ti**	**-átok**	**-étek**
3rd person **ők, maguk, önök**	**-ák**	**-ék**
1st person singular subject with 2nd person object	**-alak**	**-elek**

The following verbs trigger different endings; the relevant triggers are
indicated in brackets; their conjugations follow.

strike	**üt**	[Class A, front rounded vowel]
ask for	**kér**	[Class B, front vowel]
introduce	**bemutat**	[Class C, back vowel]

Past tense definite conjugations

	üt	kér	bemutat
én	ütöttem	kértem	bemutattam
te	ütötted	kérted	bemutattad
ő	ütötte	kérte	bemutatta
mi	ütöttük	kértük	bemutattuk
ti	ütöttétek	kértétek	bemutattátok
ők	ütötték	kérték	bemutatták

The form for verbs with the subject én 'I' and direct object téged, titeket, benneteket 'you' (familiar, sg. or pl.):

ütöttelek	I struck you
kértelek	I asked you
bemutattalak	I introduced you

4.3.4 | Past tense: usage

4.3.4.1

The past tense is used, as in English, to express actions that occurred in the past.

Tegnap bicikliztünk az erdőben.	Yesterday we were biking in the woods.
Múlt évben Franciaországban nyaraltak.	They vacationed in France last year.
Befejeztem a munkát.	I finished the work.

4.3.4.2

Hungarian has only one past tense form. The use of time expressions
and coverbs combine to express the meanings of the complex tense forms
found in English. See **4.6.3** on aspect and coverbs.

> **Elolvastam a könyvet.** (past tense, with a coverb, only
> perfective aspect)
> I read the book. / I have read the book. / I had read the book.

> **Olvastam a könyvet.** (past tense, without a coverb,
> imperfective or perfective aspect)
> I was reading the book. / I had been reading the book. / I read
> the book.

4.3.4.3

The auxiliary verb **szokott** 'usually' is found only in the past tense although
its meaning may be either past or present.

> **Reggel kávézni szoktam, este inkább teázom.**
> In the morning I usually drink coffee, in the evening I drink tea.

> **Régen korcsolyázni szoktunk télen, de most már öregek
> vagyunk.**
> In the old days we would go ice skating in the winter, but now
> we are too old.

4.3.4.4

The past tense may also be used (in compound sentences) to indicate the
completion of an action in the future.

> **Ha megebédeltem, lefekszem egy órára.**
> When I have finished my lunch, I will lie down for an hour.

> **Mihelyt megírtam a levelet, rohanok a postára.**
> As soon as I have written the letter I will rush to the post office.

4.3.5 | Subjunctive/imperative: conjugation

The subjunctive serves as the imperative as well and for the sake of brevity
will be referred to here only as the subjunctive. Its marker is -j- and it

is located between the verb stem and the personal endings. Depending on the verb stem, the -j- may be assimilated or otherwise altered. The following are the regular alternations of the subjunctive marker -j-:

1   In verb stems ending in a sibilant (**s, sz, z, dz**), the subjunctive -j- assimilates to the sibilant.[8]

    keres + -j- → keress-

2   In verb stems ending in -**st**[9] or -**szt**, the stem-final -**t** is lost and the subjunctive -j- assimilates to the sibilant.

    ébreszt + -j- → ébressz-

3   In verb stems ending in a long vowel + **t** or a consonant + **t** (except as defined in the previous paragraph), the subjunctive -j- becomes -**s**-.

    segít + -j- → segíts-

4   In verb stems ending in a short vowel + **t**, both the stem-final -**t** and the subjunctive -j- become **s**.

    mutat + -j- → mutass-

The personal endings show some variation in the subjunctive. The second person singular has both a long and short form; although the short form is becoming more common in colloquial speech, the long form expresses a somewhat milder command.

| 4.3.5.1 | Subjunctive indefinite |

The regular endings are used much more frequently with -**ik** verbs than the other optional endings found in the first and third persons singular; the optional endings are more archaic and often found in older writings.

---

[8] Compare with the -j initial personal endings in the definite conjugation of the present tense where the same assimilation occurs.

[9] Only one verb ends in -**st**: **fest** 'paint'.

Subjunctive indefinite – personal endings

Singular	Back vowel	Front vowel	
		unrounded	rounded
1st person **én**	**-ak**	**-ek**	
-ik verbs (optional)	**-am**	**-em**	
2nd person **te**	**-(ál)**	**-(él)**	
3rd person **ő, maga, ön**	**-on**	**-en**	**-ön**
-ik verbs (optional)		**-ék**	
Plural			
1st person **mi**	**-unk**	**-ünk**	
2nd person **ti**	**-atok**	**-etek**	
3rd person **ők, maguk, önök**	**-anak**	**-enek**	

The following verbs trigger different endings; the relevant triggers are indicated in brackets; their conjugations follow.

ask for   **kér**   [front unrounded vowel]

run   **fut**   [back vowel, ends in short vowel + **t**]

wake   **ébreszt**   [front unrounded vowel, ends in -**szt**]

play   **játszik**   [back vowel, -**ik** verb, stem ends in sibilant]

Subjunctive indefinite conjugations

	kér	fut	ébreszt	játszik
én	kérjek	fussak	ébresszek	játsszak (~ játsszam)
te	kérjél ~ kérj	fussál ~ fuss	ébresszél ~ ébressz	játsszál ~ játssz
ő	kérjen	fusson	ébresszen	játsszon (~ játsszék)
mi	kérjünk	fussunk	ébresszünk	játsszunk
ti	kérjetek	fussatok	ébresszetek	játsszatok
ők	kérjenek	fussanak	ébresszenek	játsszanak

4.3.5.2 | Subjunctive definite

In the definite conjugation, there is both a short and long form for the second person singular ending. The long form is given below in the table. The short form is arrived at by dropping the -j- of the subjunctive (or the consonant to which it had assimilated) and the vowel that follows it. For example,

kér + j + ed → **kérjed** (long form) ~ **kérd** (short form)

nyit + j + ad → **nyissad** (long form) ~ **nyisd** (short form)

ébreszt + j + ed → **ébresszed** (long form) ~ **ébreszd** (short form)

The one regular exception to this pattern is found in verb stems ending in a long vowel + **t** or a consonant + **t** (other than **st, szt**). For verbs of this large class, only the vowel following the subjunctive marker -j- is lost, the subjunctive marker is kept (in this class, the -j- becomes an s). For example,

tart + j + ad → **tartsad** (long form) ~ **tartsd** (short form).

Except for the short form in the second person singular, the personal endings of the subjunctive definite conjugation are identical to those for the past tense definite conjugation.

Subjunctive definite – personal endings

Singular	Back vowel	Front vowel
1st person **én**	**-am**	**-em**
2nd person **te**	**-ad**	**-ed**
3rd person **ő, maga, ön**	**-a**	**-e**
Plural		
1st person **mi**	**-uk**	**-ük**
2nd person **ti**	**-átok**	**-étek**
3rd person **ők, maguk, önök**	**-ák**	**-ék**
1st person singular subject with 2nd person object	**-alak**	**-elek**

The following verbs trigger different endings; the relevant triggers are indicated in brackets; their conjugations follow.

wait	**vár**	[back vowel]
love	**szeret**	[front unrounded vowel, ends in short vowel + **t**]
hold	**tart**	[back vowel, ends in a consonant + **t**]
frighten	**ijeszt**	[front unrounded vowel, ends in **-szt**]

Subjunctive definite conjugations

	vár	szeret	tart	ijeszt
én	**várjam**	**szeressem**	**tartsam**	**ijesszem**
te	**várjad**	**szeressed**	**tartsad**	**ijesszed**
	~ **várd**	~ **szeresd**	~ **tartsd**	~ **ijeszd**
ő	**várja**	**szeresse**	**tartsa**	**ijessze**
mi	**várjuk**	**szeressük**	**tartsuk**	**ijesszük**
ti	**várjátok**	**szeressétek**	**tartsátok**	**ijesszétek**
ők	**várják**	**szeressék**	**tartsák**	**ijesszék**

The form for verbs with the subject **én** 'I' and direct object **téged, titeket, benneteket** 'you' (familiar, sg. or pl.):

vár	wait	**várjalak**	that I wait for you
szeret	love	**szeresselek**	that I love you
tart	hold	**tartsalak**	that I hold you
ijeszt	frighten	**ijesszelek**	that I frighten you

4.3.6 | Subjunctive: usage

The subjunctive conjugation is also used for the imperative, i.e., it is the form used when giving commands. It is also used in several types of subordinate clauses.

4.3.6.1 | The subjunctive as imperative

The subjunctive is used to give commands – polite or otherwise. Any coverb is removed to a post-verb position in commands. Imperative sentences always end in an exclamation mark.

Gyere ide!	Come here!
Csukja be az ajtót, legyen szíves!	Close the door, please!
Hívjál fel később!	Call me later!
Hagyjál békén!	Leave me alone!

When giving commands in the negative, the forms **ne, se** replace **nem, sem**, respectively.

Ne menjen el!	Don't leave!
Ne edd meg azt a barackot!	Don't eat that apricot!
Senki se zavarjon!	Don't anyone bother me!

Stricter, more threatening commands can be formed by *not* removing the coverb (or other adverbial) from the preverb position.

Megcsináld!	Do it!
Lassan menjél!	Walk slowly!

Strict negative commands are formed by placing the coverb before the negative particle.

Meg ne edd azt a barackot!	Don't (you dare) eat that apricot!	Conjugation and usage
Ki ne nyissátok az ablakot!	Don't (you dare) open the window!	

The subjunctive is used in the first person plural to mean 'let's'.

Együnk már!	Let's eat already!
Menjünk moziba!	Let's go to the movies!
Ne keljünk fel korán holnap!	Let's not get up early tomorrow!

The subjunctive combines with the frozen form **hadd** 'let' to express permission.

Hadd maradjon itthon, ha akar!	Let him stay home if he wants!
Hadd vegyem meg ezt az autót!	Let me buy this car!

4.3.6.2 Subjunctive and questions

The subjunctive is used in questions in the first person singular and plural, to express 'should I/we . . .?' or 'shall I/we . . .?' In this usage, the coverb is not removed from the verb (unless other focus elements are in the clause – see focus and word order chapter 16).

Megmondjam nekik az igazat?	Should I tell them the truth?
Táncoljunk?	Shall we dance?

The subjunctive is also used in indirect questions; the meaning is similar to the previous usage, expressing 'should/shall one . . .?'

Megkérdezték, hogy felírják-e az új szavakat.
They asked whether they should write down the new words.

Megérdeklődted, hogy elinduljál-e?
Did you inquire as to whether you should leave?

4.3.6.3 Subjunctive and subordinate clauses

The following are the most common uses of the subjunctive in subordinate clauses. Careful attention must be paid to the position of the coverb.

In subordinate clauses containing requests or commands, the coverb is (usually) removed from the preverb to a post-verb position; in other subordinate clauses the coverb remains in the preverb position.

4.3.6.3.1 Clauses containing indirect requests, commands

If the desire or will of the subject of the main clause is pressed upon the subject of the subordinate clause, the subordinate clause will contain the subjunctive verb. The verb in the main clause may be one of will: **akar** 'want', **kér** 'request', 'ask', **javasol** 'suggest', **ajánl** 'recommend'; or it may be any verb of communication through which a wish is conveyed: **mond** 'say', **ír** 'write', **üzen** 'send the message', etc.

Többen javasolták Lacinak, hogy udvaroljon a szomszéd lánynak.
Several people had suggested to Laci that he date the girl next door.

Azt írták, hogy jöjjek haza.
They wrote me that I should come home.

Azt kérte a feleségétől, hogy szokjon le a dohányzásról.
He asked his wife to give up smoking.

If the main clause contains a prohibitive verb or expression, the subjunctive is used in the subordinate clause. Unless there are other focussed elements, a coverb in the subordinate clause remains in the preverb position.

Megtiltották, hogy elmenjen az országból.
They forbid him from leaving the country.

Nem engedték, hogy felhívjon.
They did not allow him to call me.

4.3.6.3.2 Clauses of purpose

The subjunctive is used to express 'in order to' or 'so that'; this is often combined with a main clause introduced by **azért** 'for that reason'.

(Azért) megyek Magyarországra, hogy meglátogathassam a rokonaimat.
I am going to Hungary so that I can visit my relatives.

Sokkal többet kell gyakorolnom, hogy igazán jól tudjak zongorázni.
I have to practice much more in order to play the piano really well.

Elviszi a pulóvert, hogy ne fázzon a kiránduláson.
She is taking the sweater so she won't be cold on the trip.

If the subjunctive clause of purpose is negated, it may begin with **hogy**
. . . **ne** or **nehogy**; with **nehogy** the coverb is not removed from the preverb
position.

Vigyázz, nehogy elessél!
Watch out that you don't fall!

Vigyázz, hogy ne essél el!
Watch out that you don't fall!

Another kind of clause of purpose – more subtle than the previous type
– is one in which the action in the subordinate clause is a desired or
expected result of the main clause:

Arra törekszik, hogy új állást kapjon.
He's trying to get a new job.

Figyelmeztetett arra, hogy ne felejtsem el.
He reminded me so I wouldn't forget.

Arra készültünk, hogy két napon belül elutazhassunk.
We were getting ready so that we could leave within two days.

Felhasználtam az alkalmat arra, hogy elszökjek.
I used the opportunity to get away.

**Sohasem lesz annyi tehetségem ahhoz, hogy három
   nyelvet beszéljek.**
I will never be talented enough to speak three languages.

4.3.6.3.3

Subordinate clauses following impersonal main clauses are also in the
subjunctive.

Fontos, hogy elolvassák a cikket.
It is important that they read the article.

Szükséges, hogy előre telefonáljak?
Is it necessary that I call in advance?

Illik, hogy pontos legyél.
It is appropriate that you be punctual.

| 4.3.6.3.4 |

The subjunctive is used in subordinate clauses where the main clause expresses a lack, absence or inability (to fulfill a goal).

Nincs kivel kártyázzak.
I have nobody to play cards with.

Nem volt lehetőségük, hogy bemutatkozzanak az új igazgatónak.
They had no opportunity to introduce themselves to the new director.

| 4.3.7 | *The conditional (non-past): conjugation*

The conditional marker is

-na/-ne for the third person singular indefinite form;

-né for the first person singular indefinite (i.e., there is no back vowel variant);

-ná/-né for all other persons.

The conditional is located between the verb stem and the personal endings. In verb stems ending in a long vowel + t or two consonants,[10] the linking vowel a/e is required before the conditional marker.

olvas + né + k → olvasnék   (no linking vowel)

BUT

tanít + ané + k → tanítanék   (linking vowel **a** required)

ért + ené + k → értenék   (linking vowel **e** required)[11]

| 4.3.7.1 | Conditional indefinite

In contrast to all the other conjugations, in this paradigm there is no vowel harmony in the regular first person singular ending. The endings

---

[10] Exceptions include **áll** 'stand', **száll** 'fly', **varr** 'sew', and **forr** 'boil'. Recall that in the past tense, these verbs also conjugated as those ending in only one consonant.
[11] This use of a linking vowel is identical to that found in forming the infinitive of the same verb types.

for -ik verbs are rarely used in colloquial Hungarian. Because of the variations found in vowel length and vowel harmony, the following table combines the conditional and personal markers; thus these endings attach directly to the verb stem.

Conditional indefinite – personal endings		
Singular	Back vowel	Front vowel
1st person **én**	**-nék**	
-ik verbs (optional)	**-nám**	**-ném**
2nd person **te**	**-nál**	**-nél**
3rd person **ő, maga, ön**	**-na**	**-ne**
-ik verbs (optional)	**-nék**	
Plural		
1st person **mi**	**-nánk**	**-nénk**
2nd person **ti**	**-nátok**	**-nétek**
3rd person **ők, maguk, önök**	**-nának**	**-nének**

The following verbs trigger different endings; the relevant triggers are indicated in brackets; their conjugations follow.

translate	**fordít**	[back vowel, ends in long vowel + **t**]
help	**segít**	[front vowel, ends in long vowel + **t**]
dare	**mer**	[front vowel]
swim	**úszik**	[back vowel, **-ik** verb]

Conditional indefinite conjugations

	fordít	segít	mer	úszik
én	fordítanék	segítenék	mernék	úsznék (~ úsznám)
te	fordítanál	segítenél	mernél	úsznál
ő	fordítana	segítene	merne	úszna (~ úsznék)
mi	fordítanánk	segítenénk	mernénk	úsznánk
ti	fordítanátok	segítenétek	mernétek	úsznátok
ők	fordítanának	segítenének	mernének	úsznának

4.3.7.2 Conditional definite

The personal endings for the definite conjugation exhibit no variation; the first and second person plural endings in the definite conjugation are identical to those in the indefinite conjugation. The following table combines the conditional marker with the personal endings; thus the endings given here attach directly to the verb stem.

Conditional definite – personal endings

Singular	Back vowel	Front vowel
1st person **én**	**-nám**	**-ném**
2nd person **te**	**-nád**	**-néd**
3rd person **ő, maga, ön**	**-ná**	**-né**
Plural		
1st person **mi**	**-nánk**	**-nénk**
2nd person **ti**	**-nátok**	**-nétek**
3rd person **ők**	**-nák**	**-nék**
1st person singular subject with 2nd person object	**-nálak**	**-nélek**

The following verbs trigger different endings; the relevant triggers are indicated in brackets; their conjugations follow.

love   **szeret**   [front vowel]

hold   **tart**   [back vowel, ends in two consonants]

give   **ad**   [back vowel]

	szeret	tart	ad
Conditional definite conjugations			
	szeret	tart	ad
én	szeretném	tartanám	adnám
te	szeretnéd	tartanád	adnád
ő	szeretné	tartaná	adná
mi	szeretnénk	tartanánk	adnánk
ti	szeretnétek	tartanátok	adnátok
ők	szeretnék	tartanák	adnák

The form for verbs with the subject **én** 'I' and direct object **téged, titeket, benneteket** 'you' familiar, sg. or pl.:

szeretnélek   I would love you.

tartanálak   I would hold you.

4.3.8 │ *The past conditional*

The past conditional is formed simply by conjugating the substantive verb in the past tense and following it with the fixed form **volna**. An example paradigm is given below where the verb **elmegy** 'leave' is conjugated in the past tense and **volna** follows it:

elmentem volna   I would have left

elmentél volna   you (sg.) would have left

elment volna   he/she would have left

elmentünk volna we would have left

elmentetek volna	you (pl.) would have left
elmentek volna	they would have left

When negating the past conditional construction, the negative particle is placed immediately before the conjugated verb; the coverb is removed to a position immediately after **volna**.

Nem mentem volna el. I would not have gone.

Nem hívott volna fel. She would not have called us.

Any other stressed or focussed element will change the word order in the same way as negation. (See section **16.4** on word order and focus.)

Kit látogattál volna meg, ha lett volna időd?
Whom would you have visited, if you'd had the time?

Because the formation of the past conditional is based on the past tense forms, full paradigms need not be listed here.

4.3.9 | Conditional: usage

4.3.9.1

The conditional is used to express hypothetical conditions in the present, future or past. When used to express 'if ... then ...' conditions, both clauses are conjugated in the conditional mood.

Ha több időm lenne, akkor többet olvasnék.
If I had more time, then I would read more.

Nagyon örülne, ha meglátogatnád.
She would be very happy if you would visit her.

Azonnal elindulna, ha megtalálná a kulcsát.
He would leave right now if he could find his keys.

4.3.9.2

The conditional is used to make a polite request.

Megkérnélek egy szívességre.
I would like to ask you a favor.

Kölcsön adnál egy ezrest?
Would you loan me a thousand forints?

Vennél nekem egy fagyit?
Would you buy me an ice cream?

Lenne egy kérdésem.
I have a question.

Bekapcsolhatnám a tévét?
Might I turn on the television?

4.3.9.3

The conditional is used to express wishes and desires; it is always used after bárcsak 'if only'.

Bárcsak esne a hó!
If only it would snow!

Szeretném, ha gyakrabban találkozhatnánk.
I wish we could meet more often.

Bár megnézhettem volna én is azt a filmet.
If only I could have seen that film, too.

4.3.9.4

The conditional is used in clauses introduced by the conjunctions anélkül 'without', ahelyett 'instead of', and mintha 'as if'.

Anélkül, hogy elbúcsúzott volna tőlünk, hirtelen elhagyta az országot.
Without saying goodbye, he suddenly left the country.

Ahelyett, hogy cukrot tenne a teába, egy kis rumot tett bele.
Instead of putting sugar in the tea, she put some rum in.

Úgy nézel ki, mintha megijesztettek volna!
You look as though you've been frightened!

The future tense

4.3.10.1

Although there is no inflectional future tense, future actions can be expressed in a number of ways. The present tense may combine with time expressions and/or coverbs to indicate the future.

Holnap felhívlak.   I'll call you tomorrow.

Jövő télen veszek egy új autót.   Next winter I will buy a new car.

4.3.10.2

The auxiliary verb **fog** is used to express the future tense – primarily with verbs with no coverbs. Word order patterns with **fog** are like those of other auxiliary verbs (see section **16.5** on word order). When used as a future auxiliary, **fog**[12] conjugates in the present tense in both definite and indefinite conjugations.

	pihenni + fog will rest' *indefinite*			**látni + fog** 'will see' *definite*		
én	**pihenni fogok**	I	will rest	**látni fogom**	I	will see him/her/ etc.,
te	**pihenni fogsz**	you	"	**látni fogod**	you	"
ő	**pihenni fog**	he/she	"	**látni fogja**	he/she	"
mi	**pihenni fogunk**	we	"	**látni fogjuk**	we	"
ti	**pihenni fogtok**	you	"	**látni fogjátok**	you	"
ők	**pihenni fognak**	they	"	**látni fogják**	they	"

Mikor lesz időm, pihenni fogok.
When I have time, I am going to rest.

Mikor fogsz találkozni vele?
When are you going to meet with her?

---

[12] The verb **fog** has another meaning 'catch'; in this meaning it conjugates in all moods and tenses.

The verb **fog** also combines with verbs that do have coverbs; in this case, the expression is somewhat more emphatic.

Meg fogom várni.   I *will* wait for him.

Ne félj, meg fogja javítani az   Don't worry, he *will* fix the
autót!   car.

| 4.3.10.3 |

The verb **lesz** 'will be', 'become' is the future of the verb **van** 'be'; it is not an auxiliary verb.

Ha felnövök, orvos leszek.
I will be a doctor when I grow up.

Később éhes leszel, ha nem reggelizel.
You'll be hungry later if you don't have breakfast.

Lesz can replace **van** in any construction to express the future.

'have' construction:

Sohasem lesz elég pénze.
He will never have enough money.

the verb **van** with adverbial participles:

Egy hét múlva be lesz fejezve a munka.
The work will be finished in a week.

4.4 Non-finite forms

| 4.4.1 | *Past, present, and future participles: formation*

| 4.4.1.1 |

The present participle is -ó or -**ő**. It is attached directly to the verb stem in regular verbs. The last vowel of fleeting-vowel verbs always elides and v-stem verbs always use the v-stem before the present participle.

ír	write	+ **ó**	→	**író**	writer; writing
játszik	play	+ **ó**	→	**játszó**	player; playing
énekel	sing	+ **ő**	→	**éneklő**	singer; singing

sző   weave + **ő** → **szövő**   weaver; weaving

4.4.1.2

The past participle is usually the same as the third person singular indefinite form of the past tense.

ad	give	**adott**	given
ismer	know	**ismert**	known
kifest	paint	**kifestett**	painted

There are some exceptions in monosyllabic verbs belonging to Class B.[13] Whereas the past tense always takes the short form -t, the past participle may take the long form o/e/ö + tt:

áll	stand	**állt ~ állott**
hal	die	**halt ~ halott**
ír	write	**írt ~ írott**
tör	break	**tört ~ törött**

4.4..1.3

The future participle is -andó/-endő. It is attached directly to the verb stem in regular verbs.

kel	sell well +	**endő**	→	**kelendő**	(easily) marketable
marad	remain +	**andó**	→	**maradandó**	enduring

4.4.2 | *Present, past, future participles: usage*

The present, past, and future participles are similar in usage, though the future participle is by far a rarer form in Hungarian.

4.4.2.1

These participles may always be used as adjectives:

---

[13] For description of Class B see 4.3.3. Past tense.

PRESENT

alszik	sleep	**alvó kutya**	sleeping dog
dolgozik	work	**dolgozó emberek**	working people
emelkedik	rise	**emelkedő árak**	rising prices
mosolyog	smile	**mosolygó gyerek**	smiling child
tanul	study	**tanuló fiú**	studying boy

PAST

ismer	know	**jól ismert író**	well known writer
kifest	paint	**kifestett szoba**	painted room
öltözik	dress	**selyembe öltözött nő**	woman dressed in silk

FUTURE

lesz	will be	**leendő anya**	mother-to-be
tesz	do	**teendő munka**	work to do

4.4.2.2

Many present and some past and future participles function as nouns:

PRESENT

fest	paint	**festő**	painter
ír	write	**író**	writer
szerkeszt	edit	**szerkesztő**	editor
tanul	study	**tanuló**	student

PAST

befő	become thick by boiling	**befőtt**	fruit preserves
felnő	grow up	**felnőtt**	grown-up
vádol	accuse	**vádlott**	defendant

FUTURE

jön	come	**jövendő**	future
tesz	do	**teendő**	task, agenda

4.4.2.3

In prose the participles are found in adjectival constructions and compare (semantically – not stylistically) with relative clauses in colloquial speech. It may help to think of them as relative clauses (modifying a previously mentioned noun) which have been condensed into adjectival constructions. Often the participial–adjectival constructions translate best into English as relative clauses, though English may also use a similar participial construction.

Az a fiú, aki integet, az öcsém.   (relative clause)
That boy who is waving is my little brother.

Az az *integető* fiú az öcsém.   (participle as adjective)
(lit.) That waving boy is my little brother.

Zsuzsa egy olyan házba akar beköltözni, ami a múlt
században épült.   (relat. clause)
Zsuzsa wants to move into a house which was built in the last century.

Zsuzsa egy múlt században *épült* házba akar beköltözni.
(participle as adjective)
Zsuzsa wants to move into a house built in the last century.

Participial-adjectival constructions can be rather lengthy in prose. When translating from Hungarian, it is best to identify the noun being modified and continue to translate from right to left.

4.4.3 | *Adverbial participle*

The adverbial participle is -va/-ve. It is attached directly to the stem.

mosolyog   smile + **va** → **mosolyogva**   (while) smiling

énekel   sing + **ve** → **énekelve**   (while) singing

The adverbial participle modifies a conjugated verb; it expresses a continuing action occurring at the time of another action.

***Mosolyogva* lépett be a szobába.**
She entered the room *smiling*.

Tegyél le! – mondta *nevetve* a kisfiú.
'Put me down!' said the boy *laughing*.

See section **17.9** for colloquial usage of the adverbial participle with **van** 'be'.

4.4.4 Infinitive

The infinitive ending is -ni and it is attached directly to verb stems. In verb stems ending in two consonants[14] or long vowel + t, the linking vowel a/e is required before suffixing.[15]

ért + eni → **érteni**	to understand
főz + ni → **főzni**	to cook
hall + ani → **hallani**	to hear
olvas + ni → **olvasni**	to read
tanít + ani → **tanítani**	to teach

Undeclined infinitives are found as the complement of other verbs:

Szeretek olvasni.	I like to read.
Aludni akarok.	I want to sleep.

If the direct object of the infinitive is definite, the definite conjugation is used on the conjugated verb unless the verb is impersonal (e.g., **kell** 'is necessary', **lehet** 'is possible') or inherently intransitive (e.g., **megy** 'go', **igyekszik** 'strive').

Szeretném befejezni ezt a dolgozatot.
I would like to finish this paper.

Nem tudom kinyitni az üveget.
I can't open the bottle.

Ki akarja elkészíteni a vacsorát ma este?
Who wants to make dinner tonight?

Note the following emphatic, topical use of the infinitive; it implies, and is usually followed by, a **de** 'but' clause.

Olvasni olvastam a könyvet, de nem volt jó.
(Well,) I *read* the book, but it wasn't good.

---

[14] Exceptions include **áll** 'stand', **száll** 'fly', **varr** 'sew', and **forr** 'boil'.
[15] Compare with the conditional where the linking vowel is required under identical conditions.

Ebédelni ebédeltem, de még éhes vagyok.
(Yes,) I did eat lunch, but I'm still hungry.

4.4.5 | Declined infinitives

Declined infinitives are used in impersonal constructions. They are formed by attaching personal (possessive) endings to infinitives. The infinitive is first reduced to (a/e)n, i.e., without the final i. The following personal endings are then attached. (See section 17.7 on the use of impersonal constructions.)

Declined infinitives – Personal endings			
		Front vowel	
Singular	Back vowel	unrounded	rounded
1st person	-om	-em	-öm
2nd person	-od	-ed	-öm
3rd person	-ia		-ie
Plural			
1st person	-unk		-ünk
2nd person	-otok	-etek	-ötök
3rd person	-iuk		-iük

tanít teach	**ad** give	**kezd** begin	**megy** go	**ül** sit
tanítani	**adni**	**kezdeni**	**menni**	**ülni**
tanítanom	**adnom**	**kezdenem**	**mennem**	**ülnöm**
tanítanod	**adnod**	**kezdened**	**menned**	**ülnöd**
tanítania	**adnia**	**kezdenie**	**mennie**	**ülnie**
tanítanunk	**adnunk**	**kezdenünk**	**mennünk**	**ülnünk**
tanítanotok	**adnotok**	**kezdenetek**	**mennetek**	**ülnötök**
tanítaniuk	**adniuk**	**kezdeniük**	**menniük**	**ülniük**

4.5 Productive derivational endings

Hungarian has three derivational endings which can be attached to most verbs before the tense and mood endings: the potential, causative, and frequentative. For more derivational endings occurring less productively, see chapter 12 on word formation.

4.5.1 The potential: formation

The potential is added to verb stems to add the meaning 'may', 'can', or 'is possible' to the verb. The potential ending is -hat/-het and may be added to all verbs. In regular verbs it attaches directly to the verb stem, thereby creating a new verb stem subject to all tenses, moods and conjugations.[16]

ad	give	**adhat**	may give
játszik	play	**játszhat**	may play
kér	ask for	**kérhet**	may ask for
kezd	begin	**kezdhet**	may begin
főz	cook	**főzhet**	may cook

When the potential is attached it redefines the verb type: once in place, the verbs then conjugate as any other verb type ending in a short vowel + t. So, for example, though játszik 'play' is considered Class A in the past tense because its stem ends in two consonants, játszhat 'may play' is Class C. The change in stem has repercussions throughout the verbal paradigm; all conjugational patterns apply to the new stem.

Sample verb conjugations with the potential -hat/-het:

---

[16] The potential form of **van** 'be' is formed from the **lesz** 'will be' root. See appendix 1 for the formation of the potential with irregular verbs.

	Present		Past	
	Indefinite	Definite	Indefinite	Definite
	játszhat, may play	adhat, may give	kezdhet, may begin	kérhet, may ask for
én	játszhatok	adhatom	kezdhettem	kérhettem
te	játszhatsz	adhatod	kezdhettél	kérhetted
ő	játszhat	adhatja	kezdhetett	kérhette
mi	játszhatunk	adhatjuk	kezdhettünk	kérhettük
ti	játszhattok	adhatjátok	kezdhettetek	kérhettétek
ők	játszhatnak	adhatják	kezdhettek	kérhették
én—téged/ benneteket		adhatlak		kérhettelek

	Subjunctive		Conditional	
	Indefinite	Definite	Indefinite	Definite
	főzhet, may cook	kereshet, may look for	tanulhat, may study	küldhet, may send
én	főzhessek	kereshessem	tanulhatnék	küldhetném
te	főzhess(él)	kereshes(se)d	tanulhatnál	küldhetnéd
ő	főzhessen	kereshesse	tanulhatna	küldhetné
mi	főzhessünk	kereshessük	tanulhatnánk	küldhetnénk
ti	főzhessetek	kereshessétek	tanulhatnátok	küldhetnétek
ők	főzhessenek	kereshessék	tanulhatnának	küldhetnék
én—téged/ benneteket		kereshesselek		küldhetnélek

4.5.2 | Use of the potential

The most common use of the potential is to denote 'may', 'is allowed'.

Bejöhetsz.	You may come in.
Mehetünk?	May we go?
Jani itt maradhat, ameddig csak akar.	Jani can stay here as long as he wants.

It can also have the meaning 'might, could' in expressions of doubt or uncertainty.

Jó film lehet.
It might be a good movie.

Mennyibe kerülhet egy belvárosi lakás?
How much might a downtown apartment cost?

Hol szerezhettem ezt a tollat?
Where could I have gotten this pen?

It is often combined with the conditional to make a request very polite.

Megnézhetném azt a könyvet?
Could I have a look at that book?

Mondhatnék valamit?
Might I say something?

Combined with the past conditional, the potential has the meaning 'could have + past participle'

Megvehetted volna azt az inget.
You could have bought that shirt.

Szorgalmasabban dolgozhattál volna a tervezeten.
You could have worked harder on the draft.

Meghívhattam volna, csak nem akartam.
I could have invited him, I just didn't want to.

The potential combines with the present participle -ó/-ő and the suffix -atlan/-etlen 'without' to form adjectives:

ért	érthető	érthetetlen
understand	understandable	incomprehensible
eszik	**ehető**	**ehetetlen**
eat	edible	inedible
hisz	**hihető**	**hihetetlen**
believe	believable	unbelievable
iszik	**iható**	**ihatatlan**
drink	drinkable	undrinkable
lát	**látható**	**láthatatlan**
see	visible	invisible
olvas	**olvasható**	**olvashatatlan**
read	legible, readable	illegible, unreadable

4.5.3 | The causative: formation

The causative is added to verb stems to denote the subject *has* something done, i.e., the action is not done by the subject directly.

The causative is -at/-et or -tat/-tet and is highly productive, though (for semantic reasons) it cannot be used on all verbs.

The -tat/-tet ending is added to verbs ending in a vowel + t and most polysyllabic verbs:

keres	look for	kerestet	have someone look for
olvas	read	**olvastat**	have someone read
rendel	order	**rendeltet**	have someone order
tisztít	clean	**tisztíttat**	have someone clean

The -at/-et ending is added to verbs ending in a consonant + t and most monosyllabic verbs:

ért	understand	értet	have someone understand
kér	ask for	**kéret**	have someone ask for
mos	wash	**mosat**	have someone wash
vár	wait	**várat**	have someone wait

The following monosyllabic verb stems take the -tat/-tet ending.

ázik	become soaked	**áztat**	soak something
bukik	fail	**buktat**	fail someone
él	live	**éltet**	keep someone alive
jár	go	**jártat**	to have someone/something walk or go
kel	rise	**keltet**	hatch
kopik	wear away	**koptat**	wear something down
lép	step	**léptet**	keep (a horse) at a slow pace
szokik	get used to	**szoktat**	accustom someone to
szopik	suck	**szoptat**	breastfeed
szűnik	cease, stop	**szüntet**	stop, interrupt
ül	sit	**ültet**	plant, have someone sit

As with the potential ending, verbs re-formed in the causative form new stem types. Once attached, the verbs conjugate as any regular verb ending in a short vowel + **t**.

Sample verb conjugations with the causative -at/-et, -tat/-tet.

	Present		Past	
	Indefinite	Definite	Indefinite	Definite
	rendeltet, have sy order	tisztíttat, have sy clean	mosat, have sy wash	kerestet, have sy look for
én	**rendeltetek**	**tisztíttatom**	**mosattam**	**kerestettem**
te	**rendeltetsz**	**tisztíttatod**	**mosattál**	**kerestetted**
ő	**rendeltet**	**tisztíttatja**	**mosatott**	**kerestette**
mi	**rendeltetünk**	**tisztíttatjuk**	**mosattunk**	**kerestettük**
ti	**rendeltettek**	**tisztíttatjátok**	**mosattatok**	**kerestettétek**
ők	**rendeltetnek**	**tisztíttatják**	**mosattak**	**kerestették**

	Subjunctive		Conditional	
	Indefinite	Definite	Indefinite	Definite
	várat, have sy wait	hívat, have sy call	küldet, have sy send	olvastat, have sy read
én	várassak	hívassam	küldetnék	olvastatnám
te	várass(ál)	hívas(sa)d	küldetnél	olvastatnád
ő	várasson	hívassa	küldetne	olvastatná
mi	várassunk	hívassuk	küldetnénk	olvastatnánk
ti	várassatok	hívassátok	küldetnétek	olvastatnátok
ők	várassanak	hívassák	küldetnének	olvastatnák

A verb formed with the causative may add the potential to its stem.

olvas + tat + hat → **olvastathat** may have someone read

rendel + tet + het → **rendeltethet** may have someone order

4.5.4 Use of the causative

The causative is used to denote that it is not the subject, rather someone else who performs the action of the verb. The one who performs the action may or may not be included in the sentence; when the performer is included, it is usually marked with the instrumental case -val/-vel.

Kivasaltattam az ingemet a férjemmel.
I had my husband iron my shirt.

A nővérem elszívatta velem az első cigarettát.
My older sister got me to smoke my first cigarette.

Mátyással hívatott egy taxit.
She had Mátyas call a taxi.

Egy új kabátot varratott az anyjával.
She had her mother sew her a new coat.

If there is no other direct object in the sentence, the performer of the activity is in the accusative case.

A tanár vizsgáztatta a diákokat.
The teacher had the students take an exam.

Minden este a szomszédom sétáltatja a kutyáját.
My neighbor walks her dog every night.

Leültettem a gyerekeket.
I had the children sit down.

The causative ending is sometimes used to make an intransitive verb transitive.

Intransitive	Transitive
bukik fail	**buktat** fail someone
fürdik take a bath	**fürdet** give someone a bath
szűnik cease, stop	**szüntet** stop, interrupt
változik change	**változtat** change

Nagyon megváltozott a férje.
Her husband has really changed.

Tilos megváltoztatni az eredményeket.
It is not allowed to change the results.

Megszűnt a szegénység.
Poverty has ended.

Megszüntették a rendeletet.
They abolished the decree.

4.5.5 *The frequentative: formation*

Frequentatives are added to verb stems to denote that the action is done repetitively, for a lengthy period of time, or without specific aim or purpose.

The most common frequentative ending is **-gat/-get** (for other, less productive frequentative suffixes, see chapter 12 on word formation). It is attached directly to the verb stem; most monosyllabic stems, however, require a linking vowel (o/e/ö) before the frequentative.

néz	watch	**nézeget**	look about
olvas	read	**olvasgat**	read a bit
rendez	organize	**rendezget**	tidy up a bit
üt	strike	**ütöget**	keep on striking

Verbs re-formed in the frequentative form new stem types. Once attached, the verbs conjugate as any verb ending in a short vowel + t.

Sample verb conjugations with the frequentative **-gat/-get**.

	Present		Past	
	Indefinite	Definite	Indefinite	Definite
	nézeget, look about	ütöget, keep striking	mosogat, wash dishes	keverget, keep stirring
én	**nézegetek**	**ütögetem**	**mosogattam**	**kevergettem**
te	**nézegetsz**	**ütögeted**	**mosogattál**	**kevergetted**
ő	**nézeget**	**ütögeti**	**mosogatott**	**kevergette**
mi	**nézegetünk**	**ütögetjük**	**mosogattunk**	**kevergettük**
ti	**nézegettek**	**ütögetitek**	**mosogattatok**	**kevergettétek**
ők	**nézegetnek**	**ütögetik**	**mosogattak**	**kevergették**

	Subjunctive		Conditional	
	Indefinite	Definite	Indefinite	Definite
	sétálgat, stroll about	hívogat, call repeatedly	rendezget, tidy up	olvasgat, read a bit
én	**sétálgassak**	**hívogassam**	**rendezgetnék**	**olvasgatnám**
te	**sétálgass(ál)**	**hívogas(sa)d**	**rendezgetnél**	**olvasgatnád**
ő	**sétálgasson**	**hívogassa**	**rendezgetne**	**olvasgatná**
mi	**sétálgassunk**	**hívogassuk**	**rendezgetnénk**	**olvasgatnánk**
ti	**sétálgassatok**	**hívogassátok**	**rendezgetnétek**	**olvasgatnátok**
ők	**sétálgassanak**	**hívogassák**	**rendezgetnének**	**olvasgatnák**

The frequentative may change the meaning of the verb more radically:

beszél	speak	**beszélget**	chat
hall	hear	**hallgat**	listen, be quiet
kér	ask for	**kéreget**	beg
lát	see	**látogat**	visit
mos	wash	**mosogat**	do the dishes

The frequentative may add the potential to its stem.

| **olvas** | read | **olvasgathat** | may read a bit |
| **néz** | look at | **nézegethet** | may look about |

4.6 Coverbs

Coverbs are prefixes that can be attached to (and subsequently separated from) verbs. Coverbs modify verbs in a variety of ways, including indicating the direction of motion, the manner of an action, and the beginning or completion of an action (aspect). By no means is this the extent of their semantic reach; sometimes coverbs change the meaning of the verb entirely.

Verbs attach only one coverb at a time. The position of coverbs in sentence word order is often affected when introducing focus, quasi-auxiliary verbs and imperatives. See chapter 16 for a complete discussion of word order and coverbs.

In this section we will first examine the general (directional, manner, and aspectual) uses of coverbs and then focus on their more individual uses.

4.6.1 Direction

The most common directional coverbs include **be** 'in', **ki** 'out', **fel** 'up', **le** 'down', **el** 'away', **oda** 'toward there', **ide** 'toward here', **vissza** 'back'. Not surprisingly, verbs of motion are particularly inclined to take coverbs of direction, e.g., **megy** 'go' and **jön** 'come':

| **bemegy** go in | **bejön** come in |
| **kimegy** go out | **kijön** come out |

felmegy go up	**feljön** come up
lemegy go down	**lejön** come down
elmegy go away, leave	**eljön** come away
odamegy go there	**idejön** come here
visszamegy go back	**visszajön** come back

Beteszi a tollat a táskába.
He puts the pen into the bag.

Visszajöttünk a szabadságról.
We have returned from vacation.

Kiszedtem a pénzt a tárcából.
I took the money out of the wallet.

A pincér elviszi a tányérokat.
The waiter takes away the plates.

Felmennek a hegyre.
They are going up the mountain.

Laci lement a boltba kenyérért.
Laci went (down) to the store for bread.

Odament a kerítéshez.
He went over toward the fence.

Kitette a széket a kertbe.
She put the chair out into the garden.

Felszállt a villamosra.
She got on the tram.

Elvették az útlevelemet tőlem.
They took my passport away from me.

Directional coverbs may also be used with verbs with no motion, thereby adding motion to them:

áll stand	**feláll** stand up	**odaáll** stand over there
ül sit	**leül** sit down	**odaül** sit over there
ad give	**visszaad** give back	**bead** turn in, deliver

Géza a széken ül.	Géza is sitting on the chair.
Leült a székre.	He sat down on(to) the chair.
Felállt a székről.	He stood up from the chair.

4.6.2 | *Manner*

Coverbs such as **végig** 'all the way', **agyon** 'all the way', 'to death', **túl** 'beyond', 'too (excessive)', **újra** 'anew' modify the verb with respect to how, or to what extent the action is executed.

ver	beat	**agyonver**	beat to death
él	live	**túlél**	survive
megy	go	**végigmegy**	go all the way
választ	elect	**újraválaszt**	re-elect

Végigmentek a piacon.
They walked all the way through the market.

A szülei túlélték a háborút.
Her parents survived the war.

Újraválasztották a népszerű elnököt.
The popular president was re-elected.

4.6.3 | *Aspect*

In English the past, present and future tenses have several forms, e.g., *I was going*, *I went*, *I have gone* are all past tense forms of the verb 'to go'. Because Hungarian has only one form for each tense, it relies on the use of coverbs and word order to indicate progressive or completed actions. The aspect of the verb is termed *imperfective* when the action is progressive or ongoing; the *perfective* aspect refers to actions that were or will be completed.

Although all coverbs can have a perfectivizing function, the two most common perfectivizing coverbs are **meg** and **el**.

In the past tense, the use of a coverb (perfective aspect) indicates that the action is complete; verbs without coverbs indicate that an action was in progress. In the present tense, the verbs with no coverbs indicate actions in progress with no comment as to completion. Present tense verbs with coverbs, however, tend to be translated into the future tense in English[17] (because for most verbs the completion of the action, in fact, comes at a time after the statement is made).

Írtam egy levelet.	I was writing a letter.	(imperfective)
Megírtam a levelet.	I wrote the letter.	(perfective)
Olvassa a könyvet.	She is reading the book.	(imperfective)
Elolvassa a könyvet.	She will read the book.	(perfective)

In the subjunctive/imperative, there is no tense; the use of coverbs still indicates perfective aspect.

Egyél valamit!	Eat something!
Edd meg a szendvicset!	Eat (up) the sandwich!

Although present tense verbs prefixed with coverbs often indicate future tense, verbs and coverbs may also combine with the future auxiliary **fog**; the aspect is perfective and the meaning is often simply one of emphasis, though it is not necessarily so.

Megtanulja a verset.	She will learn the poem.
Meg fogja tanulni a verset.	She *will* learn the poem.

Conversely, present tense verbs without coverbs combine with the future auxiliary **fog** to indicate imperfective future.

Sírok.	I am crying.
Sírni fogok.	I am going to cry.
Pihen.	She is resting.
Pihenni fog, mikor lesz ideje.	She will rest when she has time.

Imperfective aspect may co-occur with coverbs. Here word order is crucial: the coverb must be removed to a post-verb position.

Átmentem az utcán. (perfective)
I walked across the street.

---

[17] This does not mean, however, that the converse is true, i.e., you may not simply add a coverb to a verb to indicate future tense.

Mentem át az utcán, mikor eszembe jutott, hogy otthon várnak. (imperfective)

I was walking across the street when I remembered that I was expected at home.

Coverbs may also indicate the beginning of an action:

alszik	sleep	**elalszik**	fall asleep
haragszik	be angry	**megharagszik**	get angry
lát	see	**meglát**	espy, catch sight of
sír	cry	**elsírja magát**	burst into tears
szeret	like, love	**megszeret**	take a fondness or liking to

Amióta itt élek, megszerettem ezt a várost.

I have come to love this city since I've been living here.

Nagyon nehéz neki elaludni.

It is very hard for him to fall asleep.

Nagyon haragszik rám. Megharagudott, mikor későn jöttem haza.

She is very angry with me. She got angry when I came home late.

Some verbs occur only with coverbs.

megbetegszik	fall ill
megbénul	become paralyzed
megrészegszik	become drunk
megsüketül	go deaf

4.6.4 *Common uses of some common coverbs*

Coverbs have an infinite number of uses – only the most common are listed here. Simply because a coverb has one meaning with one verb does not mean that any verb can attach to the same coverb and result in the same meaning. Each verb has its own inventory of possible coverbs, and it is sometimes surprising to find what coverbs may occur with certain verbs.[18]

---

[18] One example: **akaszt** 'hang (transitive)':

4.6.4.1 *Meg*

Use **meg** to indicate the completion of an action in the past, present or future.

Megírta a könyvet.	She wrote the book.
Megmosom a kezemet.	I (will) wash my hands.
Megvárlak.	I (will) wait for you (until you come).
Az orvos megvizsgálja a betegeket.	The doctor examines/will examine the patients.

Meg may indicate the beginning of an action:

Úgy megörültem neked, amikor megláttalak!
I was so delighted when I caught sight of you!

Apám két évvel ezelőtt megbetegedett.
My father fell ill two years ago.

Megfázol, ha nem vigyázol jobban magadra.
You will catch cold if you don't take better care of yourself.

Use **meg** to indicate the single instance of an action.

Megcsillant a gyémánt a napfényben.
The diamond flashed in the sunlight.

Megzörrentek a levelek.	The leaves rustled.
Húzd meg azt a kart!	Give that lever a pull!

Meg will often indicate the expected or successful occurrence of an action.

Minden nap megjön a kenyér a sarki boltba.
Every day the bread comes to the corner store. (It is expected to come.)

Megtalálta a pénztárcáját.
He found his wallet. (The use of **meg** presumes he had been looking for it.)

---

felakaszt 'hang up' **Felakasztja a kabátját a fogasra**. He hangs his coat on the rack.

leakaszt 'unhang' **Leakasztja a kabátját a fogasról**. He takes his coat off the rack. (lit., he hangs it down.)

Meg kell keresnem a szemüvegemet.
I have to look for (and find) my glasses. (The use of **meg**
presumes finding the glasses.)

Végre megjött a tavasz!
Spring has finally arrived!

Use **meg** with verbs of communication, to (briefly) utter a statement:

Megmondtam neki a véleményemet.
I gave him my opinion.

Megüzente, hogy jöjjek haza.
She sent word for me to come home.

Megkérdeztem tőle, hogy mikor kell a pénz.
I asked her when she needed the money.

4.6.4.2 | *El*

The coverb el has the directional meaning *away*.

Eltette a meleg ruhát jövő télig.
He put the warm clothes away until next winter.

Elvették a jegyeket tőlünk.
They took (away) our tickets.

Elrúgta a labdát.
He kicked the ball away.

Elkérte tőlem a tollamat.
He asked me for my pen

Use el as a perfectivizing coverb to indicate the completion of an action.

Elolvasta a kötelező könyveket.
He read the required books.

Elvégezte a munkát.
He finished the work.

El may indicate the beginning of an action.

Elindult a vonat.   The train departed.

Elaludt a fiam a vonaton.   My son fell asleep on the train.

Elgondolkozott azon, amit mondtam.
He began to think over what I said.

Elhallgattak a madarak.
The birds fell silent.

El may combine with a verb to indicate the action occurs all the way to a place.

Ugye eljössz a buliba?
You are coming to the party, right?

A fiúk elkísértek bennünket a buszmegállóig.
The boys escorted us to the bus stop.

Use el with verbs to indicate covering over a (wide) area.

A gaz elborította a mezőt.
The field was covered with weeds.

Régen eltakarták az arcukat egy fátyollal.
In the old days they covered their faces with a veil.

El can change the meaning of the verb by indicating the action is done incorrectly.

Elírtam a címét, és most nem találom a házszámát.
I wrote down the wrong address and now I can't find her
building number.

Elnéztem a menetrendet, és lekéstem a vonatot.
I misread the schedule and missed the train.

Use el to mean *apart*.

A szüleim 1990-ben váltak el.
My parents divorced in 1990.

Elszakadt a szoknyám a villamoson.
My skirt tore on the tram.

El is found in construction with the postpositions **előtt, mellett**: the combination results in the meaning 'along'.

Az a kocsi mindig elmegy a házunk előtt.
That car is always going by our house.

Az egész város mellett folyik el a Tisza.
The Tisza flows along the side of the whole city.

Use **el** to indicate using something up.

Elkártyázta az összes pénzét.
He spent all of his money on cards. (lit., He carded away all his money.)

Elittuk az egész havi fizetését.
We drank his whole month's salary.

Elhasználták a cukrot.
They used up the sugar.

El may indicate the lengthy duration of an action.

Jól elbeszélgették a napot.
They talked the whole day through.

Jó sokáig elüldögéltek a kávéházban.
They lounged around a good long time in the coffee shop.

Used with verbs of communication, **el** indicates that something is said or otherwise communicated (all the way) to the end.

Elmesélte az egész történetet.
He told the whole story.

Elmagyarázta, hogy kellett betörni a házba.
He explained at length how he had to break into the house.

Elénekelt nekem egy gyönyörű népdalt.
He sang me a beautiful folksong.

It is useful to compare the uses of **el** and **meg** when combined with the same verbs. When combined with verbs describing a change in physical or mental condition, the coverb **el** indicates an unfortunate turn of events and **meg** indicates an expected or usual change.

Jól meghízott a disznó.	The pig got nice and fat.
Teljesen elhízott, és már alig tud menni.	He got really fat and now can hardly walk.
Megfagyott a víz a mélyhűtőben.	The water froze in the freezer.
Elfagyott a keze.	His hand got frostbite.

73

Szépen megpirult a kenyér a sűtőben.	The bread browned nicely in the oven.
Elpirultam a szégyentől.	I turned red with shame.
Megsóztam a levest.	I put salt in the soup.
Elsóztam a levest.	I put too much salt in the soup.

4.6.4.3 | *Be*

The coverb **be** has the directional meaning *in*, *into*.

Benézett a szobába.	He looked into the room.
Beszálltam a kocsiba.	I got into the car.
Betette a ruhát a szekrénybe.	She put the dress in the closet.
Beszippantotta a friss levegőt.	He breathed in the fresh air.

Be combines with verbs to mean 'cover entirely', 'envelop' by some means or action.

Betakarta a gyereket, hogy ne fázzon az éjjel.
She covered up the child, so he wouldn't get cold in the night.

Befestettem feketére a székeket.
I painted the chairs black.

Teljesen befedte a házat a hó.
The house was completely covered with snow.

Kend be az orrodat, hogy ne égjen le!
Put some cream on your nose so it doesn't burn!

Use the coverb **be** with verbs meaning 'close', 'fasten'.

Becsukta az ablakot.	He closed the window.
Begomboltam a kabátomat.	I buttoned up my coat.
Becsomagoltam az ajándékot.	I wrapped up the present.
Be kell varrni a szakadást a nadrágján.	He has to sew up the tear on his pants.
Befűztem a cipőmet.	I tied my shoes.

4.6.4.4 | *Ki*

The coverb **ki** has the directional meaning 'out'.

Kimentek a kertbe.	They went out to the garden.
Kiveszik az almát a kosárból.	They will take the apples out of the basket.
Kivitte a szemetet.	He took out the garbage.
Kinéztek az ablakon.	They looked out the window.

The coverb **ki** often combines with verbs to mean 'undo'.

Kifűztem a cipőmet.
I untied my shoes.

Kibontották az összes csomagot.
They opened up all of the packages.

Ki kell csomagolni a bőröndöket, mielőtt elmegyünk várost nézni.
We have to unpack before we go out to see the town.

Ki combines with verbs to indicate selection.

Kinéztem magamnak egy szép új autót.
I've picked out a nice new car for myself.

Kikeresték és kiírták az ismeretlen szavakat a szótárból.
They looked up and wrote out the unknown words in the dictionary.

Kiválasztotta a legszebb rózsát.
She chose the most beautiful rose.

4.6.4.5 | *Fel*

The coverb **fel** has the directional meaning 'up'.

Felmászott a hegyre.	She climbed up the mountain.
Felnéztünk a csillagokra.	We looked up at the stars.
Feltette a vázát a polcra.	She put the vase up on the shelf.
Felszaladt a lépcsőn.	He ran up the stairs.

Fel combines with verbs to mean 'on'.

Felvette a legszebb öltönyét.
He put on his best suit.

Felpróbált egy új kabátot, de nem tetszett neki.
She tried on a new coat, but she didn't like it.

Te soha nem írod fel, amit mondok neked.
You never write down (lit., write on) what I tell you.

Use fel with verbs to mean 'furnish or supply with something'.

Felfegyverezték a hadsereget.
They armed the troops.

Ebből a pénzből nem tudok felruházkodni.
I can't provide myself with clothes with this money.

Felhatalmazta az ügyvédet, hogy eladja a házát.
She gave the lawyer the authority to sell her house.

The coverb fel is used with verbs of motion to indicate 'turning over' or 'upside down'.

Felfordították a hajót.
They capsized the boat.

Az utóbbi hír felkavarta a gyomrát.
The recent news turned his stomach.

Felborította a széket.
She knocked the chair over.

Teljesen fel van fordítva a ház.
The house is a mess (lit., turned upside down).

Fel combines with verbs to mean 'appear from somewhere'.

A kislány hirtelen felbukkant a bokor mögül.
The little girl suddenly appeared from behind the bush.

Ki fedezte fel a rádiumot?
Who discovered radium?

Hirtelen felkerültek a feketelistára.
They suddenly turned up on the blacklist.

Fel is used with verbs describing the change of a mental state denoting the onset of the change.

Korán ébredtem fel.
I woke up early.

Mire feleszmélt, a rablók már eltűntek.
By the time he came to, the burglars had disappeared.

Feldühödtem, mikor hallottam, mi történt.
I became enraged when I heard what had happened.

Fel may indicate the (sudden) beginning of an action.

Felsírt, mikor az orvos beleszúrta a tűt.
He cried out when the doctor stuck in the needle.

Felragyogott az arca, mikor megpillantotta a régóta várt barátnőjét.
His face shone when he caught sight of his long awaited girlfriend.

| 4.6.4.6 | *Le*

The coverb **le** has the directional meaning 'down'.

Mikor fog leszállni a repülőgép?
When will the plane land?

Gyere le onnan!
Come down from there!

Lefeküdt az ágyra, és rögtön elaludt.
She lay down on the bed and fell asleep immediately.

Lenéztek az udvarra, hogy ott van-e a kutya.
They looked down into the courtyard to see if the dog was there.

Le combines with verbs to mean 'off'.

Lesegíted a kabátomat?
Will you help me off with my coat?

Levette a cuccait az asztalról.
She took her things off the table.

Letört az odvas ág a fáról.
The rotten branch broke off the tree.

Le akart szállni a villamosról.
He wanted to get off the tram.

Le combines with verbs meaning 'to remove or take away', 'relinquish', 'give up'.

Lefegyverezték a hadsereget.
The troops were disarmed.

Anne Boleynt 1536-ban fejezték le.
Anne Boleyn was beheaded in 1536.

Télre kellett leszerelni a hajót.
The ship had to be dismantled for winter.

Le kell szoknia a dohányzásról.
He must give up smoking.

Bármit mondasz, nem tudsz lebeszélni arról, hogy elmenjek!
No matter what you say you can not talk me out of going.

Le is used with verbs meaning 'to cover the surface of something'.

Le kell takarni az ágyat valami szebb takaróval.
We have to cover the bed with a prettier spread.

Lehunytam a szememet, hogy pihenjek egy kicsit.
I closed my eyes to rest a bit.

Use the coverb le to indicate 'copying', 'reproducing' by some means.

Leírtam a címét a noteszembe.
I wrote his address into my notebook.

Le kell fényképezned azt a szobrot!
You have to take a picture of that statue!

Bár nem lett volna szabad, lemásolta a könyvet.
She made a copy of the book though she wasn't really allowed to.

Le combines with verbs to mean 'to lessen or reduce in some way'.

Egy idő után lecsillapodott a fájdalom.
After a while the pain lessened.

Lefogytál, amióta utoljára láttalak.
You have lost weight since I last saw you.

Lelassította a lépteit, mikor megpillantotta az idegent.
He slowed his walk when he saw the stranger.

Le may provide a negative connotation to verbs.

Bár nem is ismertem a férfit, rögtön letegezett.
Even though I didn't know the man, he used the familiar te form
with me.

Az igazgató, sajnos, nagyon lenézi a kollégáit.
Unfortunately the director looks down on his colleagues.

Jól leszidta a sógorát, és azóta nem beszélnek egymással.
He really put his brother-in-law down and since then they don't
speak.

4.6.5 | More coverbs

Many more coverbs exist in addition to those outlined in the preceding
section. Coverbs are derived from all parts of speech; sometimes it is only
a writing convention that distinguishes coverbs from adverbs (i.e., they
are written as one word with the verb, not two).

Jólesett a séta.   The walk felt good.   (**jól** is a coverb)

Jól érzi magát.   He feels well.   (**jól** is an adverb)

Egyetértek veled.   I agree with you.   (**egyet** is a coverb)

Egyet sóhajtott.   She gave a sigh.   (**egyet** is an adverbial)

Some pronominalized cases may serve as coverbs; these are often restricted
to the third person singular form.

bele	**Beletette a cukrot a kávéba.**	She put the sugar into the coffee.
rá	**Ránézett a fiúra.**	He looked at the boy.
rajta	**Rajtakaptam a hazugságon**	I caught him in a lie.
hozzá	**Hozzáfordultam jó tanácsért.**	I turned to him for good advice.
neki	**Nekimentem a falnak.**	I bumped into the wall.

Many postpositions may also serve as coverbs.

át	**Kétszer kellett átírni a szöveget.** They had to rewrite the text twice.
alá	**Aláírta az oklevelet.** She signed the document.
ellen	**Makacsul ellenálltak nekem.** They stubbornly resisted me.
keresztül	**Keresztülmentek a mezőn.** They passed through the field.
körül	**Körülnéztünk az üzletben.** We looked around the shop.
mellé	**Mellébeszéltek.** They didn't speak to the issue. (lit., They spoke beside it.)
túl	**Túlbecsüli a könyv értékét.** He overestimates the value of the book.
végig	**Végigjártuk a környéket.** We walked throught the whole area.

Additional important coverbs include the following.

elő	forth	**Elővették a könyvüket.** They took out their books.
félre	aside, mis-	**Félretettek egy kis pénzt a jövőre.** They put some money aside for the future. **Félreértettem a helyzetet.** I misunderstood the situation.
fenn	above, up	**Fenntartotta magát a vízben.** He stayed afloat in the water. (lit, kept himself up)
hátra	backward	**Hátramaradtunk, mert fáradtak voltunk.** We fell behind because we were tired.
haza	homeward	**Hazajött a hétvégére.** She came home for the weekend.

oda	toward there	**Odamegyünk a kirakathoz.**
		We will walk over to the display window.
ott	there	**Szó nélkül otthagyta az állását.**
		He left his job without a word.
össze	together	**A pulóverem összement a forró vízben.**
		My sweater shrank in the hot water.
		(lit., went together)
szét	apart	**Szétesett a polc a nappaliban.**
		The shelf fell apart in the living room.
tovább	further	**Továbbadta az üzenetet.**
		She passed the message on.
utána	after	**Utána tudsz nézni az ügynek?**
		Can you look into the matter?
vissza	back	**Hat órakor jön vissza a munkahelyről.**
		She comes back from work at six o'clock.

Coverbs

Chapter 5

Nouns

5.1 Articles

5.1.1 *Definite article*

The definite article is **a** or **az** 'the', the latter reserved for use before words beginning with a vowel. It does not agree in case or number with its noun.

a ház	the house	**a házban**	in the house
az esemény	the event	**az események**	the events

5.1.1.1

The definite article is used similarly as in English with the following additional uses:

- before possessed nominals: *a* **gyerekem** 'my child' (except in 'have' constructions)

- before possessive pronouns: *az* **enyém** 'mine'

- before nominals with a demonstrative pronoun: **ez** *a* **gyerek** 'this child'

- before many abstract nouns: **Ilyen** *az* **élet**. 'Such is life.'

- before a noun in order to give it a generic connotation: **Szeretem** *a* **banánt**. 'I like bananas.'

- in colloquial speech before a person's name: **Kedves** *a* **Péter**. 'Péter is nice.'

5.1.2 | Indefinite article

The indefinite article is **egy** 'a', 'an'.

Tegnap este elolvastam egy könyvet. I read a book last night.

5.1.3 | Zero article

There are some cases where neither article is used:

5.1.3.1

Existential (there is/there are) and 'have' constructions:

Szép fa van a kertben.	There is a beautiful tree in the garden.
Neki gyönyörű háza van.	She has a beautiful house.

5.1.3.2

Before predicate nouns:

Csilla énekesnő, Tamás rendőr.	Csilla is a singer, Tamás is a policeman.

5.1.3.3

Finally, articles need not be used before indefinite subjects, objects or adverbials occurring immediately before the verb. (When occurring after the verb, however, there is usually an article.)

Minden este János levest főz.	János makes soup every night.
A Kovácsék (egy) szép lakásban laknak.	The Kovácses live in a nice apartment.
Abban a lakásban (egy) kedves család lakik.	A nice family lives in that apartment.

5.2 Nouns and suffixes

5.2.1 Suffixes

Hungarian is an agglutinative language, i.e., suffixes and prefixes can be attached to words to change their meaning and/or function in a sentence. Suffixes can be added to nouns to indicate plurality, possession, location, manner, etc. In fact, several suffixes can be added to the same word; for example we may attach two suffixes to the word **zseb** 'pocket': the plural **-k**, and a locative case **-ben** 'in' to yield **zsebekben** 'in pockets'.

5.2.2 Vowel harmony

For the most part vowel harmony is maintained when adding suffixes; most suffixes come with two or more vowel choices either within the suffix itself or as a linking vowel between the stem and the suffix. Examples are abundant: the illative case has the variants **-ban/ben**; the allative case has the variants **-hoz/-hez/-höz**.

5.2.3 Gender

There is no gender in Hungarian in either nouns or pronouns.

5.2.4 Stem alternation

Suffixes, e.g., the plural, cases, and possessive suffixes, are attached directly to the end of a word, sometimes creating a change in the word stem, e.g., **ló** 'horse' has the stem **lov-** when forming the plural. It is helpful to recognize the different types of noun stems since each type attaches endings in its own way. Sometimes the difference in the way nouns decline is subtle, hence careful attention must be paid to the differences. The rest of this chapter classifies nouns according to their stem alternations.

5.3 Noun stems and the nominative case – singular and plural

Although not all suffixes cause a change in the noun stem, many do. For example, the delative case -ról 'off' attaches to the stem ló 'horse' with no change in the stem: lóról 'off the horse'. When suffixing the plural -k, however, the noun reveals another stem, in this instance, a v-stem: lovak 'horses'.

The singular nominative case is the dictionary entry form; however, almost all of the information about a noun stem is revealed when forming the nominative plural. Therefore noun stems and the nominative plural are presented simultaneously. Throughout this book reference will be made to noun stems and how the plural is formed. Any idiosyncrasies with respect to noun stems and other suffixes are found under the individual suffix entry. A list of highly irregular noun stems not presented here is found in appendix 3.

PLURAL: The plural marker is -k. It is not used after numbers or other expressions of quantity – these are always followed by the singular. There is a separate plural paradigm for the possessive declension – there the -k plural is not used. Cases may be added to words already formed in the plural.

Depending on the stem of the noun, the plural -k may or may not need a linking vowel preceding it; the plural -k is attached to nouns according to the following rules. (For discussion of vowel harmony rules, see chapter 3.)

5.3.1 Nouns ending in a vowel

If a noun ends in a vowel, no linking vowel is needed before the plural suffix; if the final vowel is a or e, it must be lengthened to á or é before the plural -k; otherwise, simply add -k.

Word final vowel

	Noun ends in **a** or **e**		Noun ends in other vowels[1]	
	Singular	Plural	Singular	Plural
lamp	**lámpa**	**lámpák**	woman	**nő**	**nők**
bag	**táska**	**táskák**	car	**kocsi**	**kocsik**
cup	**csésze**	**csészék**	boat	**hajó**	**hajók**
lesson	**lecke**	**leckék**	gate	**kapu**	**kapuk**
			needle	**tű**	**tűk**

5.3.2 | *Nouns ending in a consonant*

When nouns end in a consonant they require linking vowels before the plural (and other suffixes, too). Most nouns require the linking vowel choice o/e/ö before these suffixes, a smaller number require the vowel choice a/e.

Some noun types also exhibit a change in the stem when adding linking vowels. The following are the most important noun stems grouped according to linking vowel choice and stem changes:

5.3.2.1 | Nouns requiring the linking vowel *a/e*

5.3.2.1.1 | *Low vowel nouns*[2]

This is a finite group of just over 100 nouns. There is no way of identifying these words by simply looking at them, hence they must be memorized. (A list of these nouns is found in appendix 3.) This group of nouns has a further subdivision: those that don't lose the length of the last vowel when suffixing and those that do. (Of course, if the word does not have a long vowel in the final syllable, loss of length is irrelevant.)

---

[1] Except **férfi** 'man' which has the plural **férfiak**.
[2] So called because the linking vowels these nouns require are the low vowel a/e. (Thus technically, v-stems and -**alom**/-**elem** volcabulary are low vowel nouns too.)

Low vowel nouns

	Loses length			No loss of length	
	Singular	Plural		Singular	Plural
hand	**kéz**	**kezek**	house	**ház**	**házak**
letter	**levél**	**levelek**	book	**könyv**	**könyvek**
glass	**pohár**	**poharak**	deer	**őz**	**őzek**
road	**út**	**utak**	pen	**toll**	**tollak**
water	**víz**	**vizek**	matter	**ügy**	**ügyek**

| 5.3.2.1.2 | *V-stems* |

These nouns have a stem quite different from the nominative. The nominative ends in a long vowel, but the stem to which the plural ending attaches ends in a **v** preceded by a short vowel;[3] this vowel may change in quality as well as length. For example, **ló** 'horse' has the stem **lov-**, but **tó** 'lake' has the stem **tav-**. There is some variation in suffixing within this group that will be pointed out for each suffix. A complete list of these nouns is found in appendix 3.

v-stems

	Singular	Plural		Singular	Plural
pipe	**cső**	**csövek**	work	**mű**	**művek**
grass	**fű**	**füvek**	maggot	**nyű**	**nyüvek**
snow	**hó**	**havak**	word	**szó**	**szavak**
stone	**kő**	**kövek**	lake	**tó**	**tavak**
horse	**ló**	**lovak**	stem	**tő**	**tövek**

---

[3] Except for **mű: műv-** where the vowel preceding v remains long.

5.3.2.1.3 -alom, -elem *nouns*

A large class of nouns ends in the derivation **-alom** or **-elem**. These decline as a combination of both fleeting vowel (see below) and low-vowel nouns,[4] i.e., the last vowel is omitted and a/e is the linking vowel choice.

-alom/-elem nouns					
	Singular	Plural		Singular	Plural
reign	**uralom**	**uralmak**	mystery	**rejtelem**	**rejtelmek**
power	**hatalom**	**hatalmak**	feeling	**érzelem**	**érzelmek**
reward	**jutalom**	**jutalmak**	mercy	**kegyelem**	**kegyelmek**

5.3.2.2 Nouns requiring the linking vowel *o/e/ö*

5.3.2.2.1 *Fleeting vowel nouns*

The last vowel of the noun is omitted when suffixing the plural **-k**. This is a large group of nouns that, like the low vowel nouns, must simply be memorized, although a pattern emerges with familiarity: fleeting vowel nouns have **o**, **e**, or **ö** in the last syllable and a final consonant of **l**, **m**, **n**, **ny**, **r**, **sz**, **s**, **k**, **g** and, less commonly, **cs** or **ly**.

Fleeting vowel					
			BACK VOWEL		
			Singular	Plural	
		bush	**bokor**	**bokrok**	
		tower	**torony**	**tornyok**	

FRONT VOWEL, LAST VOWEL UNROUNDED			FRONT VOWEL, LAST VOWEL ROUNDED		
	Singular	Plural		Singular	Plural
twin	**iker**	**ikrek**	nail	**köröm**	**körmök**
strawberry	**eper**	**eprek**	mirror	**tükör**	**tükrök**

---

[4] Except **cimbalom** 'Hungarian cymbalo' which is a fleeting vowel word.

5.3.2.2.2 | Regular nouns

Most nouns are of this type – negatively defined as not belonging to any of the previous types. The linking vowel o/e/ö is supplied before the plural suffix -k.

Regular nouns

		BACK VOWEL	
		Singular	Plural
	hat	**kalap**	**kalapok**
	paper	**papír**	**papírok**
	plate	**tányér**	**tányérok**
	drawer	**fiók**	**fiókok**

FRONT VOWEL, LAST VOWEL UNROUNDED			FRONT VOWEL, LAST VOWEL ROUNDED		
	Singular	Plural		Singular	Plural
chair	**szék**	**székek**	crime	**bűn**	**bűnök**
law	**törvény**	**törvények**	acquaintance	**ismerős**	**ismerősök**
notebook	**füzet**	**füzetek**	fruit	**gyümölcs**	**gyümölcsök**

5.3.4 | *Summary of plural formation*

Nouns: plural

Ends in a vowel		Ends in a consonant				
final vowel is **a** or **e**	other final vowel	low vowel (**v**-stems listed separately)		-alom/ -elem	fleeting vowel	regular
lengthen vowel		stem loses length	no change in stem	last vowel elides		no change in stem
add **-k**		add **a/e** + **-k**			add **o/e/ö** + **-k**	

5.4 Number and usage

5.4.1 Singular

The singular is unmarked. In addition to the standard use of the singular to mark non-plural items, the singular is used in some constructions differently than in English.

5.4.1.1

The singular is used after numbers and other expressions of quantity.

Hat *ló* van az istállóban.   There are six horses in the stable.

Hány *diák* van a teremben? How many students are in the classroom?

5.4.1.2

The singular is used with paired body parts and the clothing or accessories that accompany them.

kéz	hands	**láb**	legs; feet	**szem**	eyes
kesztyű	gloves	**cipő**	shoes	**szemüveg**	glasses
		nadrág	pants		

Koszos a cipő.   The shoes are dirty.

Drága volt a szemüveg.   The glasses were expensive.

If specific reference to only one of the pair is required, use **fél** 'half'.[5]

fél szem one eye   **fél kéz** one hand   **fél láb** one leg

Csak fél szemmel követte az eseményeket.
He followed the events only half-heartedly. (lit., 'with half an eye')

---

[5] This does not work with **cipő**, however; **félcipő** denotes a kind of shoe, not a single shoe.

5.4.1.3

The singular may be used when referring to a general category (the definite
article is usually used in these constructions).

Az *alma* a sarokban, a *körte* a polcon van.
The apples are in the corner, the pears are on the shelf.

A *bálna* a legnagyobb emlősállat.
Whales are the largest mammals.

5.4.2 | Plural

In Hungarian the plural is used as in English except for those areas
described previously in the usage of the singular. The plural -k is not
used in the possessive paradigm where another plural (-i-) is used (see
section 8.2).

The plural declension of nouns is formed by simply adding the cases to
the plural form of the noun. The temporal, distributive and sociative cases
are not used in the plural.

a diákok the students **a diákokról** about the students

a gépek the machines **a gépekben** in the machines

When forming the plural accusative, the linking vowel a/e is always
required after the plural -k.

nominative		*accusative*
kutyák	dogs	**kutyákat**
levelek	leaves	**leveleket**

Chapter 6
The case system

Hungarian has an extensive case system. Cases are used to mark the grammatical function of words in a sentence: the nominative case marks the subject; the accusative case marks the direct object. They are also used adverbially: they may indicate place, time, manner. Most often case-marked words correspond to prepositional phrases in English (Hungarian has no prepositions): for example **könyv** 'book' marked with the inessive case **-ben** 'in' becomes **könyvben** 'in (a) book'.

Cases attach to the ends of words; they may follow the plural suffix **-k** or possessive suffixes. Although one or more suffixes may precede them, cases are always the final suffix of a word: **könyv + ek + ben** 'book + plural suffix + inessive case' → **könyvekben** 'in books'. Cases may also be attached to nouns already marked for possession: **a könyvem** 'my book' plus the inessive case yields **a könyvemben** 'in my book'. Although most commonly used with nouns, cases may also attach to adjectives, numerals, and demonstrative and interrogative pronouns. Cases do not attach to most personal pronouns – there is a separate paradigm for these (see section 7.1.2). The complete paradigm of cases is called a declension.

Cases attach directly to the end of a word; the following stem alternations occur regularly:

(a) word-final **a** or **e** lengthens to **á, é**, respectively[1]
(b) the accusative **-t**, superessive **-n**, distributive **-nként**, sociative **-stul/ -stül**, and distributive-temporal **-nta/-nte** all require linking vowels when suffixing to consonant-final stems. This may trigger other changes in the word stem.

---

[1] The two exceptions are the temporal (**-kor**) and the essive-formal (**-ként**); here there is no lengthening of the final vowel.

The Hungarian case system

Grammatical cases

nominative	——	*no ending; marks the subject*
accusative	**-t**	*marks the direct object*

Locative cases

illative	**-ba/-be**	into
inessive	**-ban/-ben**	in
elative	**-ból/-ből**	out of, out from
sublative	**-ra/-re**	onto
superessive	**(-o/-e/-ö)-n**	on, at
delative	**-ról/-ről**	off, from, about
allative	**-hoz/-hez/-höz**	toward
adessive	**-nál/-nél**	near, at
ablative	**-tól/-től**	(away) from

Oblique cases

dative	**-nak/-nek**	to, for
instrumental	**-val/-vel**	with
translative	**-vá/-vé**	(turning) into
causal-final	**-ért**	for the purpose of
essive-formal	**-ként**	as
terminative	**-ig**	until, up to
distributive	**(-o/-a/-e/-ö) -nként**	per, each

Less productive cases

temporal	**-kor**	at (plus time expression)
distributive-temporal	**(-o/-e/-ö)-nta**	per, every (plus time expression)
sociative	**(-o/-a/-e/-ö/) -stul/-stül**	(together) with
locative	**-t/(-o/-e/-ö)-tt**	at

Vowel harmony is maintained when suffixing cases. Several cases have a three-way vowel harmony choice (e.g., the allative **-hoz/-hez/-höz**); most cases, however have only a front or back vowel choice (e.g., the elative **-ból/-ből** or the adessive **-nál/-nél**) and several cases offer no choice in vowel harmony (e.g., the terminative **-ig**).

The many cases in Hungarian may be divided into three groups: (1) the grammatical cases (nominative and accusative), (2) the locative cases (indicating place and/or motion to or from a place) and (3) the oblique cases (all the rest). All the locative and oblique cases will be referred to by both their name and shape (e.g., 'adessive **-nál/-nél**').

In addition to the productive cases, there are several more unproductive cases found in only limited use. These are dealt with at the end of the chapter.

6.1 Grammatical cases

6.1.1 Nominative

The nominative is the 'zero' case, i.e., there is no case-marking on the word. It is the citation form for nouns and adjectives in the dictionary.

6.1.1.1

Subjects are in the nominative case.

Elindult a vonat.	The train departed.
A lányok az egyetemen találkoztak.	The girls met at the university.

6.1.1.2

The nominative case is used as a modifier of quantity.

Egy korsó sört rendelt.	She ordered a mug of beer.
Egy fej salátát kellett vennem.	I had to buy a head of lettuce.
Megivott egy csésze teát.	He drank a cup of tea.

6.1.1.3

The objects of most postpositions are in the nominative. (See section 9.4 for exceptions.)

A függöny mögött találtam egy ceruzát.
I found a pencil behind the curtain.

Betette a táskát az asztal alá.
She put her bag down under the table.

6.1.1.4

If, in a possessive construction, the possessor immediately precedes the possessed item, the possessor may be in the nominative case. (See chapter 8 for complete rules on possession.)

Elkértem Zsuzsa tollát.
I asked for Zsuzsa's pen.

Kíváncsi volt a gyerek véleményére.
He was interested in the child's opinion.

6.1.1.5

Some time expressions use the nominative case.

Time expressions ending in the word **nap** 'day':

Minden nap/egész nap/vasárnap tanul.
She studies every day/all day/on Sunday.

Time expressions of 'ago' and 'since' formed with the possessive:

Már három hete van itt.   He's been here for three weeks already.

Hét hónapja utazott el.   He left seven months ago.

6.1.2 | Accusative: -t

6.1.2.1 Formation

The accusative -t is attached in much the same way as the plural -k with one difference: within the group of regular nouns there is a division.

Regular nouns ending in the consonants **j, l, ly, n, ny, r, s, sz, z, zs** require no linking vowel when suffixing the accusative case.[2] Regular nouns ending in any other consonant still require the linking vowel **o/e/ö**.

The table opposite gives the accusative for the different noun stem types. The plural nominative forms are provided here to illustrate the similarities and differences in suffixing (note that the only difference is found where the regular nouns require no linking vowel).

When suffixing the accusative case to a plural noun, the linking vowel **a/e** is always required.

6.1.2.2 Usage

6.1.2.2.1

The accusative case marks the direct object of the verb.

Felolvastam a leveleket az apámnak.
I read the letters to my father.

Jó napot kívánok.
Good day! (I wish you a good day.)

Meleg ruhát vettünk fel.
We put on warm clothes.

6.1.2.2.2

The accusative case may also be used in some time expressions:

Egy hetet töltöttünk a Balatonon.
We spent a week at the Balaton.

6.1.2.2.3

The accusative may modify a verb:

Nagyot sóhajtott.   He gave a big sigh.

Jót aludtak.   They slept well.

---

[2] Note that it does not matter what the final consonant is for low vowel or fleeting vowel words – they always require a linking vowel.

Accusative case suffixing

Noun stem types		Nominative singular	Accusative singular	Nominative plural
stems ending in	lamp	**lámpa**	**lámpát**	**lámpák**
a or **e**:	cup	**csésze**	**csészét**	**csészék**
stems ending in	woman	**nő**	**nőt**	**nők**
other vowels	car	**kocsi**	**kocsit**	**kocsik**
	boat	**hajó**	**hajót**	**hajók**
	gate	**kapu**	**kaput**	**kapuk**
	needle	**tű**	**tűt**	**tűk**
low vowel nouns	road	**út**	**utat**	**utak**
(lose length)	hand	**kéz**	**kezet**	**kezek**
low-vowel nouns	house	**ház**	**házat**	**házak**
(no loss of length)	pen	**toll**	**tollat**	**tollak**
	book	**könyv**	**könyvet**	**könyvek**
	deer	**őz**	**őzet**	**őzek**
v-stems[3]	lake	**tó**	**tavat**	**tavak**
	pipe	**cső**	**csövet**	**csövek**
-alom/-elem	reward	**jutalom**	**jutalmat**	**jutalmak**
	mystery	**rejtelem**	**rejtelmet**	**rejtelmek**
fleeting vowel	bush	**bokor**	**bokrot**	**bokrok**
	strawberry	**eper**	**epret**	**eprek**
	mirror	**tükör**	**tükröt**	**tükrök**
regular noun	plate	**tányér**	**tányért**	**tányérok**
ending in **j, l, ly,**	painting	**festmény**	**festményt**	**festmények**
n, ny, r, s, sz, z, zs	acquaintance	**ismerős**	**ismerőst**	**ismerősök**
other regular	hat	**kalap**	**kalapot**	**kalapok**
nouns	chair	**szék**	**széket**	**székek**
	fruit	**gyümölcs**	**gyümölcsöt**	**gyümölcsök**

---

[3] Two exceptions are: **szó** 'word' **szót** *(acc.)*, **jó** 'good' **jót** *(acc.)*

6.2 Locative case system

The locative cases serve mostly as adverbials and answer the question 'where', although they have other semantic uses as well.

6.2.1 Formation

The locative cases are attached directly to the end of the word. They may be attached to words already formed for the plural or the possessive. All the locative cases require that words ending in **a** or **e** lengthen the vowel to **á**, **é**, respectively; for words ending in any other vowel, the cases attach directly with no change in the stem.

With the exception of the superessive case **-n**, all the locative cases attach directly to stems ending in a consonant without requiring a linking vowel or making any changes in the stem of the word.

The superessive case requires the linking vowel **o/e/ö** when suffixed to all words ending in a consonant (the superessive makes no distinction between low vowel and regular nouns). For **v**-stem vocabulary, the **v**-stem is required; **-alom/-elem** vocabulary and fleeting vowel words omit the last vowel before suffixing the superessive case.

The table opposite illustrates the suffixing of locative cases with respect to noun type. Because the superessive **-n** case suffixes differently it is in a column of its own; all other locative cases suffix identically and are represented in the table by the inessive case **-ban/-ben**.

6.2.2 Usage

The locative cases of Hungarian form a system with respect to three parameters of motion: **motion toward, no motion, motion away,**[4] and three parameters of space: **interior, exterior, near.** Thus there is a case ending corresponding to the English prepositions 'into', 'in', 'out of', 'from', 'onto', 'on', 'off'.

---

[4] Here, 'no motion' means there is no explicit motion *to* or *from* a place; there may, however be motion within the space defined under 'no motion', e.g.,

Sétálnak a parkban. They are walking in the park.

Suffixing of locative cases

Noun stem types		Nominative singular	Superessive -n	All other locative cases e.g., -ban/-ben
stems ending in	lamp	**lámpa**	**lámpán**	**lámpában**
a or **e**	cup	**csésze**	**csészén**	**csészében**
stems ending in	woman	**nő**	**nőn**	**nőben**
other vowels	car	**kocsi**	**kocsin**	**kocsiban**
	boat	**hajó**	**hajón**	**hajóban**
	gate	**kapu**	**kapun**	**kapuban**
	needle	**tű**	**tűn**	**tűben**
low-vowel	road	**út**	**úton**	**útban**
	hand	**kéz**	**kézen**	**kézben**
and	house	**ház**	**házon**	**házban**
	book	**könyv**	**könyvön**	**könyvben**
regular nouns	plate	**tányér**	**tányéron**	**tányérban**
	chair	**szék**	**széken**	**székben**
	fruit	**gyümölcs**	**gyümölcsön**	**gyümölcsben**
v-stems	lake	**tó**	**tavon**	**tóban**
	pipe	**cső**	**csövön**	**csőben**
alom/-elem	reward	**jutalom**	**jutalmon**	**jutalomban**
	mystery	**rejtelem**	**rejtelmen**	**rejtelemben**
fleeting vowel	bush	**bokor**	**bokron**	**bokorban**
	strawberry	**eper**	**epren**	**eperben**
	mirror	**tükör**	**tükrön**	**tükörben**

Locative system: parameters of motion and space			
	motion toward ⇨ ⇨ ●	no motion ●	motion away ● ⇨ ⇨
interior	**-ba/-be** *illative*	**-ban/-ben** *inessive*	**-ból/-ből** *elative*
exterior	**-ra/-re** *sublative*	**-(o/e/ö) n** *superessive*	**-ról/-ről** *delative*
near	**-hoz/-hez/-höz** *allative*	**-nál/-nél** *adessive*	**-tól/-től** *ablative*

6.2.2.1 | Interior

The interior set of cases correspond to the English prepositions *in*, *into*, *out of*, *from (the inside of)*. They are used with

(a) geographic names including countries; **Angliában** 'in England' (except **Magyarország** 'Hungary');
(b) most cities outside of Hungary, **Párizsból** 'from Paris';
(c) cities within Hungary whose final consonant is **m, n, ny, j, r**: **Debrecenbe** 'to Debrecen'; **Tihanyba** 'to Tihany';
(d) interiors of objects, buildings, and other spaces; **a fiókban** 'in the drawer', **a szívemben** 'in my heart'.

6.2.2.1.1

The illative case **-ba/-be** is used to express motion to the interior of a place.

Bemegyek a régi házba.   I am going into the old house.

Imre elment Olaszországba.   Imre went to Italy.

Zsuzsa betett egy tollat a zsebébe.   Zsuzsa put a pen into her pocket.

6.2.2.1.2

The inessive case -**ban**/-**ben** is used to express no motion in(side) a place.

Géza olvas a kertben. Géza is reading in the garden.

Kétemeletes házban lakom. I live in a two-storey house.

Három könyv van a There are three books in my
táskámban. bag.

6.2.2.1.3

The elative case -**ból**/-**ből** is used to express motion out from the interior
of a place:

A gyerekek kifutottak az teremből.
The children run out of the classroom.

Kitéptem egy lapot a füzetemből.
I tore a page out of my notebook.

Melyik városból jössz?
From which city are you coming?

6.2.2.2 Exterior

The exterior cases correspond to the English prepositions 'on', 'at', 'onto',
'off', 'from (the surface of)'. They are used with

(a) most place names within Hungary (or places that used to be
governed by Hungary): **Budapesten** 'in Budapest';
(b) the name of Hungary itself: **Magyarországról** 'from Hungary';
(c) public transportation: **villamoson** 'on a tram';
(d) events: **sportmérkőzésen** 'at a sports match'; **hangversenyre** 'to a
concert';
(e) surfaces and open spaces: **az asztalra** 'onto the table', **falon** 'on a
wall', **jégen** 'on ice'.

6.2.2.2.1

The sublative case -**ra**/-**re** is used to express motion toward an exterior.

Elmegyünk Budapestre. We are going to Budapest.

A táskám leesett a földre.	My bag fell to the floor.
Felszállok erre az autóbuszra.	I will get on this bus.

6.2.2.2.2

The superessive case (o/e/ö) is used to express a position on or at an exterior.

Híres egyetemen dolgozunk.	We work at a famous university.
Ilona Magyarországon lakik.	Ilona lives in Hungary.
A szótár az asztalon van.	The dictionary is on the table.

6.2.2.2.3

The delative case -ról/-ről is used to express motion away from an exterior.

A szótár leesett az asztalról.	The dictionary fell off the table.
Tegnap feljöttek Pécsről.	They came up from Pécs yesterday.
Levette a hirdetést a falról.	She took the advertisement off the wall.

6.2.2.3 | Near

The near cases correspond roughly to the English prepositions 'near(by)', 'at', 'with', 'toward', 'away from'. They are used to express positions at, near, or away from the vicinity of

(a) vertical objects: **ajtóhoz** 'toward a door' **a fánál** 'by the tree';
(b) people: **Kingához** 'toward Kinga';
(c) a person's home: **Dénesnél** 'at Dénes' place/house';
(d) a person's place of business: **az orvosnál** 'at the doctor's office'.

6.2.2.3.1

The allative case -hoz/-hez/-höz expresses motion toward the vicinity of someone/something.

Elmentünk a fogorvoshoz. We went to the dentist('s office).

Leültünk az asztalhoz. We sat down at the table.

Odafutottak a kerítéshez. They ran up to the fence.

6.2.2.3.2

The adessive case -nál/-nél expresses a position near or in the vicinity of someone/something:

A kulcs Imrénél van.
Imre has the key. (lit.: The key is by Imre.)

A kutya az ágynál fekszik.
The dog is lying near the bed.

A Kovácséknál voltam két hétig.
I stayed with the Kovácses for two weeks.

6.2.2.3.3

The ablative case -tól/-től expresses motion away from the vicinity of someone/something:

Erzsébettől kaptam a könyvet.
I got the book from Erzsébet.

Boldogan jöttek el az orvostól.
They came happily from the doctor's (office).

Felkeltünk az asztaltól.
We stood up from the table.

6.3 Non-locative usage of locative cases

The locative cases may have more abstract meanings as well. They can be used in time expressions and other adverbial, not strictly spatial, expressions. Often, a verb or adjective will require the use of a specific case. Examples of some abstract or metaphoric uses of the locative cases are given below.

6.3.1 | Illative -ba/-be

6.3.1.1

Verbs with the coverb **bele** 'into' take an illative complement:

Belefáradt a munkába.	He got tired of the work.
Mária beleszeretett Jánosba.	Mária fell in love with János.

6.3.1.2

The illative may be used with a condition somebody gets into:

Az a fiú mindig nagy bajba kerül.
That boy always gets into big trouble.

Dühbe jött, mikor meglátta a jegyét.
She flew into a rage when she saw her grade.

6.3.2 | Inessive -ban/-ben

6.3.2.1

The inessive is used in time expressions:

A születésnapom decemberben van.
My birthday is in December.

Melyik évben laktál külföldön?
Which year did you live abroad?

6.3.2.2

Some verbs and adjectives require an inessive complement:

Biztos vagy benne?	Are you sure of it?
Nem vettünk részt a vitában.	We did not take part in the debate.
Hiszel Istenben?	Do you believe in God?
Miben vagyunk bűnösek?	What are we guilty of?
Rákban halt meg.	He died of cancer.

6.3.2.3

The inessive is used with the condition or state a person is in.

Bajban vagyunk.   We are in trouble.

Jóban vagyok a főnökkel.   I'm in good with (I have a
                                 good relation with) the boss.

6.3.2.4

The inessive may express the means by which an action occurs.

Dollárban fizetnek.   They pay us in dollars.

Nagy pelyhekben hullott a hó. The snow fell in large flakes.

6.3.3 | Elative -ból/-ből

6.3.3.1

The elative may mark the origin of something – whether concerning persons, material or time.

Fizikus lett a bátyámból.
My elder brother became a physicist.

Milyen anyagból készült a ruha?
What material is the dress made of?

Melyik korból való az a festmény?
What era is that painting from?

6.3.3.2

The elative may mark the cause or manner of an action.

Nemcsak szerelemből házasodnak az emberek.
It is not only out of love that people get married.

Tévedésből vettem ezt a könyvet.
I bought this book by mistake.

Csak kíváncsiságból kérdeztem.
I only asked out of curiosity.

6.3.3.3

The elative has a partitive use.

Csak keveset evett a halból, mert nem ízlett neki.
He only ate a little of the fish because he didn't like it.

Kérsz még a süteményből?
Would you like some more pastry?

6.3.4 | Sublative -ra/-re

6.3.4.1

The sublative is used in time expressions to indicate the time by which an action is done.

Hat órára jön haza.	He'll be home by six o'clock.
Jövő hétre lehűl az idő.	The weather will cool down by next week.
Mához egy évre megint találkozunk.	We'll meet again a year from today.

6.3.4.2

Some verbs (especially those with the coverb rá) and adjectives require a sublative complement.

Büszke a gyerekeire.	She is proud of her children.
Kíváncsi vagyok Szabó új filmjére.	I am curious about Szabó's new movie.
Nem emlékszel rám?	Don't you remember me?
Mire van szükségetek?	What do you need?
Sokat gondol a barátnőjére.	He thinks about his girlfriend a lot.
Ránéztem az ablakra.	I glanced at the window.
A rendőr rámutatott a jelzőtáblára.	The policeman pointed to the sign.

6.3.4.3

The sublative may be used to mark the result or goal of an action.

Apró darabokra vágtam a hagymát.
I cut the onion into small pieces.

Magyarra fordította a könyvet.
He translated the book into Hungarian.

Könnyekre fakadt, mikor megnyerte a lottót.
She burst into tears when she won the lottery.

Fehérre festettünk minden falat.
We painted every wall white.

6.3.5	*Superessive -(o/e/ö)n*

6.3.5.1

The superessive is used with the days of the week and other time expressions.

Minden héten találkoznak.
They meet every week.

Hétfőn, szerdán és pénteken jár a francia órára.
He goes to French class on Mondays, Wednesdays and Fridays.

6.3.5.2

The following postpositions require that the noun preceding them be in the superessive case.

alul below	**fölül** above	**kívül** outside, besides
át across	**innen** this side of	**túl** beyond
belül within	**keresztül** across	**végig** along, to the end

Egy órán belül készült el a leves.
The soup was ready within an hour.

Imrén kívül senki sem volt pontos.
Besides Imre, nobody was on time.

6.3.5.3

Many verbs (especially those using the above postpositions as coverbs)
take a superessive complement.

Melyik terven dolgozol?
Which plan are you working on?

Sokáig gondolkozott az ügyön.
She thought about the matter for a long time.

Átment az utcán.
He walked across the street.

6.3.6 | *Delative -ról/-ről*

6.3.6.1

The delative often has the meaning 'about'.

Nem szeret magáról beszélni.
She doesn't like to talk about herself.

Miről szól a cikk?
What is the article about?

Nem tudnak sokat Budapestről.
They don't know much about Budapest.

6.3.6.2

The delative is found in adverbial constructions with the sublative -ra/-re.

napról napra	from day to day
szóról szóra	word by word
időről időre	from time to time
magyarról angolra	from Hungarian into English

6.3.7 | Allative -hoz/-hez/-höz

6.3.7.1

The allative is used with expressions of attaching something to, adding to, or communicating to someone or something (especially with verbs having the coverb **hozzá**).

Hozzászólt a kérdéshez.	He addressed the question.
Melyik párthoz akarsz csatlakozni?	Which party do you want to join?
Mit iszol a vacsorához?	What will you drink with dinner?

6.3.7.2

Some verbs, adverbs, adjectives, and postpositions require an allative complement.

Mihez van kedved ma?	What are you in the mood for today?
Közel lakik a Nemzeti Múzeumhoz.	She lives near the National Museum.
Nem értek a geometriához.	I am not good at geometry.
Udvarias volt hozzám.	He was polite to me.
Nagyon hasonlít az anyjához.	She resembles her mother very much.

6.3.8 | Adessive -nál/-nél

6.3.8.1

The adessive is used in comparative constructions:

Dénes magasabb Péternél.	Dénes is taller than Péter.
Az idei barack édesebb a tavalyinál.	This year's apricots are sweeter than last year's.

6.3.8.2

The adessive combines with plural pronouns to mean 'in one's country or part of the world'.

Nálunk sokan csak kint dohányoznak, nálatok hogy van?
Where I live many people smoke only outside, how is it in your country?

6.3.8.3

The adessive may be used in expressions of a person's condition or state.

Nem vagy észnél!   You are out of your mind!

Most már magánál van.   He's conscious now.

6.3.9 | *Ablative -tól/-től*

6.3.9.1

The ablative is used with verbs expressing fear or separation.

Nem félek a kutyáktól.   I am not afraid of dogs.

Megijedtünk a csontváztól.   We were frightened by the
                                  skeleton.

Elváltak egymástól.   They separated from each other.

6.3.9.2

The ablative is used to express the origin of an object or action in time and space (often used in conjunction with the terminative -**ig**).

Kettőtől otthon leszek.
I'll be home from two o'clock on.

Reggeltől estig dolgozik.
He works from morning till night.

Kitől kaptad a virágokat?
From whom did you get the flowers?

Budapesttől Párizsig beszélgettek a vonaton.
They talked on the train from Budapest to Paris.

6.3.9.3

The ablative may be used to denote the cause of an action.

Reszket a hidegtől.	She is shivering from the cold.
Kivagyok a sok gondtól.	I am worn out with all the worry.
Elájult a hőségtől.	He fainted from the heat.

6.4 Oblique cases

In addition to the locative cases, there are cases denoting the English prepositions 'for', 'with', 'as', 'until', 'per', 'at' (with respect to time) and more.

6.4.1 Formation

The oblique cases are added to stems in the same way as the inessive with the following exceptions:

(a) The initial **v-** of the instrumental **-val/-vel** and translative **-vá/-vé** always assimilates to the stem-final consonant to which it suffixes.

víz + vé → vízzé	(turning) into water
bor + vá → borrá	(turning) into wine
barátok + val → barátokkal	with friends
barátom + val → barátommal	with my friend

If the consonant to which the case assimilates is a digraph, only the first letter of the digraph is doubled.

lány + val → lánnyal	with (a) girl
ész + vel → ésszel	with (a) mind

If the consonant to which the case assimilates is a double consonant, the resulting tri-consonant cluster is simplified to a double consonant.

toll + val → tollal	with (a) pen
orr + val → orral	with (a) nose

(b) The causal-final **-ért**, the terminative **-ig**, the essive-formal **-ként**, and the temporal **-kor** have no vowel harmony counterparts.

(c) The temporal **-kor** and the essive-formal **-ként** attach to words ending in **a** and **e** without lengthening the vowel.

(d) The distributive **-nként,** the sociative **-stul/-stül,** and the distributive-temporal **-nta**[5] require a linking vowel when suffixing to stems ending in consonants. This is the same linking vowel required when forming the plural; all the stem alternations effected in the plural are found when forming these cases as well.

6.4.2 | Usage of oblique cases

6.4.2.1 | Dative -nak/-nek

6.4.2.1.1

The dative case marks the indirect object or the beneficiary of an action.

Csillának adtam egy könyvet.
I gave a book to Csilla.

Megmutatja Nórának a fényképeit.
She shows her pictures to Nóra.

Kinek telefonálsz?
Whom are you calling?

6.4.2.1.2

Many verbs and some adjectives take a dative complement.

Fekete Gyulának hívják.
His name is Gyula Fekete.

Fáradtnak látszol.
You look tired.

Jó barátomnak tartalak.
I consider you a good friend.

Unalmasnak találtam a cikket.
I found the article boring.

---

[5] **hó** 'month', **havonként, havonta** 'monthly', 'per month' are exceptions.

Ez a lakás nem alkalmas nagy családnak.
This apartment does not suit a large family.

6.4.2.1.3

The dative is also used in impersonal constructions (see section 17.7 for more on impersonal constructions):

Gábornak tanulnia kell ma este.
Gábor must study this evening. (lit.) It is necessary for Gábor to study this evening.

Zsófiának fontos minden nap zongoráznia.
It is important for Zsófia to play the piano every day.

6.4.2.1.4

The dative marks the possessor in 'have' constructions (see section 17.4 for more on 'have' constructions):

Gyulának két húga van.   Gyula has two younger sisters.

Láza van a lányomnak.   My daughter has a fever.

6.4.2.1.5

The dative may mark the possessor in possessive constructions (see chapter 8 on possessives for discussion of obligatory and optional uses of the dative).

Ennek az árát nem tudom.
I don't know the price of this/its price.

Annak a férfinak a kocsija eladó.
That man's car is for sale.

Kinek a labdája ez?
Whose ball is this?

Gábornak fáj a lába.
Gábor's leg hurts.

6.4.2.2 | Instrumental *-val/-vel*

6.4.2.2.1

The instrumental denotes the person, material, manner or means of transportation with which an action is done.

Inkább ceruzával írok, mint tollal.	I prefer to write with a pencil than a pen.
Eljössz velem?	Are you coming with me?
Már régóta jár Évával.	He's been going with Éva for a long time.
Busszal vagy metróval menjünk?	Shall we go by bus or metro?
Örömmel!	With pleasure! (I'd be delighted.)

6.4.2.2.2

The degree of comparison and other measures are expressed with the instrumental.

Imre két évvel fiatalabb, mint Kornél.
Imre is two years younger than Kornél.

Régen sokkal hosszabb volt a hajam.
My hair was much longer in the old days.

Vizet iszol? Én is kérek egy pohárral.
Are you drinking water? I would also like a glassful.

6.4.2.2.3

The agent of causative constructions is in the instrumental.

A szabóval varrattam egy új öltönyt.
I had the tailor sew me a new suit.

Jánossal hívattunk egy taxit.
We had János call a taxi.

6.4.2.2.4

Many verbs, adverbs, adjectives, and the two postpositions **együtt** 'together' and **szemben** 'across' take an instrumental complement.

Mikor találkoztok az elnökkel?
When are you meeting the president?

A láda tele van régi ruhával.
The chest is full of old clothes.

A házzal szemben van egy gyönyörű park.
There is a beautiful park across from the house.

6.4.2.3 | Translative -vál/-vé

The translative has a fairly limited use; it combines with the verbs denoting a change in state, e.g., **válik** 'become', 'turn into', **lesz** 'become', **tesz** 'make' and **változtat** 'change' to express what something or someone changes *into*.

Hallgatag emberré vált, miután meghalt a felesége.
He become a quiet man after his wife died.

Ezt a kunyhót valódi palotává változtatták.
They have changed this shack into a real palace.

6.4.2.4 | Causal-final -ért

6.4.2.4.1

The causal-final denotes cause, reason or purpose; it is often translated as 'for'.

Mindent megtesz a családjáért.
He does everything for his family.

Elküldtem a boltba kenyérért.
I sent him to the store for bread.

Zsuzsa eljön a repülőtérre értem.
Zsuzsa is coming for (to meet) me at the airport.

6.4.2.4.2

It is used in financial transactions, marking either the price or merchandise – whichever is in the 'for' phrase in English.

Hatezer forintot fizetett a cipőért.
She paid six thousand forints for the shoes.

Hatezer forintért vette a cipőt.
She bought the shoes for six thousand forints.

Mennyiért lehet kapni egy jó üveg bort?
How much (money) can you get a good bottle of wine for?

6.4.2.4.3

The demonstrative pronoun in the causal-final case **azért** 'for the (following) reason' introduces clauses of purpose.

Azért megyünk a hegyekbe, hogy végre pihenhessünk egy kicsit.
The reason we are going to the mountains is so we can finally rest a bit.

Azért tanul angolul, hogy többet keressen a munkahelyén.
The reason he is studying English is to earn more money at work.

6.4.2.5 | Essive-formal -ként

The essive-formal means 'as' and can be used instead of a clause introduced by **mint** 'as'.

Egy évig tanárként dolgozott.	She worked as a teacher for a year.
Egy évig dolgozott, mint tanár.	"
Rabszolgaként bánnak velem.	They treat me like a slave.
Úgy bánnak velem, mintha rabszolga lennék.	They treat me as if I were a slave.

6.4.2.6 Terminative -ig

The terminative is used in both temporal and spatial expressions to denote 'until'. It is often paired with the ablative -tól/-től.

Elkísért bennünket a sarokig.   He accompanied us to the
                                                            corner.

Nyolctól ötig dolgozik.   She works from eight until five.

Az út csak egy óráig tartott.   The trip lasted only an hour.

6.4.2.7 Distributive -nként

The distributive expresses a regular division and can be translated as 'per', 'by', 'every'.

Mennyibe kerül a vacsora fejenként?
How much does the dinner cost per person?

Óránként fizetnek.
They pay by the hour.

Egyenként léptek be a terembe.
They entered the hall one by one.

6.5 Less productive cases

The following cases are limited in use.

6.5.1 Temporal -kor

This denotes 'at' for time expressions only.

Hat órakor jön haza.
He is coming home at six o'clock.

Szép, ha karácsonykor esik a hó.
It's pretty when it snows at Christmas.

Éjfélkor szoktam lefeküdni.
I usually go to bed at midnight.

6.5.2 | Distributive-temporal -nta/-nte

This suffix attaches to words denoting time expressions to mean 'per', 'every'.

Hetente háromszor van magyar óra.
Hungarian class is three times per week.

Óránta közlik a híreket.
They broadcast the news every hour.

6.5.3 | Sociative -stul/-stül

The sociative denotes 'with' with people or objects closely associated with each other.

Mindig családostul utazik.
He always travels with his family.

Mindenestül érkezett meg.
She arrived with all her belongings/bag and baggage.

6.5.4 | Locative -t/-ott/-ett/-ött

A few towns and several words may use this locative case to mean 'in'.[6]

Pécsett	in Pécs
Győrött	in Győr
Kolozsvárt or **Kolozsvárott**	in Kolozsvár

oldal	side	**oldalt**	sideways
egyenes	straight	**egyenest**	straight ahead

---

[6] This is the same ending as found in some adverbs of place: **itt** 'here', **ott** 'there', **másutt** 'elsewhere'; and postpositions: **alatt** 'under', **előtt** 'in front of', etc.

The above examples illustrate how cases can have several meanings; of course words and phrases change in meaning when adding different cases; this is comparable to the use of different prepositional phrases in English.

Hiszek Jánosban.	I believe in János.
Hiszek Jánosnak.	I believe János.
Istvánról beszélek.	I am speaking about István.
Istvánnal beszélek.	I am speaking with István.

In the preceding examples, the meaning of the verb doesn't change, only the complement of the verb. Often, however, the meaning of a verb can change depending upon which case it governs.

Nem értem a leckét.	I don't understand the lesson.
Nem értek a fizikához.	I am no good at physics.
Sokáig tartott az előadás.	The lecture lasted a long time.
Sokáig tartotta a síró gyereket.	He held the crying child for a long time.
Attól tartok, hogy rossz jegyet fogok kapni.	I'm afraid I will get a bad grade.

Because the meaning of the verb can change so much, it is important to use a dictionary carefully; a good one will list the meanings of a verb (or other expression) according to the case it governs.

6.7 Plural declension

The plural declension is arrived at by simply forming the plural first and then adding the case suffix to the plural form. A case suffix is added directly to the plural form with the following exceptions:

(a) The linking vowel a/e is required after the plural form when suffixing the accusative case.
(b) The linking vowel o/e/ö is required after the plural when suffixing the superessive case -n.
(c) The temporal -kor, distributive -nként, distributive-temporal -nta/ -nte, and sociative -stul/-stül are not used in the plural.

Examples of the plural paradigm

	Back vowel	Front unrounded vowel	Front rounded vowel
	lány	**kert**	**ismerős**
	girl	garden	acquaintance
nominative	**lányok**	**kertek**	**ismerősök**
accusative	**lányokat**	**kerteket**	**ismerősöket**
inessive	**lányokban**	**kertekben**	**ismerősökben**
superessive	**lányokon**	**kerteken**	**ismerősökön**
instrumental	**lányokkal**	**kertekkel**	**ismerősökkel**

6.8   Full declension of select nouns

For declensions of all noun types, see appendix 2.

	Singular 'family'	Plural 'families'	Singular 'cup'	Plural 'cups'	Singular 'hour'	Plural 'hours'
nominative	család	családok	csésze	csészék	óra	órák
accusative	családot	családokat	csészét	csészéket	órát	órákat
illative	családba	családokba	csészébe	csészékbe	órába	órákba
inessive	családban	családokban	csészében	csészékben	órában	órákban
elative	családból	családokból	csészéből	csészékből	órából	órákból
sublative	családra	családokra	csészére	csészékre	órára	órákra
superessive	családon	családokon	csészén	csészéken	órán	órákon
delative	családról	családokról	csészéről	csészékről	óráról	órákról
allative	családhoz	családokhoz	csészéhez	csészékhez	órához	órákhoz
adessive	családnál	családoknál	csészénél	csészéknél	óránál	óráknál
ablative	családtól	családoktól	csészétől	csészéktől	órától	óráktól
dative	családnak	családoknak	csészének	csészéknek	órának	óráknak
instrumental	családdal	családokkal	csészével	csészékkel	órával	órákkal
translative	családdá	családokká	csészévé	csészékké	órává	órákká
causal-final	családért	családokért	csészéért	csészékért	óráért	órákért
essive-formal	családként	családokként	csészeként	csészékként	óraként	órákként
terminative	családig	családokig	csészéig	csészékig	óráig	órákig
distributive	családonként	—	csészénként	—	óránként	—
temporal	—	—	—	—	órakor	—
sociative	családostul	—	csészéstül	—	órástul	—
locative	(Kolozsvárt)	—	—	—	—	—

Chapter 7

Pronouns[1]

Pronouns replace nouns; personal pronouns refer to people; demonstrative pronouns usually refer to things. Reflexive and reciprocal pronouns refer back to the subject(s) of a sentence. The personal pronouns of Hungarian include both familiar and several formal forms. The demonstrative pronouns have important discourse functions not found in English.

7.1 Personal pronouns

The formation and usage of pronouns in the grammatical cases is different from their formation and usage from the locative and oblique cases.

7.1.1 Nominative and accusative cases

	I	you (sg.)[2]	she/he	we	you (pl.)	they
nom.	én	te	ő	mi	ti	ők
acc.	engem ~ (engemet)	téged ~ (tégedet)	őt	minket ~ bennünket	titeket ~ benneteket	őket

The first and second person singular pronouns have the option of omitting the accusative ending; it is common to do so – especially in the Budapest dialect. The first and second persons plural have two accusative

---

[1] Adverbial pronouns are treated in chapter 11.
[2] The second person forms discussed here are familiar forms. The polite pronouns are discussed in 7.2.

forms; they are used in free variation with no difference in style or meaning. All first and second person pronoun direct objects are considered indefinite.

Hungarian sentences do not require the use of a personal pronoun in the nominative or accusative case unless the pronoun is emphasized, contrasted, or referred to specifically. Otherwise it is most often omitted. Third person direct objects are implicit in the definite conjugation of the verb; it is common however to use the pronoun **őket** and omit the pronoun **őt** (unless otherwise emphasized).

As there is no gender marking in Hungarian, there is only one pronoun for *he* and *she*. In the nominative case, the third person pronouns can refer only to people; in the accusative, **őket** may refer to animals or objects, though **őt** is usually reserved for humans only; non-human direct objects may be referred to by the demonstrative pronouns, **azt, azokat, ezt, ezeket**.

Nominative pronouns:

Én egy sört fogok rendelni, te mit iszol?
I will order a beer, what will you have?

Mi angolul beszélünk, ők meg magyarul.
We speak English and they speak Hungarian.

Ő is, ti is jöttök szombaton.
Both he and you are coming on Saturday.

Accusative pronouns:

Látsz engem?
Do you see me?

Jánost is, téged is látlak.
I see both you and János.

Ott van Kati, most őt is látom.
There is Kati, now I see her, too.

Várom.
I am waiting for him/her/it.

Szeretem (őt).
I love him/her.

Szeretem őket.
I love them.

Mikor hívsz meg minket/bennünket vacsorára?
When will you invite us to dinner?

Holnap elviszlek titeket/benneteket a moziba.
I'll take you (pl.) to the movies tomorrow.

Because pronouns are often omitted, in the absence of context sentences with no overt direct objects are ambiguous in meaning.

Látsz?
Do you see me? Do you see us? Do you have the ability to see?

Látod?
Do you see him/her/it? Do you see them?

Várunk.
We are waiting for you (singular or plural). We are waiting.

Várnak.
They are waiting for me/us/you (singular or plural). They are waiting.

7.1.2 | Locative and oblique cases

The pronouns of the non-grammatical cases are formed by using the case as a stem and suffixing the possessive endings. Pronominal forms do not exist for all cases; the existing pronominalized case forms are given here.

Declension of personal pronouns

	sg. 1	sg. 2	sg. 3	pl. 1	pl. 2	pl. 3
Illat.	belém	beléd	bele, belé(je)	belénk	belétek	beléjük
Iness.	bennem	benned	benne	bennünk	bennetek	bennük
Elat.	belőlem	belőled	belőle	belőlünk	belőletek	belőlük
Sublat.[3]	rám	rád	rá(ja)	ránk	rátok	rájuk
Superess.	rajtam	rajtad	rajta	rajtunk	rajtatok	rajtuk
Delat.	rólam	rólad	róla	rólunk	rólatok	róluk
All.	hozzám	hozzád	hozzá(ja)	hozzánk	hozzátok	hozzájuk
Adess.	nálam	nálad	nála	nálunk	nálatok	náluk
Abl.	tőlem	tőled	tőle	tőlünk	tőletek	tőlük
Dat.	nekem	neked	neki	nekünk	nektek	nekik
Instr.	velem	veled	vele	velünk	veletek	velük
Caus.-fin.	értem	érted	érte	értünk	értetek	értük

[3] Also, less colloquially, reám, reád, reá(ja), reánk, reátok, reájuk.

Beszélünk róluk.	We are speaking about them.	Polite forms of address
Hiszek benned.	I believe in you.	
Rám vársz?	Are you waiting for me?	
Mikor jöttök hozzánk?	When will you come to our place?	
Adok neki egy rózsát.	I'll give him/her a rose.	
Nincs sok pénz nálam.	I don't have much money with me.	

Emphasis of the pronominalized cases is obtained by prefixing the nominative pronoun to the case form; the third person plural prefix, however, is **ő** (without the final **k**):[4]

énbennem, tebenned, őbenne, mibennünk, tibennetek, őbennük, etc.

Terád várok, senki másra.
I am waiting for *you* and nobody else.

Énnekem küldd el a pénzt, ne a bátyámnak!
Send the money to *me*, not my brother!

Tiveletek akarok menni!
I want to go with *you*!

Őbennük egyáltalán nem lehet hinni!
You can not believe in *them* at all!

7.2 Polite forms of address

7.2.1 Usage

The pronouns **te** and **ti** are used to address friends, relatives, children and animals. The pronouns **maga** (singular) and **maguk** (plural) are used to address people you are not as familiar with as well as strangers with whom you wish to maintain a reserved but not too formal relation. They can, however, be quite rude or condescending and it is best to wait until someone addresses you as such before using them. The pronouns **ön** (singular) and **önök** (plural) are used to address people with whom you wish to maintain a formal relation. In letters, the polite pronouns are

---

[4] Recall that this is also true with the postpositions and possessive constructions.

capitalized. As with all pronouns, when they are subjects or direct objects they may be omitted.

(Maga) milyen könyvet keres?
What kind of book are you (singular) looking for?

(Maguk) felszállnak a buszra?
Are you (plural) getting on the bus?

Kérdezhetek öntől valamit?
May I ask you (singular) a question, sir/ma'am?

Önök ott lesznek a tárgyaláson?
Will you (plural) be at the meeting?

Another common and polite form of address uses no pronoun at all. Instead the person's name or title is used with the third person conjugations of the verb.

Siet a professzor úr?   Are you in a hurry, professor?

Finally, the use of the verb tetszik (plural: tetszenek) plus the infinitive is a polite form often used by children with adults or by adults with much older adults. It uses no pronouns.

Nem tetszik/tetszenek tudni, mennyi az idő?
Do you (singular/plural) know what time it is?

7.2.2 | Declension of polite pronouns

The polite pronouns are considered third person pronouns; as such they conjugate with the third person forms of the verb (both singular and plural); when they are direct objects (either overtly stated or implied) they are considered definite (see definite conjugation, section 4.2).

Maga and **maguk** are identical with the reflexive pronouns and decline as any possessed noun. **Ön** and **önök** decline as regular nouns. None of the polite pronouns decline as personal pronouns, rather as nouns.

Declension of polite pronouns

Nom.	maga	maguk	ön	önök
Acc.	magát	magukat	önt	önöket
Illat.	magába	magukba	önbe	önökbe
Iness.	magában	magukban	önben	önökben
Elat.	magából	magukból	önből	önökből
Sublat.	magára	magukra	önre	önökre
Superess.	magán	magukon	önön	önökön
Delat.	magáról	magukról	önről	önökről
All.	magához	magukhoz	önhöz	önökhöz
Adess.	magánál	maguknál	önnél	önöknél
Abl.	magától	maguktól	öntől	önöktől
Dat.	magának	maguknak	önnek	önöknek
Instr.	magával	magukkal	önnel	önökkel
Caus.-fin.	magáért	magukért	önért	önökért

7.2.3 | *Possessive constructions with polite pronouns*

The polite pronouns, in keeping with their 'nounness', form possessives
identical to the nominal possessive constructions:

your (sg.) book **a maga könyve ~ magának a könyve**
az ön könyve ~ önnek a könyve

your (pl.) book **a maguk könyve ~ maguknak a könyve**
az önök könyve ~ önöknek a könyve

your (sg.) books **a maga könyvei ~ magának a könyvei**
az ön könyvei ~ önnek a könyvei

your (pl.) book **a maguk könyvei ~ maguknak a könyvei**
az önök könyvei ~ önöknek a könyvei

7.3 Reflexive pronouns

The reflexive pronouns are used when the subject is referred to again in the same clause. It translates as *myself, yourself, himself/herself/oneself*, etc. Some idioms require the use of the reflexive pronoun where English does not.

The reflexive pronouns are the possessive forms of a stem **mag-**; as such they attach suffixes as any possessed noun and are considered definite when a direct object. It is common in the Budapest dialect to omit the accusative endings on the **magam** and **magad** forms.[5]

Declension of reflexive pronouns

	sg.1	sg.2	sg.3	pl.1	pl.2	pl.3
Nom.	magam	magad	maga	magunk	magatok	maguk
Acc.	magam(at)	magad(at)	magát	magunkat	magatokat	magukat
Illat.	magamba	magadba	magába	magunkba	magatokba	magukba
Iness.	magamban	magadban	magában	magunkban	magatokban	magukban
Elat.	magamból	magadból	magából	magunkból	magatokból	magukból
Sublat.	magamra	magadra	magára	magunkra	magatokra	magukra
Superess.	magamon	magadon	magán	magunkon	magatokon	magukon
Delat.	magamról	magadról	magáról	magunról	magatokról	magukról
All.	magamhoz	magadhoz	magához	magunkhoz	magatokhoz	magukhoz
Adess.	magamnál	magadnál	nagánál	magunknál	magatoknál	maguknál
Abl.	magamtól	magadtól	magától	magunktól	magatoktól	maguktól
Dat.	magamnak	magadnak	magának	magunknak	magatoknak	maguknak
Instr.	magammal	magaddal	magával	magunkkal	magatokkal	magukkal
Caus.-fin.	magamért	magadért	magáért	magunkért	magatokért	magukért

[5] Recall that this is true of the first and second person singular personal pronouns as well.

Jól érezzük magunkat ebben a városban.
We feel (ourselves) comfortable in this city.

Vidd el magaddal a pénzt!
Take the money with you.

Ilona nem szeret magáról beszélni.
Ilona doesn't like to speak about herself.

7.4 Reciprocal pronoun

The reciprocal pronoun is **egymás** and is translated as 'each other', 'one another'. The same pronoun is used regardless of person. **Egymás** declines as a regular noun; when it is the direct object, it is considered definite.

Gyakran látogatjuk egymást. We visit each other often.

Egymás mellett ülnek. They are sitting next to each other.

Sokat várunk egymástól. We expect a lot of each other.

7.5 Possessive pronouns

Possessive pronouns translate as 'mine', 'yours', 'his/hers', etc. In Hungarian forms exist for plural as well as singular possession. They must always be preceded by the definite article. Possessive pronouns decline as any possessed noun; the possessive endings for polite pronouns are the same as those for regular nouns (see section 8.8).

Possessor	Singular possession	Plural possession
mine	**az enyém**	**az enyéim ~ az enyémek**
yours (te)	**a tied (tiéd)**	**a tieid**
his/hers	**az övé**	**az övéi**
yours (maga)	**a magáé**	**a magáéi**
yours (ön)	**az öné**	**az önéi**
ours	**a mienk (miénk)**	**a mieink**
yours (ti)	**a tietek (tiétek)**	**a tieitek**
theirs	**az övék**	**az övéik**
yours (maguk)	**a maguké**	**a magukéi**
yours (önök)	**az önöké**	**az önökéi**

Megmutattam neked az én fényképeimet, most mutasd meg *a tieidet!*
I showed you my pictures, now you show me yours.

Ezek a könyvek *az övéi.*
These books are his/hers.

Ez *a tied?*
Is this yours (singular)?

A ti lakásotokban öt szoba van, *a mienkben* csak négy.
In your apartment there are five rooms, in ours there are only four.

7.6   Demonstrative pronouns

Hungarian has demonstrative pronouns to replace nouns, adjectives, number and adverbs. (The adverbial pronouns are treated in chapter 11 on adverbs.)

7.6.1 | Ez/Az

The demonstratives **ez** 'this' and **az** 'that' have some anomalies in their declension.

> In the singular declension of the non-grammatical cases, the final **-z** of the demonstrative pronouns assimilates to the initial consonant of most suffixed cases.

> Because the initial **v-** of the instrumental case (**-val/-vel**) regularly assimilates to the consonants to its left, two forms exist for the demonstrative pronoun in the singular of this case.

> Note the irregularity (**-dd-**) in the terminative **-ig** case formation.

The plurals and accusatives are formed regularly.

Declension of demonstrative pronouns **ez, az**

	Singular		Plural	
Nom.	ez	az	ezek	azok
Acc.	ezt	azt	ezeket	azokat
Illat.	ebbe	abba	ezekbe	azokba
Iness.	ebben	abban	ezekben	azokban
Elat.	ebből	abból	ezekből	azokból
Sublat.	erre	arra	ezekre	azokra
Superess.	ezen	azon	ezeken	azokon
Delat.	erről	arról	ezekről	azokról
All.	ehhez	ahhoz	ezekhez	azokhoz
Adess.	ennél	annál	ezeknél	azoknál
Abl.	ettől	attól	ezektől	azoktól
Dat.	ennek	annak	ezeknek	azoknak
Instr.	ezzel, evvel	azzal, avval	ezekkel	azokkal
Caus.-fin.	ezért	azért	ezekért	azokért
Termin.	eddig	addig	ezekig	azokig
Transl.	ezzé	azzé	ezekké	azokké
Ess.-form.	ekként	akként	ezekként	azokként
Temp.	ekkor	akkor	——	——

7.6.2 | *Usage of* ez *and* az

7.6.2.1

The demonstrative pronouns may be used to replace a noun or have a deictic function.

Azt láttam. | I saw that/it.

Ezeket megvesszük. | We will buy these (things).

Demonstrative pronouns may also modify nouns. As modifiers the demonstrative pronoun must (1) agree in case and number with the noun it is modifying and (2) the noun must always be immediately followed by the definite article.

Azt a filmet akarom megnézni.
I want to watch that movie.

Ennek a lánynak fekete a haja.
This girl's hair is black.

Erre a buszra szállunk fel.
We are getting on this bus.

Azokról az emberekről beszéltünk.
We were talking about those people.

Whether used as a modifier or a noun replacement, the demonstrative pronoun is considered definite when it is the direct object.

7.6.2.3

A more literary demonstrative pronoun is **e**. This pronoun is used only attributively. Unlike its regular counterpart **ez**, it does not decline nor is the noun it modifies preceded by the definite article.

E házban lakott az egész család.
The entire family lived in this house.

E nagyszerű lovon ült a herceg.
The prince sat on this magnificent horse.

7.6.2.4

Demonstrative pronouns may also combine with the prefix **ugyan-** to connote 'the same'. As with the unprefixed forms, they can replace nouns or modify them.

János megnézte a Szerelem című filmet. Ugyanezt láttam én is.
János saw the movie titled 'Love'. I saw the same one.

Ugyanazt a térképet vettem meg, mint te.
I bought the same map as you.

7.6.3 | Adjectival demonstrative pronouns

7.6.3.1

The following pronouns can modify nouns or replace adjectives:

ilyen[6]	such, this kind	**olyan**[6]	such, that kind
ugyanilyen	the same kind (as this)	**ugyanolyan**	the same kind (as that)
efféle, ilyenféle	this sort of	**afféle, olyanféle**	that sort of
ekkora	this big	**akkora**	that big, so big
ugyanekkora	the same size (as this)	**uganakkora**	the same size (as that)

Ilyen az élet.
Such is life.

Olyanokat tud mondani, hogy nem hiszek a fülemnek.
She says such things, that I can't believe my ears.

Akkora a háza, mint egy kastély.
Her house is as big as a castle.

Ugyanekkora házat vettem én is.
I bought a house the same size.

7.6.3.2

The pronouns **ilyesmi** 'such a thing (as this)' and **olyasmi** 'such a thing (as that)' are demonstrative pronouns. They are very common in colloquial usage and decline as regular nouns.

Ilyesmit soha életemben nem hallottam.
I never heard such a thing in my life.

Nem szokott olyasmiket mondani.
She doesn't usually say things like that.

---

[6] Less colloquial forms include **ily, emilyen** 'such', 'this kind' and **oly, amolyan** 'such', 'that kind'.

7.6.4 Numerical demonstrative pronouns

These demonstrative pronouns replace expressions of quantity.

ennyi this much/many **annyi** so/that much/many

ugyanennyi this same amount/ **ugyanannyi** that same amount/
number number

Én ugyanannyit fizettem az autóért, mint te.
I paid as much for the car as you did.

Sohasem láttam ennyi embert egy helyen!
I have never seen this many people in one place!

7.7 Interrogative pronouns

7.7.1

The interrogative pronouns **ki** 'who' and **mi** 'what' decline exactly as
regular nouns. They can be singular or plural. When direct objects, they
are considered indefinite.

Kit láttál tegnap este az étteremben?
Who did you see last night in the restaurant?

Mik azok a kezedben?
What are those in your hand?

Kitől kaptad azt a könyvet?
From whom did you receive that book?

Miről szól a film?
What is the movie about?

Kire vártok?
Who are you waiting for?

7.7.2

The interrogative pronoun **melyik** 'which' is considered definite when a
direct object. Its plural is **melyek**, and otherwise declines regularly.

Melyik tollat kéred? Which pen would you like?

It can also take the plural possessive suffixes:

melyikünk	which of us
melyiketek, melyikőtök	which of you
melyikük	which of them

Melyikőtök Kis György?
Which one of you is György Kis?

7.7.3

The adjectival interrogative pronouns are:

milyen	what kind of	**mely**	which
miféle, mifajta	what sort of	**mekkora**	how large

Milyen húst veszel ma?	What kind of meat are you buying today?
Mekkora a lakása?	How big is her apartment?
Miféle filmet szeret?	What sort of movie do you like?

7.7.4

The numerical interrogative pronouns are **mennyi** 'how much', **hány** 'how many', **hányadik** 'what ordinal number'. They may either modify nouns or replace numerals.

Mennyi pénz van nálad?
How much money do you have on you?

Mennyibe kerül a vonatjegy?
How much does the train ticket cost?

Hány kiló krumplit kér?
How many kilos of potatoes would you like?

Hányadik emeleten laknak?
Which floor (lit., what numbered floor, fourth?, fifth?, etc.) do they live on?

7.8 Relative pronouns

The relative pronouns **aki** 'who', **ami** 'what', 'which', 'that' decline exactly as their corresponding interrogative pronouns. **Amely** is another relative pronoun with the same meaning as **ami**; **ami** is more common in colloquial speech. When direct objects, these pronouns are always considered indefinite. Relative pronouns are always preceded by a comma.

Ismered a lányt, akiről beszélek?
Do you know the girl (who) I'm talking about?

Elolvastam a könyvet, amit küldtél nekem.
I read the book that you sent me.

A kedvenc szobrom, amelyet Varga Imre alkotott, Óbudán áll.
My favorite statue, which Imre Varga sculpted, is in Óbuda.

Additional relative pronouns are formed by prefixing **a-** to the interrogative pronoun; they decline as their corresponding pronouns do: **amelyik, amilyen, amekkora, ahány, amennyi.**

Nem keresünk annyit, amennyit szeretnénk.
We do not earn as much as we would like.

Nem ismered a színdarabot, amelyikről beszélek?
Don't you know the play which I am talking about?

7.9 Cataphoric use of pronouns

Demonstrative pronouns (of nouns, adjectives and number) are commonly used cataphorically, i.e., to refer ahead or refer back to something previously mentioned. Most commonly, the back vowel forms (**az, olyan, annyi,** etc.) refer to a later, forthcoming clause; the front vowel forms (**ez, ilyen, ennyi,** etc.) refer to an earlier clause, sentence or utterance. English does not have a close equivalent to these pronouns; they are often left untranslated or another circumlocution is employed. Their importance in clear Hungarian prose cannot be underestimated.

János nem szerette azt, hogy beszéltek róla. Ezt én sem szeretem.
János didn't like (the fact) that they were talking about him. I don't like it either.

Annak örülök, hogy hazamehetek karácsonyra.
I am glad (of the fact) that I can go home for Christmas.

Megnyerte a lottót, és ekkor kezdődött a baj.
He won the lottery and that is when the trouble started.

Annyi cipője van neki, hogy nem fér el a szekrényben.
She has so many shoes that they don't fit in the closet.

7.10   Indefinite pronouns

Indefinite pronouns are formed by adding the prefix **vala-** to the interrogatives.

nouns:

valami	something
valaki	someone
valamelyik	one or the other

adjectives:

valamilyen	some kind of
valamiféle	some kind of
valamekkora	of some size

numerical expressions

valamennyi[7]	some amount of
valahány	some number of

Other indefinite pronouns are formed by attaching the prefixes **akár-** '(just) any', 'no matter (who, what,' etc.), **bár** 'any' to the interrogative pronouns.

Akármit mondasz, elindulok holnap.
No matter what you say, I'm leaving tomorrow.

**Melyik CD-t akarja hallgatni?   Bármelyiket, nekem
                                   mindegy.**
Which CD would you like to   Any one at all, it's all the
listen to?   same to me.

---

[7] **valamennyi**, paradoxically, also means 'every', 'all': **Valamennyien jöttek.**
'Everyone came.'

There can be a slight difference in the meaning between the two prefixes:

Akárki jöhet a konferenciára.
Bárki jöhet a konferenciára.
Anyone may come to the conference.

The first sentence has the meaning that any type of individual may come to the conference; the second that the conference is open to all, i.e., the first sentence says more about the pronoun subject, the second says more about the whole situation.

7.11 Negative and universal pronouns

The negative pronouns are formed by attaching the prefix se-/sem- to the interrogative pronoun. The universal pronouns are usually formed by prefixing the word **minden**. There are several exceptions in prefixing as the table below shows. The negative and universal pronouns decline exactly as their corresponding pronouns (except **minden**, which declines as a regular noun).

nouns:

ki	who	**mindenki**	everyone	**senki**	nobody
mi	what	**minden/ mind**	everything, all	**semmi**	nothing
melyik	which	**mindegyik**	each, every	**semelyik**	not one

adjectives:

milyen	what kind			**semmilyen**	no kind
miféle	what kind	**mindenféle**	all kinds	**semmiféle**	no kind
mekkora	how big			**semekkora**	of no size

numerical expression:

mennyi	how much	**minden, mind**	everything, all
semennyi	none at all	**hány**	how many

Double negation is always required in sentences containing a negative pronoun. The negatives **nem/ne/nincs** can be replaced by **sem/se/sincs** if a negative pronoun precedes it in the sentence; otherwise, **nem/ne/nincs** must be used.

Itt mindenki magyarul beszél.

Everyone speaks Hungarian here.

Itt senki sem/nem beszél magyarul.

No one speaks Hungarian here.

Nem találkoztam senkivel az úton.

I didn't meet anybody on the trip.

Senkivel nem/sem találkoztam az úton.

I didn't meet anybody on the trip.

Nincs semmi a szekrényben.

There is nothing in the closet.

Semmi nincs/sincs a szekrényben.

There is nothing in the closet.

Chapter 8

Possession

Hungarian indicates possession with a personal possessive ending attached to the noun. Thus, for example, in the word **autóm** the ending **-m** 'my' is attached to the word **autó** 'car' to mean 'my car'. Cases may subsequently follow possessive endings: **autóm + ban** 'in my car'. The plural **-k** may not be used with possessive endings; instead there is a separate plural possessive paradigm which uses the plural marker **-i**: **autóim** 'my cars'.

Although the possessive is usually attached to nouns, it may sometimes attach to adjectives being used as nouns: **drága** 'dear'; **drágám** 'my dear (one)'.

Nouns marked with a possessive ending are usually preceded by the definite article. Although the definite article is rarely omitted in colloquial speech, it is often omitted in writing – especially at the beginning of sentences.

For emphasis or purposes of contrast, the personal pronoun may precede the possessed word. In this case, the definite article is always used. The personal pronouns are always in the nominative form with one exception: the third person plural pronoun is **ő** (not **ők**!), i.e., it is identical with the third person singular pronoun.[1] In the following tables the personal pronouns are used for the sake of clarity.

8.1 Singular possessive endings

Possessive endings (as with the plural and accusative endings) may effect a change in the word stem and may or may not need a linking vowel when suffixed. The third person endings are the trickiest (and least predictable) to form; the first and second person endings are stable.

---

[1] Compare with the postpositions and declension of personal pronouns.

8.1.1 | Vowel-final stems

For words ending in a vowel, the possessive endings are always

my	**-m**	our	**-nk**
your (sg.)	**-d**	your (pl.)	**-tok, -tek, -tök**
his/her	**-ja, -je**	their	**-juk, -jük**

For words ending in **a** or **e** the vowel is lengthened to **á, é**, respectively, when adding the possessive ending. Other vowel-final words have no change in the stem.

Vowel-final stems-possessive singular					
		táska	csésze	autó	bábu	cipő
		bag	*cup*	*car*	*puppet*	*shoe*
my	**az én**	**táskám**	**csészém**	**autóm**	**bábum**	**cipőm**
your (sg.)	**a te**	**táskád**	**csészéd**	**autód**	**bábud**	**cipőd**
his/her	**az ő**	**táskája**	**csészéje**	**autója**	**bábuja**	**cipője**
our	**a mi**	**táskánk**	**csészénk**	**autónk**	**bábunk**	**cipőnk**
your (pl.)	**a ti**	**táskátok**	**csészétek**	**autótok**	**bábutok**	**cipőtök**
their	**az ő**	**táskájuk**	**csészéjük**	**autójuk**	**bábujuk**	**cipőjük**

8.1.2 | Consonant-final stems

For words ending in a consonant the possessive endings are somewhat different than for those ending in a vowel.

The same noun classes recognized for the nominative plural must be recognized here. (See section 5.3 for a review of noun classes.) The noun classes determine both the shape of the stem and the linking vowel choice when suffixing the possessive.

stems which require the linking vowel choice **a/e**:
   low vowel nouns (both classes: loss of length/no loss of length)
   v-stem (**v**-stem is required when suffixing possessive)
   -alom/-elem class (omits the last vowel when suffixing)

all other nouns require the linking vowel choice **o/e/ö**:
   fleeting vowel nouns (omit last vowel when suffixing)
   regular nouns

Possessive endings for consonant-final stems (*V* stands for linking vowel)

my	**-Vm**	*our*	**-unk, -ünk**
your (sg.)	**-Vd**	*your (pl.)*	**-Vtok, -Vtek, -Vtök**
his/her	**-(j)a, -(j)e**	*their*	**-(j)uk, -(j)ük**

As the table illustrates, the én, te, and ti forms require a linking vowel (which is determined by stem-type).

regular noun:	**barát**	friend	**a barátom**	my friend
low vowel noun:	**toll**	pen	**a tollad**	your (sg.) pen
regular noun:	**testvér**	sibling	**a testvéretek**	your (pl.) sibling

The mi possessive ending begins with a vowel; therefore, no linking vowel is required.

szomszéd	neighbor	**a szomszédunk**	our neighbor
hely	place	**a helyünk**	our place

The third person forms do not use a linking vowel; here, however, it must be determined whether the ending includes a j. (Both the third person singular and plural suffixes behave identically, i.e., if one includes the j in the suffix, then so does the other.) There are some rules, tendencies and much free variation in determining the presence or absence of j.

Rules:

Words ending in **j, gy, ly, ny, ty, s, sz, z, zs, c, cs** do not take a **j** (except **nagy**).

Low vowel words (including **v-**stems) do not take a **j** (the exceptions are **kád, nád, vad, rúd, lúd, út, kút, föld**[2]).
Fleeting vowel words do not take a **j**.
Nouns ending in **f** and **ch** do take a **j**.

Tendencies:

Nouns formed with the derivational ending **-at/-et** rarely take a **j**.
Back vowel words ending in **p, t, k, b, d, g** usually take a **j**.
Words ending in consonant clusters often take a **j**.
Words ending in **h** usually do not take a **j** (exceptions are **pléh, sah**).

Examples of third person possessives

	description	his/her	their
festmény painting	ends in **ny**	**a festménye**	**a festményük**
garázs garage	ends in **zs**	**a garázsa**	**a garázsuk**
tál bowl	low vowel word	**a tála**	**a táluk**
kosár basket	low vowel word	**a kosara**	**a kosaruk**
ló horse	**v-**stem	**a lova**	**a lovuk**
tükör mirror	fleeting vowel word	**a tükre**	**a tükrük**
feladat task	derivation **-at**	**a feladata**	**a feladatuk**
szomszéd neighbor	back vowel, ends in **d**	**a szomszédja**	**a szom0-szédjuk**
barát friend	back vowel, ends in **t**	**a barátja**	**a barátjuk**
kert garden	ends in consonant cluster	**a kertje**	**a kertjük**

[2] Note that these exceptions all end in the dentals **d** or **t**; with the exception of **hát** 'back', we may say that all low vowel words ending in **d** or **t** require the **j**-initial third person possessive suffixes. Also note that the words, **híd, rúd, lúd, út** and **kút**, which customarily lose length of the vowel when adding the plural, accusative, and first and second person possessive suffixes, do *not* lose length when adding the third person possessive suffixes.

For any stem-type not described above there is no consistent way to guess whether the third person suffixes include a **j** or not. In addition, there is free variation in some vocabulary where the suffix takes either the **j**-initial or the **j**-less suffix; however, the **j**-initial suffix is becoming more common in the modern language.

8.1.2.1 Possessive paradigms according to stem-type

Low vowel possessive singular

		(No loss of length)		(Loss of length)	
		váll	könny	pohár	ész
		shoulder	*tear*	*glass*	*mind*
my	**az én**	**vállam**	**könnyem**	**poharam**	**eszem**
your (sg.)	**a te**	**vállad**	**könnyed**	**poharad**	**eszed**
his/her	**az ő**	**válla**	**könnye**	**pohara**	**esze**
our	**a mi**	**vállunk**	**könnyünk**	**poharunk**	**eszünk**
your (pl.)	**a ti**	**vállatok**	**könnyetek**	**poharatok**	**eszetek**
their	**az ő**	**válluk**	**könnyük**	**poharuk**	**eszük**

---

v-stem possessive singular

		ló	cső
		horse	*pipe*
my	**az én**	**lovam**	**csövem**
your (sg.)	**a te**	**lovad**	**csöved**
his/her	**az ő**	**lova**	**csöve**
our	**a mi**	**lovunk**	**csövünk**
your (pl.)	**a ti**	**lovatok**	**csövetek**
their	**az ő**	**lovuk**	**csövük**

-alom/-elem stems possessive singular

		jutalom *reward*	érzelem *feeling*
my	**az én**	**jutalmam**	**érzelmem**
your (sg.)	**a te**	**jutalmad**	**érzelmed**
his/her	**az ő**	**jutalma**	**érzelme**
our	**a mi**	**jutalmunk**	**érzelmünk**
your (pl.)	**a ti**	**jutalmatok**	**érzelmetek**
their	**az ő**	**jutalmuk**	**érzelmük**

Fleeting vowel possessive singular

		álom *dream*	terem *hall*	ököl *fist*
my	**az én**	**álmom**	**termem**	**öklöm**
your (sg.)	**a te**	**álmod**	**termed**	**öklöd**
his/her	**az ő**	**álma**	**terme**	**ökle**
our	**a mi**	**álmunk**	**termünk**	**öklünk**
your (pl.)	**a ti**	**álmotok**	**termetek**	**öklötök**
their	**az ő**	**álmuk**	**termük**	**öklük**

Regular possessive singular

		nadrág *pants*	szék *chair*	ismerős *acquaintance*
my	**az én**	**nadrágom**	**székem**	**ismerősöm**
your (sg.)	**a te**	**nadrágod**	**széked**	**ismerősöd**
his/her	**az ő**	**nadrágja**	**széke**	**ismerőse**
our	**a mi**	**nadrágunk**	**székünk**	**ismerősünk**
your (pl.)	**a ti**	**nadrágotok**	**széketek**	**ismerősötök**
their	**az ő**	**nadrágjuk**	**székük**	**ismerősük**

8.2 Plural possessive endings

The plural possessive paradigm marks the plurality of the possessed item,[3] e.g., my dog*s*, his sister*s*.

In the possessive paradigm the plural suffix is -i (never -k), followed by the personal endings. The personal endings are slightly different in the plural paradigm, but unlike the singular paradigm, they are unchanging:

my	**-i-m**	our	**-i-nk**
your (sg.)	**-i-d**	your (pl.)	**-i-tok/-i-tek**[4]
his/her	**-i**	their	**-i-k**

8.2.1 | Vowel-final words

The plural -i attaches directly to words ending in a vowel. If the vowel is a or e, it is lengthened to á or é.

Vowel-final stems – possessive plural

		óra *clock*	csésze *cup*	szeplő *freckle*	kapu *gate*
my	**az én**	**óráim**	**csészéim**	**szeplőim**	**kapuim**
your (sg.)	**a te**	**óráid**	**csészéid**	**szeplőid**	**kapuid**
his/her	**az ő**	**órái**	**csészéi**	**szeplői**	**kapui**
our	**a mi**	**óráink**	**csészéink**	**szeplőink**	**kapuink**
your (pl.)	**a ti**	**óráitok**	**csészéitek**	**szeplőitek**	**kapuitok**
their	**az ő**	**óráik**	**csészéik**	**szeplőik**	**kapuik**

---

[3] Note that (unlike English) if each possessor has only one of a particular item, then the singular possessive paradigm is used.

Az orvos megvizsgálta a torkukat.
The doctor examined their throats (they each have one throat).

[4] There is no -**tök** option here because in the plural there is never a front rounded vowel immediately preceding the personal ending.

8.2.2 | Consonant-final words

The plural -i can not attach directly to words ending in a consonant. Instead, it must be preceded by -(j)a/-(j)e (identical with the third person possessive singular). As a rule, if the third person possessive includes a j in the singular paradigm for consonant-final words, then the j-initial suffix is employed throughout the plural paradigm as well.[5]

Consonant-final stems – possessive plural						
		toll *pen*	kert *garden*	bűn *crime*	köröm *(finger/toe) nail*	kalap *hat*
my	az én	tollaim	kertjeim	bűneim	körmeim	kalapjaim
your (sg.)	a ti	tollaid	kertjeid	bűneid	körmeid	kalapjaid
his/her	az ő	tollai	kertjei	bűnei	körmei	kalapjai
our	a mi	tollaink	kertjeink	bűneink	körmeink	kalapjaink
your (pl.)	a ti	tollaitok	kertjeitek	bűneitek	körmeitek	kalapjaitok
their	az ő	tollaik	kertjeik	bűneik	körmeik	kalapjaik

8.3 | ó~a and ő~e stems

Several nouns display an alternation in their final vowel in the third person forms of possession: in back-vowel stems the word-final ó becomes a before the third person possessive suffixes. Similarly, in front-vowel stems, word-final ő becomes e before the suffix. Because the plural possessive is based on the singular possessive third person forms, this alternation may be continued there as well.

---

[5] There are, however, numerous exceptions, e.g., **barátjuk** 'their friend' ~ **barátaik** 'their friends'.

		idő *time*	ajtó *door*	*doors*	szülő *parent*	*parents*
my	az én	időm	ajtóm	ajtaim ~ ajtóim	szülőm	szüleim
your (sg.)	a te	idődd...				

		idő *time*	ajtó *door*	*doors*	szülő *parent*	*parents*
my	az én	időm	ajtóm	ajtaim ~ ajtóim	szülőm	szüleim
your (sg.)	a te	időd	ajtód	ajtaid ~ ajtóid	szülőd	szüleid
his/her	az ő	ideje	ajtaja ~ ajtója	ajtai ~ ajtói	szüleje~ szülője	szülei
our	a mi	időnk	ajtónk	ajtaink ~ ajtóink	szülőnk	szüleink
your (pl.)	a ti	időtök	ajtótok	ajtaitok ~ ajtóitok	szülőtök	szüleitek
their	az ő	idejük	ajtajuk ~ ajtójuk	ajtaik ~ ajtóik	szülejük~ szülőjük	szüleik

There is much free variation among these forms. Other nouns which exhibit this alternation are:

csikó	foal	erdő	forest	vessző	stick
disznó	pig	erő	force	vő	son-in-law
hintó	carriage	esztendő	year		
hordó	vat	fő	head, person		
koporsó	coffin	mező	field		
orsó	spindle	tető	roof		
tinó	steer	tüdő	lung		
zászló	flag	velő	marrow		

nouns formed with the suffix **-ső**
belső interior, **első** (the) first, **felső** upper (part), **külső** exterior

8.4 Kinship terms

The following terms are irregular in forming the possessive:

		apa[6] *father*	anya *mother*	bátya *older brother*		öcs *younger brother*	
				sg.	*pl.*	*sg.*	*pl.*
my	az én	apám	anyám	bátyám	bátyáim	öcsém	öcséim
your (sg.)	a te	apád	anyád	bátyád	bátyáid	öcséd	öcséid

[6] An older form for 'father', **atya**, used mostly in religious terminology, declines exactly as **apa**.

his/her	az ő	apja	anyja	bátyja	bátyái	öccse	öcséi
our	a mi	apánk	anyánk	bátyánk	bátyáink	öcsénk	öcséink
your (pl.)	a ti	apátok	anyátok	bátyátok	bátyáitok	öcsétek	öcséitek
their	az ő	apjuk	anyjuk	bátyjuk	bátyáik	öccsük	öcséik

		fiú[7]		néne	
		son		aunt	
		sg.	pl.	sg.	pl.
my	az én	fiam	fiaim	néném	nénéim
your (sg.)	a te	fiad	fiaid	nénéd	nénéid
his/her	az ő	fia	fiai	nénje	nénéi
our	a mi	fiunk	fiaink	nénénk	nénéink
your (pl.)	a ti	fiatok	fiaitok	nénétek	nénéitek
their	az ő	fiuk	fiaik	nénjük	nénjeik

8.5 Nominal possession

In addition to pronouns indicating possession (my book, our garden, etc.) other nouns may possess items (John's book, the story of his life, etc.).

8.5.1 Marking the possessor

In Hungarian the nominal possessive relationship has two variants: (1) the possessor is unmarked (i.e., in the nominative case) and (2) the possessor is marked with the dative case. In both instances, the possessed item is marked with a third person possessive ending.

Kornél kalapja ~ Kornélnak a kalapja   Kornél's hat

**egy anya gyerekei ~ egy anyának a
gyerekei**   a mother's children

---

[7] When **fiú** means 'boy', the possessive declension is regular; it is only irregular with the meaning 'son'.

| Magyarország fővárosa ~ | the capital of |
| Magyarországnak a fővárosa | Hungary |

8.5.1.1

When the possessor is in the nominative case, the possessed noun is not preceded by the definite article and the possessor must immediately precede the possessed noun or noun phrase.

Nem értettem a szöveg lényegét.
I did not understand the point of the text.

Gyula kutyája nem harap.
Gyula's dog does not bite.

A lakosság húsz százaléka a fővárosban lakik.
Twenty percent of the population lives in the capital.

8.5.1.2

When the possessor is in the dative case the possessed noun is most often preceded by the definite article and the possessor may occur before or after the possessed noun (or may be entirely displaced).

Imrének fáj a lába. ~ Fáj a lába Imrének. ~ Imrének a lába fáj.
Imre's foot hurts.

The definite article is not used if the possessed noun is otherwise determined.

A lakosságnak húsz százaléka a fővárosban lakik.
Twenty percent of the population lives in the capital.

8.5.1.3

The possessor must be in the dative case if

(a) it is **ez, az, ezek,** or **azok:**

   Annak a címét elfelejtettem.
   I forgot its title.

(b) it is modified by **ez, az, ezek,** or **azok:**

   Ezeknek a szobáknak fehérek a falai.
   The walls of these rooms are white.

Ennek az iskolának a homlokzata nagyon régi.
This school's facade is very old.

(c) it is **ki/kik** or **mi/mik**.

Kinek a kutyája ez?
Whose dog is this?

Minek az ára ez?
What is this the price of?

8.5.2 | Marking the possessed

The following table illustrates the possessive endings for singular and plural nominal possession. Note that, unlike the pronominal paradigm, the number (singular or plural) of the possessor is indicated on the possessor, the number of the possessed is indicated on the possessed.

	Singular possessed	Plural possessed
Singular possessor	the boy's book (one boy, one book) **a fiú könyve ~ a fiúnak a könyve**	the boy's books (one boy, several books) **a fiú könyvei ~ a fiúnak a könyvei**
Plural possessor	the boys' book (several boys, one book) **a fiúk könyve ~ a a fiúknak a könyve**	the boys' books (several boys, several books) **a fiúk könyvei ~ a fiúknak a könyvei**

Note the difference in the way **anya** is marked in the following. In both sentences **anya** 'mother' is possessed by a plurality of individuals; in the first sentence, however, it is possessed by a pronoun, in the second, by a noun.

Pronominal possession:	Nominal possession:
Ismerem az (ő) anyjukat.	**Ismerem a fiúk anyját.**
I know their mother.	I know the boys' mother.

8.6 Possession and formal forms of address

The terms **maga, maguk, ön,** and **önök** form their possessives as nominal possession.

Meleg a maga kabátja ~ magának a kabátja?
Is your coat warm?

Ezek az önök fényképei ~ önöknek a fényképei?
Are these your pictures?

8.7 Possessive declension

8.7.1 Accusative

Third person singular possessive forms end in a vowel and therefore do not require a linking vowel; **a** and **e** are lengthened to **á** and **é** before the accusative.

Keressük a kocsiját/szemüvegét/leveleit.
We are looking for his car/glasses/letters.

The linking vowel for the accusative case is **a** or **e** after all other possessive endings.

Elkérték a jegyünket.   They asked for our tickets.

Elveszik a kabátotokat.   They'll take your coats.

The accusative is optional after nouns possessed by the first or second persons singular; after all other possessive endings it may not be omitted.[8]

Ismerem a bátyád ~ bátyádat.
I know your brother.

Meglátogattuk az egyik ismerősöm ~ ismerősömet.
We visited a friend of mine.

Otthon hagytam a könyveim ~ könyveimet.
I left my books at home.

---

[8] Compare with the accusative case of the personal and reflexive pronouns.

| **8.7.2** | **Other cases** |

All other cases suffix regularly. For complete paradigms, see appendix 2.

Beszálltunk a kocsijába.	We got into his car.
Olvastam a sikereidről.	I've read about your successes.
Állandóan gondol a barátaira.	She is always thinking about her friends.
Sokat fizetett a házáért.	She paid a lot for her house.

8.8 Non-attributive possession: é, éi

The suffix é, plural éi, is attached to nouns to denote 'belonging to'. It is added directly to nouns; it lengthens final vowels a, e to á, é; otherwise no other stem changes occur. It can attach to singular, plural, or possessed nouns and may be followed by a case. The interrogative form is kié in the singular; the plural kiéi is seldom used.[9]

friend		*non-attributive possessive*	
		singular	*plural*
	barát	**baráté**	**barátéi**
sg1poss	**barátom**	**barátomé**	**barátoméi**
sg2poss	**barátod**	**barátodé**	**barátodéi**
sg3poss	**barátja**	**barátjáé**	**barátjáéi**
pl1poss	**barátunk**	**barátunké**	**barátunkéi**
pl2poss	**barátotok**	**barátotoké**	**barátotokéi**
pl3poss	**barátjuk**	**barátjuké**	**barátjukéi**
friends			
	barátok	**barátoké**	**barátokéi**
sg1poss	**barátaim**	**barátaimé**	**barátaiméi**
sg2poss	**barátaid**	**barátaidé**	**barátaidéi**
sg3poss	**barátai**	**barátaié**	**barátaiéi**
pl1poss	**barátaink**	**barátainké**	**barátainkéi**
pl2poss	**barátaitok**	**barátaitoké**	**barátaitokéi**
pl3poss	**barátaik**	**barátaiké**	**barátaikéi**

---

[9] In the plural, a question form with a nominal possession construction is preferred: **Kinek a táskái azok?** 'Whose bags are those?' replaces **Kiéi azok a táskák?** 'Whose are those bags?'.

**Ez a lakás Zsuzsáé. Zsuzsa lakását már béreltem, de
Imréét sohasem.**

This apartment is Zsuzsa's. I have rented Zsuzsa's apartment, but
never Imre's.

**Ezek a kulcsok a barátodéi. Ezek a kulcsok az övéi, de
nem találom az apáméit.**

These keys are your friend's. These keys are hers, but I can't find
my father's.

Chapter 9

Postpositions

Postpositions supplement the case system and provide additional ways of expressing temporal, spatial, or other abstraction realtionships. As the name implies, postpositions follow a noun phrase instead of preceding it. The noun phrase is usually in the nominative case, though some postpositions require a noun phrase marked with a different case.

Postpositions share several characteristics with cases. In addition to the abstract postpositions there is a locative system; postpositions may be used as roots to which personal suffixes are attached; demonstrative pronouns exhibit a pattern of agreement as similarly found with cases; verbs may govern postpositional phrases; and like phrases marked with the oblique cases, postpositional phrases function as adverbials, thus they also share word order patterns.

9.1 Some postpositions of time

közben	during
múlva	in, after (+ time expression)
óta	since
tájt	around, about

Három nap múlva jövök haza.
I'll come home in three days.

Az előadás közben senki sem beszélt.
No one spoke during the lecture.

9.2 Postpositions with possessive suffixes

Possessive suffixes attach to postpositions ending in consonants as they would to low-vowel noun stems. Added emphasis may be supplied by prefixing the personal pronoun to the postposition. As with the possessive declension of nouns, the third person plural possessive pronoun in this case is **ő** (not **ők**).

9.2.1 Some postpositions taking possessive suffixes

által	by (means of)	**miatt**	because of
ellen	against	**nélkül**	without
helyett	instead of	**szerint**	according to
iránt	towards, for	**után**	after
kívül	besides, except		

9.2.2 Sample possessive paradigms of postpositions[1]

	(emphatic)		
szerintem	**énszerintem**	according to	me
szerinted	**teszerinted**	"	you (sg.)
szerinte	**őszerinte**	"	him/her
szerintünk	**miszerintünk**	"	us
szerintetek	**tiszerintetek**	"	you (pl.)
szerintük	**őszerintük**	"	them

---

[1] Recall that for most purposes the formal forms of address behave like nouns; thus the postposition paradigms for **maga, maguk, ön, önök** are like those for nouns: **Maga nélkül** 'without you', **önök után** 'after you', etc.

(emphatic)

miattam	énmiattam	because of me	
miattad	temiattad	"	you (sg.)
miatta	őmiatta	"	him/her
miattunk	mimiattunk	"	us
miattatok	timiattatok	"	you (pl.)
miattuk	őmiattuk	"	them

Velem vagy, vagy ellenem?
Are you with me or against me?

János nélkül nem megyünk, ő se megy nélkülünk.
We will not go without János, he won't go without us either.

Ne aggódjatok őmiattuk!
Don't worry on account of *them*!

9.3 Postpositions of location

The following are postpositions that adhere to the same tri-part directional system as found with the locative cases.

Motion toward ⇨●	No motion ●	Motion away ●⇨	
elé	előtt	elől	in front of
mögé	mögött	mögül	behind
fölé	fölött/felett	fölül	above
alá	alatt	alól	below
mellé	mellett	mellől	next to
közé	között	közül	between
köré	körül	——	around
felé	——	felől	in the direction of

Négy szék van az asztal körül.
There are four chairs around the table.

Felakasztotta a festményt a két ablak közé.
She hung the painting up between the two windows.

A szőnyeg alá seperte a port.
He swept the dust under the rug.

9.3.1

These postpositions may also add possessive suffixes. Note that with post-positions ending in a vowel (elé, mögé, fölé, alá, közé, köré, and felé), the third person singular forms may occur with or without the -ja/-je suffix.

elém, eléd, elé(je), elénk, elétek, eléjük
toward in front of me, you (sg.), him/her/it . . .

előttem, előtted, előtte, előttünk, előttetek, előttük
in front of me, you (sg.), him/her/it . . .

előlem, előled, előle, előlünk, előletek, előlük
from in front of me, you (sg.), him/her/it . . .

alám, alád, alá(ja), alánk, alátok, alájuk
toward beneath me, you (sg.), him/her/it . . .

alattam, alattad, alatta, alattunk, alattatok, alattuk
beneath me, you (sg.), him/her/it . . .

alólam, alólad, alóla, alólunk, alólatok, alóluk
from beneath me, you (sg.), him/her/it . . .

Gyere ide mellém!
Come here next to me!

Ki áll mögötted?
Who is standing behind you?

Elénk tárult a balatoni táj.
The Balaton landscape unfolded before us.

9.4 Postpositions governing cases

The following postpositions govern cases other than the nominative.

superessive **(-o/-e/-ö)-n** +	**alul**	at the bottom
	át	across, through
	belül	within
	felül/fölül	at the top
	innen	this side of
	keresztül	through
	kívül[2]	besides, outside of, except for
	túl	beyond

Egy órán belül elkészül.
It will be ready within an hour.

Tiszán innen, Dunán túl . . .
This side of the Tisza, beyond the
Danube . . . (folk song)

sublative **-ra/-re** +	**nézve**	with respect to

**Rám nézve végtelenül nehéz
volt az út.**
The trip was extremely difficult for
me.

delative **-ról/-ről** +	**nézve**	as seen from

**Közelebbről nézve láttuk, hogy
az aláírás hamis volt.**
Upon closer inspection we saw
that the signature was fake.

---

[2] kívül has two paradigms with personal endings:

kívülem, kívüled, kívüle, kívülünk, kívületek, kívülük as well as
**rajtam kívül, rajtad kívül, rajta kívül, rajtunk kívül, rajtatok kívül, rajtuk
kívül.**

| allative | **-hoz/-hez/-höz +** | **hasonlóan** | similar to |
| | | **képest** | compared to |

Hozzád képest Ilona gyakran megy moziba.
Compared you, Ilona goes to the movies a lot.

| ablative | **-tól/-től +** | **fogva** | from, since |
| | | **kezdve** | starting from |

Januártól kezdve szorgal-masabban tanul.
He has been studying more diligently ever since January.

| instrumental **-val/-vel +** | | **együtt** | together |
| | | **szemben** | opposite to, facing |

A házzal szemben van egy gyönyörű gesztenyefa.
There is a beautiful chestnut tree across the way from the house.

9.5 Complex postpositions

9.5.1

Some postpositions are formed of a root, a possessive suffix, and a case.[3]
The third person singular forms can be used nominally as well as pronom-inally, thus the preceding noun phrase may be in either the nominative or dative case.

(az én)	**számomra**	for my part
(a te)	**számodra**	for your (sg.) part
(az ő), valaki, mindenki, etc.	**számára**	for his/her, someone's, everyone's part

---

[3] Structurally these are simply nominal possessive constructions; they are included here as postpositions by convention only.

(a mi)	**számunkra**	for our part
(a ti)	**számotokra**	for your (pl.) part
(az ő)	**számukra**	for their part

The following postpositions pattern identically:

ellenemre, ellenedre, ellenére,etc.
in spite of me, you, him/her/it . . .

kedvemért, kedvedért, kedvéért, etc.
for my, your, his/her sake . . .

részemre, részedre, részére, etc.
for my, your, his/her part . . .

javamra, javadra, javára, etc.
in my, your, his/her favor . . .

Számomra is lesz hely?
Will there be room for me too?

**Annak ellenére, hogy esett az eső, a fiúk tovább fociztak
a kertben.**
Despite the fact that it was raining, the boys continued to play
soccer in the yard.

A maga kedvéért tettem meg.
I did it for your sake.

9.5.2

The following postpositions occur with the third person possessive suffix
only, i.e., they are not used with pronouns:

folyamán	in the course of
jóvoltából	thanks to, due to
következtében	as a consequence of
mentén	along
révén	through, by means of
során	in the course of
útján	through, by means of

A patak mentén találtam egy aranygyűrűt.
I found a gold ring along by the stream.

A hosszú tárgyalás folyamán mindenki el tudta mondani a véleményét.
Everyone was able to voice his opinion in the course of the long discussion.

9.6 Demonstratives and postpositions

In the same way that demonstratives agree in case and number with the noun they modify, so do they agree in postposition. Compare the following:

ezek előtt a házak előtt	**ezekben a házakban**
in front of these houses	in these houses

Similarly, the final -z of the demonstratives is not tolerated before postpositions (and cases) beginning with a consonant:[4]

e mögött a ház mögött	**ebben a házban**
behind this house	in this house

As is found with cases, postpositional phrases with **ez, ezek** may be reduced:

ez alatt a szék alatt → e szék alatt
under this chair

ezek között a szekrények között → e szekrények között
between these cupboards

9.7 Postpositions as prepositions

The following postpositions may also be used as prepositions. They require the same cases as when used as postpositions.

---

[4] Although the spelling does not reveal it, correct pronunciation of these phrases is like those of case-marked demonstratives where the final -z assimilates to the following consonant: compare ez + ben → ebben with e + mögött → [emmögött], a + fölött → [affölött], i.e., in both instances the pronunciation includes a doubling of the consonant: the written down form of the postposition, however, does not indicate this doubling.

át	through, across	**szemben**	facing, opposite
együtt	together	**túl**	beyond
keresztül	through		

Túl a Tiszán van egy csikós ...
There is a cowboy beyond the Tisza river ... (folksong)

Chapter 10

Adjectives

Adjectives qualify nouns and pronouns. When used attributively, adjectives in Hungarian precede the noun they modify and do not agree in case or number with the noun.

Hosszú szoknyákat viselnek.	They are wearing long skirts.
Érdekes cikkről beszélnek.	They are talking about an interesting article.

10.1 Declension of adjectives

Adjectives, when not used as modifiers, decline for case and number.

Predicate adjectives must agree in number with their subjects:

A fiú magas.	The boy is tall.
A fiúk magasak.	The boys are tall.

Adjectives may occur in all cases (though never when used attributively).

Kérem a pirosat.	I would like the red one.
A barnáról beszél.	He is speaking about the brunette.
Megitta a feketét.	She drank the coffee (lit., the black one).
Fáradtnak látszol.	You seem tired.

10.1.1 Nominative plural of adjectives

The plural suffix **-k** is added to adjectives in a slightly different manner than nouns. When required, the linking vowel choice is **a/e** (exceptions are listed below).

| 10.1.1.1 | Adjectives ending in a vowel |

10.1.1.1.1 *Adjectives ending in a/e*

Word-final **a** or **e** is lengthened to **á**, **é**, respectively.

	singular	plural		singular	plural
brown	**barna**	**barnák**	black	**fekete**	**feketék**
dear	**drága**	**drágák**	gray	**szürke**	**szürkék**

10.1.1.1.2 *Adjectives ending in -i/-ú/-ű*

These adjectives require the linking vowel **a/e**.

	singular	plural		singular	plural
Canadian	**kanadai**	**kanadaiak**	one from Pest	**pesti**	**pestiek**
long	**hosszú**	**hosszúak**	simple	**egyszerű**	**egyszerűek**

10.1.1.1.3 *Some exceptions*

	singular	plural
small	**kicsi**	**kicsik**
vain	**hiú**	**hiúk**
thick	**sűrű**	**sűrűk**

10.1.1.1.4

Adjectives ending in **ó** or **ő** witness some variation in forming the plural. Participles, for example, allow both variants – with or without the linking vowel:

	singular	plural
visible	**látható**	**láthatóak ~ láthatók**
intelligible	**érthető**	**érthetőek ~ érthetők**
permanent	**állandó**	**állandóak ~ állandók**

10.1.1.1.5

Other adjectives ending in -ó/-ő never take a linking vowel:

	singular	plural
good	jó	jók
tiny	apró	aprók
cheap	olcsó	olcsók

10.1.1.2 Adjectives ending in a consonant

10.1.1.2.1

Adjectives require the linking vowel a/e before the plural -k.

	singular	plural
pretty	csinos	csinosak
worthwhile	érdemes	érdemesek
strong	erős	erősek
interesting	érdekes	érdekesek
patient	türelmes	türelmesek
hardworking	szorgalmas	szorgalmasak

10.1.1.2.2

Exceptionally, the following adjectives require the linking vowel o before the plural -k.

	singular	plural		singular	plural
big	nagy	nagyok	happy	boldog	boldogok
rich	gazdag	gazdagok	blind	vak	vakok
thick	vastag	vastagok	base	aljas	aljasok
free	szabad	szabadok	other	más	mások

10.1.1.2.3

Adjectives formed with the derivation -atlan/-etlen or its variants decline
as nouns; therefore they use o/e[1] for the linking vowel in the plural.

	singular	*plural*
unhealthy	**egészségtelen**	**egészségtelenek**
unhappy	**boldogtalan**	**boldogtalanok**
impatient	**türelmetlen**	**türelmetlenek**
invisible	**láthatatlan**	**láthatatlanok**

10.1.1.2.4

Ethnonyms are the words used to indicate someone's ethnicity, home
country or city. In Hungarian these words are not capitalized. Ethnonyms
that do not end in -i decline as nouns and require the o/e/ö linking vowel
choice. Ethnonyms ending in -i decline as adjectives and require the linking
vowel a/e.

	singular	*plural*
Hungarian	**magyar**	**magyarok**
Spaniard/Spanish	**spanyol**	**spanyolok**
Greek	**görög**	**görögök**
Czech	**cseh**	**csehek**
Pole/Polish	**lengyel**	**lengyelek**
Turk/Turkish	**török**	**törökök**
one from Budapest	**pesti**	**pestiek**
one from Vienna	**bécsi**	**bécsiek**
American	**amerikai**	**amerikaiak**
Londoner	**londoni**	**londoniak**

---

[1] The ö linking vowel option found with nouns is never used since these adjectives never have a last vowel that is front and rounded.

10.1.2 | The accusative of adjectives

The accusative is suffixed to adjectives slightly differently than to nouns.

10.1.2.1 | Adjectives ending in vowels

Adjectives ending in vowels suffix the accusative case -t in the same way as nouns ending in vowels.

10.1.2.1.1

Adjectives end in **a** or **e** lengthen to **á**, **é**, respectively, when adding the accusative **-t**.

	nominative	accusative
yellow	**sárga**	**sárgát**
ugly	**csúnya**	**csúnyát**
weak	**gyenge**	**gyengét**
blond	**szőke**	**szőkét**

10.1.2.1.2

Adjectives ending in any other vowel add the accusative **-t** directly to the end of the word.[2]

	nominative	accusative
awful	**borzasztó**	**borzasztót**
edible	**ehető**	**ehetőt**
dense	**sűrű**	**sűrűt**
sad	**szomorú**	**szomorút**
old	**régi**	**régit**
curious	**kíváncsi**	**kíváncsit**

---

[2] Note how this differs from the formation of *plural* adjectives: in the plural, a linking vowel is needed before adjectives ending in **-i/-ú/-ű**.

10.1.2.2 Adjectives ending in consonants

10.1.2.2.1

Regular adjectives ending in a consonant require the linking vowel a/e before the accusative -t.[3]

	nominative	accusative
blue	**kék**	**kéket**
valuable	**értékes**	**értékeset**
ready	**kész**	**készet**
tall	**magas**	**magasat**
low	**alacsony**	**alacsonyat**
sure	**biztos**	**biztosat**

10.1.2.2.2

The following adjectives are exceptions and require the linking vowel o before the accusative -t.

	nominative	accusative			nominative	accusative
big	**nagy**	**nagyot**	happy		**boldog**	**boldogot**
rich	**gazdag**	**gazdagot**	blind		**vak**	**vakot**
thick	**vastag**	**vastagot**	free		**szabad**	**szabadot**

10.1.2.2.3

Adjectives formed with the derivation -atlan/-etlen or its variants decline as nouns; since they end in -n they take no linking vowel before the accusative.

	nominative	accusative
unnecessary	**szügségtelen**	**szügségtelent**
unknown	**ismeretlen**	**ismeretlent**

---

[3] Note how this differs from the formation of the accusative in the *noun*: in the noun no linking vowel is required if the word ends in **j, l, ly, n, ny, r, s, sz, z, zs.**

	nominative	*accusative*
unchangeable	**megváltozhatatlan**	**megváltozhatatlant**
carefree	**gondtalan**	**gondtalant**

10.1.2.2.4

Ethnonyms ending in a consonant decline as nouns: there is no linking vowel after the consonants j, l, ly, n, ny, r, s, sz, z, zs; otherwise, the linking vowel is o/e/ö before the accusative -t. (See section 6.1.2.1 on the accusative of nouns.)

	nominative	*accusative*
Croat	**horvát**	**horvátot**
Dutch	**holland**	**hollandot**
German	**német**	**németet**
Serbian	**szerb**	**szerbet**
Turk	**török**	**törököt**
Greek	**görög**	**görögöt**
Finn	**finn**	**finnt**
Hungarian	**magyar**	**magyart**
Albanian	**albán**	**albánt**
Pole	**lengyel**	**lengyelt**

10.1.3 | *Other irregularities in the accusative and plural of adjectives*

10.1.3.1

The following adjectives witness a change in the stem when forming the plural and accusative:

	nominative		accusative
	sg.	plural	
difficult	**nehéz**	**nehezek**	**nehezet**
honest	**derék**	**derekak**	**derekat**
few	**kevés**	**kevesek**	**keveset**
brave	**bátor**	**bátrak**	**bátrat**

| 10.1.3.2 | *kicsi—kis*

The adjective **kicsi** 'small' has a short form **kis**. The short form is used when it is used attributively; otherwise the long form **kicsi** is used. (Similarly **kettő** – **két** 'two', see section 14.1.2.)

Kis lakásban lakom.   I live in a small apartment. (attribute)

Egy kis kávét kérek.   I would like a little coffee. (attribute)

A lakásom kicsi.   My apartment is small.   (predicate adjective)

Csak egy kicsit tudok franciául.   I only know a bit of French.   (accusative)

10.2   Adjectives used as nouns

Adjectives may function as nouns; when they do, they decline as nouns.

Azok az épületek ismerősek.
Those buildings are familiar.

Azok ismerősök.
They are acquaintances.

| 10.2.1 | *Full declension of adjectives*

Other than in the accusative, adjectives suffix cases exactly as nouns.

Declension of adjectives

	singular	plural	singular	plural
	'high, tall'		'kind'	
nominative	magas	magasak	kedves	kedvesek
accusative	magasat	magasakat	kedveset	kedveseket
illative	magasba	magasakba	kedvesbe	kedvesekbe
inessive	magasban	magasakban	kedvesben	kedvesekben
elative	magasból	magasakból	kedvesből	kedvesekből
sublative	magasra	magasakra	kedvesre	kedvesekre
superessive	magason	magasakon	kedvesen	kedveseken
delative	magasról	magasakról	kedvesről	kedvesekről
allative	magashoz	magasakhoz	kedveshez	kedvesekhez
adessive	magasnál	magasaknál	kedvesnél	kedveseknél
ablative	magastól	magasaktól	kedvestől	kedvesektől
dative	magasnak	magasaknak	kedvesnek	kedveseknek
instrumental	magassal	magasakkal	kedvessel	kedvesekkel
translative	magassá	magasakká	kedvessé	kedvesekké
causal-final	magasért	magasakért	kedvesért	kedvesekért
essive-formal	magasként	magasakként	kedvesként	kedvesekként
terminative	magasig	magasakig	kedvesig	kedvesekig

10.3   Forming the comparative

The comparative expresses the degree of an adjective, e.g., old: older. To form the comparative the suffix -bb is added to the adjective.

10.3.1

If the adjective ends in the vowels a or e, the vowel is lengthened when adding -bb; adjectives ending in other vowels witness no change in the stem.

drága	dear, expensive	**drágább**	dearer, more expensive	
érthető	understandable	**érthetőbb**	more understandable	
fekete	black	**feketébb**	blacker	
keserű	bitter	**keserűbb**	more bitter	
olcsó	cheap	**olcsóbb**	cheaper	
régi	old	**régibb**	older	
szomorú	sad	**szomorúbb**	sadder	

10.3.2

The following adjectives lose their final vowel -ú/-ű (compare these with their adverbial forms):

hosszú	long	**hosszabb**	longer
ifjú	young	**ifjabb**	younger
könnyű	easy	**könnyebb**	easier
lassú	slow	**lassabb**	slower
szörnyű	awful	**szörnyebb**	more awful

10.3.3

The linking vowel a/e is used to link the suffix to adjectives ending in a consonant.

édes	sweet	**édesebb**	sweeter
különös	special	**különösebb**	more special
piros	red	**pirosabb**	redder

10.3.4

The following are some common exceptions:

jó	good	jobb	better
kicsi	small	kisebb	smaller
sok	many, a lot	több	more
szép	beautiful	szebb	more beautiful

10.3.5

Of the exceptional adjectives forming their plural and accusative with the linking vowel o, only **nagy** 'big', **nagyobb** 'bigger' is exceptional in the comparative.

10.3.6

Adjectives with a v-stem[4]

bő	abundant	bővebb	more abundant
hű	faithful	hűbb ~ hívebb	more faithful

10.3.7

Note the stem changes in the following:

bátor	brave	bátrabb	braver
derék	decent	derekabb	more decent
kevés	few, little	kevesebb	fewer, less
nehéz	difficult, heavy	nehezebb	more difficult, heavier

10.3.8

Some stems are already a comparative degree:

alsó	lower	felső	upper
belső	inner	külső	outer

---

[4] Compare with the adverbial forms where the v-stem is also evident.

10.3.9

Adjectives with the comparative suffix decline as regular adjectives.

10.4   Using the comparative

10.4.1

Comparative statements are commonly made with the conjunction **mint** 'than'.

Pál érdekesebb történeteket mesél, mint Attila.
Pál tells more interesting stories than Attila.

Az apám jobban főz, mint én.
My father cooks better than I.

10.4.2

If the noun in the **mint** clause is in the nominative case, it can instead be inflected with -**nál/-nél**; the conjunction **mint** is subsequently omitted.

Pál érdekesebb történeteket mesél Attilánál.
Pál tells more interesting stories than Attila.

Az apám jobban főz nálam.
My father cooks better than I.

10.4.3

If the compared item or action is something other than a pronoun or noun in the nominative, comparison can only be made with the **mint** construction.

Rózsa szebben ír, mint rajzol.
Rózsa writes more beautifully than she draws.

István kevesebb húst eszik, mint zöldséget.
István eats less meat than vegetables.

10.4.4 egyre

Used before the comparative degree, this means 'more and more'/'less and less'.

Péter egyre magasabb lesz. Péter is getting taller and taller.

Zsuzsa egyre jobban síel. Zsuzsa is skiing better and better.

Egyre kevesebbet beszél az órán. He speaks less and less in class.

10.4.5 minél . . ., annál . . .

Used before the comparative degree, these words join two clauses of comparison:

Minél szorgalmasabban tanul István, annál jobban szereti a matematikát.
The more diligently István studies, the more he likes mathematics.

Minél többet eszem, annál éhesebb leszek.
The more I eat, the hungrier I get.

10.4.6 Degree of comparative

The degree of a comparison, e.g., *three meters higher*, uses the -val/-vel case on the degree preceding the comparative form:

három méterrel magasabb	three meters higher
sokkal boldogabb	much happier
mennyivel könnyebben?	how much more easily?
két órával hosszabb	two hours longer

10.5 Superlative

The superlative (old: oldest) is formed by attaching the prefix **leg-** to the comparative. No changes are otherwise effected in the stem.

wider	**szélesebb**	widest	**legszélesebb**
cheaper	**olcsóbb**	cheapest	**legolcsóbb**
upper	**felső**	uppermost	**legfelső**
lower	**alsó**	lowermost	**legalsó**

10.6　Demonstrative adjectives[5]

(These are also used pronominally, see 7.6.3.)

	nominative singular	nominative plural	accusative singular	
such, like that	**olyan**	**olyanok**	**olyat**	(less common: **olyant**)
such, like this	**ilyen**	**ilyenek**	**ilyet**	(less common: **ilyent**)
what kind of	**milyen**	**milyenek**	**milyet**	(less common: **milyent**)

10.7　Interrogative adjectives

(These are also used pronominally, see 7.7.3.)

10.7.1　milyen ('what kind of', 'what is (something) like')

When used as a predicate adjective, **milyen** translates as 'what is (something) like'.

Milyenek azok a férfiak?　　What are those men like?

Milyen az a könyv?　　What is that book like?

Otherwise, attributively, **milyen** translates as 'what kind of'.

Milyen gyümölcsöt akarsz vásárolni?
What kind of fruit do you want to buy?

---

[5] See section 7.6.3.1 for more on the use of these adjectival demonstratives.

10.7.2

For emphasis, **milyen** may be used to modify adjectives.

Milyen jó zongorista a Tamás!   What a good pianist Tamás is!

Milyen szép ez a virág!   What a beautiful flower this is!

10.7.3

When modifying adverbs, **milyen** translates into English as 'how' – both interrogatively and emphatically.

Milyen gyorsan fut?   How fast does she run?

Milyen gyorsan fut!   How fast she runs!

10.8   Relative adjectives

(These are also used pronominally, see 7.8.) Subordinate clauses with relative adjectives may begin with the conjunction **mint** 'as'; they may omit **mint**; or the clause may begin with **mint** and omit the relative adjective.

amilyen as, such as

> **Olyan fekete a szeme, mint amilyen a korom.**
> **Olyan fekete a szeme, amilyen a korom.**
> **Olyan fekete a szeme, mint a korom.**
> Her eyes are as black as soot.

10.9   Indefinite adjectives

10.9.1   *'Some'*

When modifying mass nouns, the word 'some' is implied in Hungarian; the phrase **egy kis** 'a little', 'some' may also be used.

> **Kávét és vajat szeretnék venni. ~ Egy kis kávét és vajat szeretnék venni.**
> I would like to buy (some) coffee and butter.

Kérsz teát?
Would you like some tea?

When modifying count nouns, use **néhány** 'several', 'a few', 'some' or egy pár 'a couple'.

Néhány körtét evett.	She ate several pears.
Tegnap este írtam egy pár levelet.	I wrote a couple of letters last night.

10.9.2 | **'Any'**

Hungarian does not have the equivalent of English 'any' (found in negative sentences). It is already implied in the negative sentence.

Sohasem olvas újságot.
He never reads (any) newspapers.

Ezen a nyáron nem veszek új ruhát.
I am not buying (any) new clothes this summer.

For emphasis, the constructions **egy ... sem** 'not one' or **egyetlen ... sem** 'not a single ...' may be used.

Egy szót sem szólt.
He didn't say one word.

Ebben az évben egyetlen jó filmet sem láttunk.
We haven't seen one good film this year.

Egyetlen rossz tanítványom sincs.
I don't have a single bad student.

10.10   Numerical adjectives

Numbers may be used as adjectives by suffixing -s. (See section **12.2.2** for forming and using -s.)

Az ötvenes években született.
She was born in the fifties (lit., the fifty-ish years).

Az egyes villamos ma nem jár.
The number 1 tram is not running today.

A 408-as irodában dolgozik.
He works in Room 408.

Chapter 11

Adverbs

Adverbs are the part of speech addressing manner, place and time of an action.

11.1 Adverbs of manner: *Hogy(an)? . . .* How?

11.1.1 -an/-en

Most adverbs of manner are made by adding the suffix -(a)n/-(e)n to the corresponding adjective. No linking vowel is required when suffixing to adjectives ending in -a/-e; this vowel, however, is lengthened to á/é:

csúnya	ugly	**csúnyán**	not nicely
drága	dear, expensive	**drágán**	dearly, expensively
fekete	black	**feketén**	pessimistically, on the black market
furcsa	strange	**furcsán**	strangely
ritka	rare	**ritkán**	rarely, seldom

The linking vowel a/e is usually used when combining with adjectives ending in -í/-ú/-ű:

célszerű	expedient	**célszerűen**	expediently
keserű	bitter	**keserűen**	bitterly
kíváncsi	curious	**kíváncsian**	curiously
savanyú	sour	**savanyúan**	sourly
szomorú	sad	**szomorúan**	sadly

There is some variation in the use of linking vowels when combining with adjectives (these are mostly participles) ending in -ó/-ő. With some exceptions, however, the linking vowel is preferred:

érthető	understandable	**érthetően**	understandably
forró	hot, boiling	**forrón**	hotly
kiváló	outstanding	**kiválóan**	outstandingly
látható	visible	**láthathóan**	visibly
olcsó	inexpensive	**olcsón**	inexpensively

The linking vowel a/e is always required when suffixing to adjectives ending in a consonant:

aranyos	sweet, cute	**aranyosan**	sweetly, charmingly
biztos	sure	**biztosan**	surely
boldog	happy	**boldogan**	happily
kedves	nice	**kedvesen**	nicely
szép	beautiful	**szépen**	beautifully

Exceptions:

The following adjectives cannot combine with **-an/-en**:

derék	honest, good	**derekul**	honestly
jó	good	**jól**	well
remek	splendid	**remekül**	splendidly
rossz	bad, poor	**rosszul**	badly, poorly
vad	wild	**vadul**	wildly

The following adjectives form their adverbs with **-on**:

gazdag	rich	**gazdagon**	richly
nagy	big	**nagyon**	very, greatly, strongly
szabad	free	**szabadon**	freely
vastag	thick	**vastagon**	thickly

The following adjectives lose their final vowel when forming the adverb:[1]

hosszú	long	**hosszan**	at length
ifjú	young	**ifjan**	young, at an early age
könnyű	easy, light	**könnyen**	easily, lightly
lassú	slow	**lassan**	slowly
szörnyű	awful	**szörnyen**	awfully

Other stem changes:

bátor	brave	**bátran**	bravely
bő	abundant	**bőven**	abundantly
hű	faithful	**híven**	faithfully (or **hűen**)
nehéz	heavy, difficult	**nehezen**	heavily, with difficulty

11.1.2 -lag/-leg

The suffix **-lag/-leg** also forms adverbs from adjectives (and participles). Although it is difficult to predict when adverbs are formed with **-lag/-leg** as opposed to **-an/-en**, the former is most often used with adjectives formed with **-i**, and the two variants are rarely used with the same adjective.

eredeti	original	**eredetileg**	originally
gyakorlati	practical	**gyakorlatilag**	in practice, practically
lehető	possible	**lehetőleg**	possibly
politikai	political	**politikailag**	politically
valószínű	probable	**valószínűleg**	probably

Ezt a konferenciát eredetileg csak évente egyszer tartották.
Originally this conference was held only once a year.

---

[1] Compare with the comparative.

Mária politikailag jól ismeri Kínát, de nyelvismerete gyenge.
Mária knows China well politically, but her knowledge of the language is poor.

This suffix is sometimes attached to nouns as well:

arány	proportion	**aránylag**	proportionately
eset	case, instance	**esetleg**	perhaps
tény	fact	**tényleg**	really
viszony	relation	**viszonylag**	relatively

| **11.1.3** | *The essive -ul/-ül* |

This ending lengthens word-final **a** and **e** to **á** and **é**, respectively; otherwise there are no changes in the stem when suffixing.

The essive case **-ul/-ül** is used to form adverbs from adjectives ending in (a)tlan/-(e)tlen:

Váratlanul toppant be a sógorom.
My brother-in-law showed up unexpectedly.

Egészségtelenül táplálkozol.
You eat unhealthy foods (lit., 'not healthily').

Ismeretlenül is üdvözlöm a férjedet.
My regards to your husband though we haven't even met yet.

The essive case is required when expressing an action '*in* a language': **magyarul** 'in Hungarian', **görögül** 'in Greek'. Note in the following examples that the English expressions may translate as direct objects, not adverbs:

Tudok magyarul, angolul és franciául.
I know Hungarian, English and French.

Zsuzsa már jól beszél oroszul, és most németül is tanul.
Zsuzsa speaks Russian well and is studying German now, too.

This case may also be added to nouns to denote how the noun is used.

István feleségül vette a húgomat.
István married my younger sister (lit., took her *as a wife*).

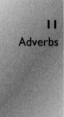

Ez a régi épület iskolául szolgál.
This old building serves as a school.

Segítségül kellett hívnom a szomszédomat.
I had to call my neighbor for (lit., as) help.

11.1.4 | The essive-formal case -ként

Similar to the essive, -ként is used with nouns to denote how the noun is used. This is usually translated as 'as' in English.

Mérnök, de egyelőre tanárként dolgozik.
She is an engineer, but for the time being she is working as a teacher.

Egy emberként beszéltek a tárgyalások alatt.
They spoke as one man during the negotiations.

Laci önként jelentkezett a rendőrségen.
Laci turned himself in voluntarily at the police station. (lit., 'as himself')

11.1.5 | -képp(en)

The suffix -képp(en) has the same meaning as the essive-formal and is found in a few forms:

aképpen	in that way
eképp(en)	in this way
mindenképpen	in any case
tulajdonképpen	actually, really, properly

11.1.6 | More adverbs of manner

alig	hardly	**igen**	indeed
általában	in general, usually	**ingyen**	free, gratis
annyira	so much, to such an extent	**is is**	so so

bizony	surely, certainly	**kevéssé**	a little, somewhat	Adverbs of manner
csak	only	**körülbelül**	approximately	
csaknem	almost	**külön**	separately	
csupán	merely, only	**majdnem**	almost	
egyáltalán nem	not at all	**még**	still, yet	
egyedül	alone	**méltán**	deservedly, worthily	
elég	fairly, rather	**önként**	voluntarily	
eléggé	fairly, rather	**össze-vissza**	randomly, confusedly	
egészen	entirely, completely	**pusztán**	merely, only	
egyébként	otherwise	**részint**	partly, to a certain extent	
egy kicsit	a little	**sőt**	moreover	
egyúttal	at the same time, in addition	**szinte**	almost, all but	
együtt	together	**teljesen**	fully, completely	
éppen	just, exactly	**többé-kevésbé**	more or less	
folyton	incessantly	**túl**	too, over-	
hiába	in vain	**valahogy**	somehow	

11.1.7

With some expressions, the accusative case is used adverbially:

elég	enough	**eleget**	**Eleget hallottam már róla.**
			I have heard enough about him.
jó	good	**jót**	**Jót aludtam.**
			I had a good sleep./I slept well.
kevés	few	**keveset**	**Keveset sportolsz.**
			You play (very) few sports.

nagy	big	nagyot	**Nagyot nevettünk.**
			We had a good laugh.
sok	many	**sokat**	**Sokat beszél a barátnőjéről.**
			He talks a lot about his girlfriend.

11.1.8

Verbs of seeming, sounding like, looking like, feeling, may take an adverbial complement – not an adjective, as in English. The adverbial may be an adverb of manner or an adjective or noun marked in the dative case.

Jól nézel ki.	You look good.
Jól esett ez a séta.	That walk felt good.
Rosszul érzi magát.	He feels bad, poorly, not well.
Ez nekem jól hangzik.	That sounds good to me.
Jó ötletnek hangzik.	It sounds like a good idea.
Fáradtnak látszol.	You seem tired.
Eleinte könnyűnek tűnt.	It seemed easy at first.

11.1.9 | *Adverbial participles*

Adverbial participles are adverbs of manner made from verbs. See section 4.4.3 on how to form them.

Tréfálkozva mondta, hogy tíz gyereket akar.
She said jokingly that she wants ten children.

Ásítva kávézott.
He drank his coffee yawning.

11.2   Comparative and superlative of adverbs of manner

The comparative and superlative of adverbs of manner are formed by adding the adverbial suffix -an/-en to adjectives already formed for the comparative and superlative (See sections 10.3 and 10.5 to form the comparative and superlative of adjectives.)

	adjective		adverb	
	positive	comparative	comparative	superlative
beautiful	szép	szebb	szebben	legszebben
rare	ritka	ritkább	ritkábban	legritkábban
loud	hangos	hangosabb	hangosabban	leghangosabban
good	jó	jobb	jobban	legjobban
few	kevés	kevesebb	kevesebben	legkevesebben
much, many	sok	több	többen	legtöbben

Kati sokkal szebben énekel nálam, de Csilla énekel a legszebben.
Kati sings much more beautifully than I, but Csilla sings the most beautifully.

Ebben az évben többen iratkoztak be a magyar tanfolyamra, mint tavaly.
This year more people signed up for the Hungarian course than last year.

Hol lehet legolcsóbban benzint venni?
Where can one buy gas most cheaply?

Csinosabban öltözködik most, mint régen.
She dresses more prettily now than before.

Note also the following irregular adverbial forms:

positive	comparative	superlative
nagyon very much	**inkább** more so, rather	**leginkább** mostly, most of all
egy kicsit a little	**kevésbé** less	**legkevésbé** least
rosszul badly	**rosszabbul** worse	**legrosszabbul** worst

Nagyon szeretem a svájci csokoládét is, de leginkább a belga csokoládét szeretem.
I like Swiss chocolate very much, but I like Belgian chocolate most of all.

Márta egy kicsit tud németül, kevésbé tud franciául, és legkevésbé olaszul tud.
Márta knows a little German, less French and knows the least Italian.

11.2.1

Adjectives with the derivational suffix (a)tlan/-(e)tlen (or its variants) and comparative or superlative affixes use the adverbial ending -ul/-ül.

cruel	**kegyetlen**	**kegyetlenebb**
	kegyetlenebbül	**legkegyetlenebbül**
unhappy	**boldogtalan**	**boldogtalanabb**
	boldogtalanabbul	**legboldogtalanabbul**

Az öreg még kegyetlenebbül is bánik a szomszédjaival most, hogy beteg lett.
The old man treats his neighbors even more cruelly now that he has become ill.

11.2.2 egyre

Use egyre with the comparative form of adverbs to mean *more and more so* or *less and less so*.

A szülei egyre gyakrabban utaznak külföldre.
His parents travel abroad more and more frequently.

Egyre többen tanulnak angolul az iskolában.
More and more people study English in school.

Imre egyre korábban kel fel.
Imre gets up earlier and earlier.

11.2.3 | minél . . ., annál . . .

Use this with the comparative of adverbs to compare clauses.

**Minél jobban tudsz főzni, annál többen jönnek hozzád
vacsorázni.**
The better you know how to cook the more people come to
your house for dinner.

**Minél ritkábban írsz nekem, annál ritkábban gondolok
rád.**
The more seldom you write me, the more seldom I think about
you.

11.2.4

The instrumental case -val/-vel is used to express the degree of comparison of the adverb.

Sokkal kedvesebben bánik velem, mint régen.
She treats me much more nicely than before.

Péter egy kicsivel jobban tud svédül, mint a húga.
Péter knows Swedish a little bit better than his sister.

11.3   Adverbs of number

Expressions of quantity can be used as adverbs when denoting the number
of people in the subject. In these constructions the subject is translated
into English as either a pronoun or 'people'.

Százan álltak a sorban.
A hundred people stood in line.

Hányan mentek Szentendrére vasárnap?
How many of you are going to Szentendre on Sunday?

Kevesen voltunk az előadáson.
There were few of us at the lecture.

11.4   Adverbs of space

Most expressions of space are formed with the case system and are discussed in chapter 6.

11.4.1   Locative system

Consistent with the locative system in case-marking, adverbs of space have a tri-part distinction with respect to motion toward, no motion, and motion away. The following table illustrates the locative system for deixis and interrogatives of place.

Motion toward (comparative) ⇨●	Motion toward ⇨●	No motion ●	Motion away ●⇨
	hova? (to) where?	**hol?** where?	**honnan?** from where?
idébb more toward here	**ide** (toward) here	**itt** here	**innen** from here
odább ~ odébb more toward there	**oda** (toward) there	**ott** there	**onnan** from there
	merre? in which direction?	**merre?** where about?	**merről?** from which direction?
errébb further this way	**erre** in this direction, this way		**erről** from this direction
arrább ~ arrébb further that way	**arra** in that direction, that way		**arról** from that direction

Hol van a táskam? Itt van az asztal alatt.
Where is my bag? Here it is under the table.

Merre vezet ez az ösvény? Menjünk arra!
Where does this path lead? Let's go in that direction.

Honnan jössz?
Where do you come from?

Hova mentek fürödni?
Where are you going swimming?

The following common adverbs occur with one or more directional pendants, some with comparative or superlative forms as well. As can be seen in the table, the paradigm is not as complete as with the other deictic elements.

	Motion toward	No motion	No motion comparat./superlative	Motion away
home	**haza**	**itthon**[2]		**itthonról**
home	**haza**	**otthon**		**otthonról**
together	**együvé**	**együtt**		
together	**össze**	**össze összébb**	**összébb**	
inside	**bentre**	**benn~bent**	**beljebb**	**bentről**
inside, within	**belülre**	**belül**	**legbelül**	**belülről**
outside	**kintre**	**kinn~kint**	**kijjebb**	**kintről**
outside, besides	**kívülre**	**kívül**	**legkívül**	**kívülről**
down(stairs)	**lentre**	**lenn~lent**	**lejjebb**	**lentről**
up (above), upstairs	**fentre föntre**	**fenn~fent ~fönn~fönt**	**fejjebb~följebb legfejjebb~legföljebb**	**fentről föntről**
above	**felülre**	**felül**	**legfelül**	**felülről**
below, bottom	**alulra**	**alul**	**alább legalul**	**alulról**
near	**közelre**	**közel**	**közelebb legközelebb**	**közelről**
front	**előre**	**elől**	**legelől**	**elölről**
back	**hátra hátrébb**	**hátul**	**leghátul**	**hátulról**
side	**félre**	**oldalt**		**oldalról**
elsewhere	**máshova**	**másutt máshol**		**máshonnan**
far	**messzire**	**messze**	**messzebb legmesszebb**	**messziről**
distant	**távolra**	**távol**	**távolabb legtávolabb**	**távolról**

[2] **itthon** refers to home when the speaker is at the home; **otthon** refers to home when the speaker is elsewhere.

Compass points

		from the ...	in the ...	to the ...
north	**észak**	**északról**	**északon**	**északra**
south	**dél**	**délről**	**délen**	**délre**
east	**kelet**	**keletről**	**keleten**	**keletre**
west	**nyugat**	**nyugatról**	**nyugaton**	**nyugatra**
northwest	**észak-nyugat**			
northeast	**észak-kelet**			
southwest	**dél-nyugat**			
southeast	**dél-kelet**			

11.5 Time expressions

Time expressions may be conveyed with the use of cases, postpositions, a combination of the two, or no marking at all.

Many time expressions are fixed – requiring no further case marking or postpositions:

addig	up until then	**máskor**	at some other time
akkor	at that time; then	**még**	yet, still
az előbb	just a moment ago	**még nem**	not yet
az idén	this year	**még mindig**	still
azonnal	immediately	**mindig**	always
eddig	up until now	**mindjárt**	soon, immediately
ekkor	at this time; then	**most**	now
eleinte	at first	**mostanában**	nowadays

először	first, the first time	**múltkor**	last time, recently	Time expressions
egyelőre	for the time being	**néha**	sometimes	
egy pillanat	(in) a moment	**nemrég**	recently	
éppen (most)	just now	**nemsokára**	soon	
gyakran	often	**nyomban**	at once	
hamar	soon	**örökké**	forever	
holnap	tomorrow	**régen**	a long time ago	
holnapután	day after tomorrow	**régóta**	since a long time	
jövőre	next year	**ritkán**	rarely	
később	later	**rögtön**	immediately	
későn	late	**sokáig**	for a long time	
korán, korábban	early, earlier	**tavaly**	last year	
ma	today	**tegnap**	yesterday	
majd	soon, in a while, later	**tegnapelőtt**	day before yesterday	
már	already, now	**többé nem**	no longer	
már nem	no more, no longer	**többé soha**	never more	

Holnap Budapesten leszek, és holnapután Prágába utazom.
Tomorrow I will be in Budapest and the day after tomorrow I travel to Prague.

Tavaly rengeteget havazott, de az idei évre inkább esőt jósolnak.
Last year it snowed a lot, but this year they are predicting more rain.

Nemsokára otthon leszünk.
We'll be home soon.

Majd felhívlak, mikor több időm lesz.
I'll call you (soon, later) when I have more time.

Régen gyakran szokta mondani, hogy szeret, de most már nagyon ritkán mondja.
A long time ago he would often tell me that he loved me, but now he says it very rarely.

Mikor először volt Londonban, nem tudott még angolul.
The first time he was in London he didn't yet speak English.

11.5.2 | Vague time

akármikor   whenever

bármikor   anytime, whenever

valaha   once, in the past

valamikor   at some time, sometime

Bármikor jöhetsz, csak gyere!
You can come any time, just come!

Valaha egy hatalmas kastély volt itt.
Once there was an enormous castle here.

Valamikor biztosan hallottam már azt a darabot, csak nem emlékszem, hogy mikor.
I'm sure I've heard that piece at some time, I just don't remember when.

11.5.3 | Dates

Dates are expressed by giving the year first, then the month, and finally the day of the month expressed as the ordinal number with the third person singular possessive suffix. There is a period after the year and the month is not capitalized.

1989. október 23-a (Ezerkilencszáznyolcvankilenc október huszonharmadika)

2000. június 17-e   (Kétezer június tizenhetedike)

To indicate 'on' a certain date, add the superessive case (o/e/ö-n) to the date:

Június 17-én születtem.	I was born on June 17.	Time expressions	
Január elsején pihenni szoktunk.	We usually relax on the first of January.		
Hatodikán jön.	He's coming on the sixth.		

11.5.4 Times of day

hajnal	dawn	**reggel**	(in the) early morning
délelőtt	morning, before noon	**nappal**	during the day
délután	(in the) afternoon	**alkony**	twilight
este	(in the) evening	**éjszaka**	(at) night

11.5.5 Days of the week

Use the superessive case (o/e/ö-n) to indicate 'on'. (Except for **vasárnap** 'on Sunday'.) Note that the days of the week are not capitalized.

hétfő	Monday	**hétfőn**	on Monday
kedd	Tuesday	**kedden**	on Tuesday
szerda	Wednesday	**szerdán**	on Wednesday
csütörtök	Thursday	**csütörökön**	on Thursday
péntek	Friday	**pénteken**	on Friday
szombat	Saturday	**szombaton**	on Saturday
vasárnap	Sunday	**vasárnap**	on Sunday

Hétfőn megyünk vissza dolgozni.
We are going back to work on Monday.

Szerdán lesz a zongoraórám.
My piano lesson will be on Wednesday.

Vasárnap meglátogatjuk a szüleinket.
On Sunday we'll visit our parents.

Only when modified by ez 'this' or az 'that' does **vasárnap** 'Sunday' require the superessive (**-n**).

Ezen a vasárnapon lemegyünk Szegedre.
This Sunday we are going to Szeged.

11.5.6 | Months

The inessive case (**-ban/-ben**) is used to express 'in', 'during' a month. Note that names of the months are not capitalized in Hungarian.

január	**januárban**	in January
február	**februárban**	in February
március	**márciusban**	in March
április	**áprilisban**	in April
május	**májusban**	in May
június	**júniusban**	in June
július	**júliusban**	in July
augusztus	**augusztusban**	in August
szeptember	**szeptemberben**	in September
október	**októberben**	in October
november	**novemberben**	in November
december	**decemberben**	in December

Júliusban lemegyünk a Balatonra.
In July we are going to the Balaton.

Decemberben jönnek a barátaim.
My friends are coming in December.

Novemberben esni szokott az eső.
It usually rains in November.

11.5.7 | Time expressions using cases

These are sometimes limited to certain lexical items.

11.5.7.1 | Superessive: (o/e/ö)-n

Use with the following words to mean 'during' or 'in'.

hét	week	**héten**	during the week
nap	day	**napon**	on (a) day
nyár	summer	**nyáron**	in/during the summer
tél	winter	**télen**	in/during the winter

Minden héten írok a szüleimnek.
I write my parents every week.

Múlt nyáron Japánba utaztunk.
We traveled to Japan last summer.

Télen korcsolyázni lehet a tavon.
In the winter one can skate on the lake.

Melyik napon jössz?
What day are you coming?

11.5.7.2 | Inessive (-ban/-ben)

Use with the following words to mean 'during' or 'in'.

hónap	month	**év**	year
század	century	**pillanat**	moment
perc	minute	**másodperc**	second
idő	time	**kor**	age
dél	noon		

Melyik hónapban születtél?
(In) which month were you born?

Rossz időben érkeztek.
They arrived at a bad time.

Ebben az évben kezdett iskolába járni.
She began school this year.

Délben ebédelni szoktak.
They usually eat lunch at noon.

| 11.5.7.3 | Sublative (-ra/-re)

Use this case to indicate 'by' a specified time:

Hatra/Hat órára otthon leszek.
I'll be home by six.

Hétfőre kell befejezni a munkát.
The work must be done by Monday.

Use to indicate 'intended' time (note the opposition with the -ig case):

Egy hétre mentem, de egy hónapig maradtam.
I went for a week, but I stayed a month.

Mennyi időre utazol el?
How long are you traveling for?

Use in tandem with the allative (-hoz/-hez/-höz) in the following construction:

mához egy hétre   a week from today

Use with the delative (-ról/-ről) in the following construction:

napról napra   from day to day

időről időre   from time to time

| 11.5.7.4 | Terminative -ig

Use this case to mean 'for' or 'until' a terminal point of time (often used in conjunction with the ablative -tól/-től).

3-tól 6-ig leszek az irodámban.
I will be in my office from 3 to 6.

Reggeltől estéig beszéltek.
They spoke from morning until night.

Két évig laktunk Debrecenben.
We lived in Debrecen for two years.

A tanfolyam egy hónapig tartott.
The course lasted one month.

Reggelig vártak.
They waited until morning.

| 11.5.7.5 | Instrumental *-vall/-vel* |

Use this case with the following words to mean 'during' or 'in'.

tavasz	spring	**tavasszal**	in the spring
ősz	fall	**ősszel**	in the fall
éj	night	**éjjel**	at night
nap	day	**nappal**	during the day.

Tavasszal találkoztunk.
We met in spring.

Ősszel sokat esik az eső.
It rains a lot in the fall.

Ebben a városban az autóbuszok éjjel-nappal járnak.
In this city the buses run day and night.

| 11.5.7.6 | Distributive (*-Vnként*) |

(See section 6.4.1 on how to suffix the distributive.) This case is used to express regularly recurring time.

Hetenként hívja fel az édesanyját.
He calls his mother every week.

Óránként közlik a híreket.
They announce the news every hour.

A buszok tíz percenként járnak.
The buses run every ten minutes.

| 11.5.7.7 | Temporal (*-kor*) |

This case is used with the hours of the day and some holidays.

Karácsonykor a gyerekek aranyosan viselkednek.
At Christmas children behave nicely.

Hétkor fog telefonálni.
She will call at seven o'clock.

11.5.7.8 Temporal-distributive (*-nta/-nte*)

Use with the following words to mean 'per', 'every'.

nap	day	**naponta**	daily, every day
hó	month	**havonta**	monthly, every month
hét	week	**hetente**	weekly
óra	hour	**óránta**	hourly

Havonta fizetnek.
I get paid monthly.

Hetente háromszor találkoznak.
They meet three times per week.

11.5.7.9 Multiplicative (*-szor/-szer/-ször*)

Add this case to numbers and some expressions of quantity to indicate the number of times.

egyszer	once	**hétszer**	seven times
kétszer	twice	**nyolcszor**	eight times
háromszor	three times	**kilencszer**	nine times
négyszer	four times	**tízszer**	ten times
ötször	five times	**sokszor**	many times
hatszor	six times	**többször**	several times

Milliószor puszillak.
I send you a million kisses. (lit., I kiss you a million times.)

Csak egyszer voltam Lengyelországban.
I've only been to Poland once.

Naponta többször telefonál.
He calls several times a day.

Add -szor/-szer/-ször to fractions to indicate the 'first', 'second', 'third', etc. time. Note the irregular form for 'first'.

először (the) first time   **harmadszor** (the) third time

másodszor (the) second time   **negyedszer** (the) fourth time

Most először vagyok Tahitin.
I am in Tahiti now for the first time.

Csak akkor értettem, mikor másodszor mondta.
I only understood it the second time he said it.

| 11.5.7.10 | Accusative (-t)

This case has a limited use in time expressions, usually occurring with only a few verbs.

Két hetet töltöttünk Spanyolországban.
We spent two weeks in Spain.

Egy órát vártunk.
We waited one hour.

| 11.5.8 | *Time expressions with postpositions*

(Note that some postpositions require a case on the time expression preceding them.)

közben during   **Senki nem beszél az előadás közben.**
No one speaks during the performance.

alatt during   (With this meaning **alatt** is a synonym of **közben**.)
A háború alatt sokan éheztek.
Many people went hungry during the war.

alatt under/   (With this meaning **alatt** is a synonym of **belül**.)
(with)in   **Egy óra alatt fejeztem be a házi feladatot.**
I finished the homework in (under) an hour.

után after   **Hívjál fel tíz óra után.**
Call me after ten o'clock.

előtt before   **Magyar óra előtt mindig találkoznak.**
They always meet before Hungarian class.

fogva/ **kezdve**	from/ since	Use with the ablative case **-tól/-től**: **Januártól kezdve/fogva már nem jár az** **előadásra.** She has not been coming to the lecture since January.
során/ **folya-** **mán**	in the course of	**A tárgyalások során sokat tanultak** **egymásról.** They learned a lot about each other in the course of the negotiations.
belül	(with)in	Use with the superessive case **o/e/ö-n**. **A fiunk egy hónapon belül jön haza.** Our son will be home (with)in a month.
át/keresz **-tül**	through	Use with the superessive case **o/e/ö-n**: **Egész életen át vártam rá.** I waited a lifetime for her.
között	between	**Négy és öt óra között az irodámban leszek.** I'll be in my office between four and five o'clock.
hosszat	long	**Hét óra hosszat dolgoztak a házi** **feladatukon.** They worked for seven hours long on their homework.
múlva	in, after	**Három nap múlva kezdődik a vizsgaidőszak.** The exam term begins in three days.
felé	toward	**Tíz óra felé kezd fáradt lenni.** Towards ten o'clock he starts to get tired.
körül, **tájban,** **táján**	about, around	These are all synonyms. **Nyolc óra körül vacsorázunk.** We eat dinner around eight o'clock. **Éjfél tájban szokott hazajönni.** She usually comes home around midnight. **Az ünnepek táján jön meglátogatni.** He will come to visit us around the holidays.
-számra	for . . . on end	Though not a true postposition, **-számra** combines with nouns similarly. **A régi barátok óraszámra tudtak beszélni.** The old friends could talk for hours on end.

Hétszámra várták a hivatalos engedélyt.
They waited for weeks on end for official
permission.

11.5.9 'Since'

Hungarian has two ways of expressing 'since' or 'for' a period of time.
Note that because the action continues into the present, the verb must
be in the present tense.

the postposition **óta**:

> **1995 óta Budapesten lakunk.**
> We have been living in Budapest since 1995.
>
> **Két év óta vagyok itt.**
> I have been here for two years.
>
> **Mióta tanulsz magyarul?**
> How long have you been studying Hungarian?

the third person singular possessive **(j)a/(j)e**:

> **Két éve vagyok itt.**
> I have been here for two years.
>
> **Három hónapja dolgozunk rajta.**
> We have been working on it for three
> months.
>
> **Mennyi ideje tanulsz magyarul?**
> How long have you been studying Hungarian?

11.5.10 'Ago'

Two constructions can be used to express 'ago'. The verb must be in the
past tense.

The posposition **ezelőtt** with -val/-vel:

Egy évvel ezelőtt kezdtem magyarul tanulni.
I began to study Hungarian one year ago.

Itt volt három perccel ezelőtt.
He was here three minutes ago.

The third person singular possessive (j)a/(j)e:

Egy éve kezdtem magyarul tanulni.
I began to study Hungarian one year ago.

Itt volt három perce.
He was here three minutes ago.

Since both the 'since' and 'ago' constructions use the third person singular possessive the verb tense may be the only way to distinguish between the meaning of the two:

Három hónapja dolgozunk rajta.
We have been working on it for three months.

Három hónapja dolgoztunk rajta.
We worked on it three months ago.

11.5.11 | Every

The word 'every', can be expressed with either the distributive case (-Vnként) or the word **minden** may be used before the time expression.

Minden kedden/Keddenként találkoztak.
They met every Tuesday.

**Minden hónapban/Havonként legalább egyszer mennek
  hangversenyre.**
Every month they go to at least one concert.

11.5.12 | Usually

The word 'usually' may be expressed by either the adverbial **általában** or the verbal construction with **szokott**. **Szokott** may conjugate for any person in both the indefinite and definite conjugations; though it means 'usually', **szokott** is only used in the past tense conjugation. It takes an infinitival complement.

Reggel teázni szoktam.
I usually drink tea in the morning.

Hétkor szokott felkelni.
She usually gets up at seven o'clock.

Tavasszal esős idő szokott lenni.
In the spring the weather is usually rainy.

Mit szoktál csinálni a szabad idődben?
What do you usually do in your free time?

| 11.5.13 | Clock time

The question **Mennyi az idő?** or **Hány óra van?/Hány óra?** 'What time is it?' may be answered using quarter-hour segments. The expressions refer to the coming full hour. The word **óra** 'hour' cannot be used with any fraction of the hour. The word **van** 'is' is always optional.

It is 1:00. **Egy óra (van).**

It is 1:15. **Negyed kettő (van).** (lit.) a quarter (on the way) to two

It is 1:30. **Fél kettő (van).** (lit.) half (on the way to) two

It is 1:45. **Háromnegyed kettő** (lit.) three quarters (on the way)
 (van). to two

Otherwise clock time is expressed with reference to the nearest quarter using the following pattern of postpositions:

X perc múlva = in X minutes

X perccel múlt = X minutes past

5:55 **öt perc múlva hat (óra)** (lit.) in five minutes it will be
 6:00

These postpositional patterns are also used with quarter-hour time segments:

2:13 **két perc múlva negyed három**
(lit.) in two minutes it will be 2:15

3:47 **két perccel múlt háromnegyed négy**
(lit.) it is two minutes past 3:45

7:33 **három perccel múlt fél nyolc**
(lit.) it is three minutes past half of eight

Official times may be stated using the full numbers. The 24-hour clock may be used:

15:55 **tizenöt óra ötvenöt perc**
(lit.) fifteen hours fifty-five minutes

3:47 **három óra negyvenhét perc**
(lit.) three hours forty-seven minutes

In response to the question **Mikor?** 'when', **Hánykor?/Hány órakor** 'at what time (on the clock)' the temporal case **-kor** must be added to the end of the time expression.

Hánykor jöttek?   **Hétkor/Hét órakor.**
When did they come?   At seven/seven o'clock.

Tizenhárom óra negyvenhárom perckor indul a vonat.
The train leaves at 13:43.

| **11.5.14** | *Interrogatives of time* |

Mikor?	When?
Hánykor?	At what time (on the clock)?
Mennyi időre?	For how long? By what time?
Mikorra?	By what time?
Mikortól (kezdve/fogva)?	Since when? From what time?
Mettől (kezdve/fogva)?	Since when? From what time?
Meddig?	Until when? For how long? How much time?
Mennyi ideig?	Until when/for how long?
Mennyi időt?	How much time?
Mióta?	Since when?
Mennyi idő múlva?	In (after) how much time?
Miközben?	During what time? When?
Mennyi idővel ezelőtt?	How long ago?
Mennyi idő alatt?	During how much time?
Mennyi időn belül?	Within how much time?
Mennyi időn keresztül?	For how long a time?

11.6 Adverbial pronouns

The adverbial pronouns reflect all the meanings of manner, space and time found among the adverbs. The following chart summarizes the possible adverbial pronouns. (The relative adverbials are formed by prefixing **a-** to the interrogatives.)

Adverbial pronouns

Interrogative	Demonstrative	Negative	Indefinite	Indefinite-2	Universal
hova where to	**ide** to here **oda** to there	**sehova** from nowhere	**valahova** to somewhere	**akárhova** **bárhova** to anywhere	**mindenhova** **mindenüvé** to everywhere
hol where	**itt** here **ott** there	**sehol** nowhere	**valahol** somewhere	**akárhol** **bárhol** anywhere	**mindenhol** **mindenütt** everywhere
honnan where from	**innen** from here **onnan** from there	**sehonnan** from nowhere	**valahonnan** from somewhere	**akárhonnan** **bárhonnan** from anywhere	**mindenhonnan** **mindenünnen** from everywhere
merre in which direction	**erre** this way **arra** that way	**semerre** in no direction	**valamerre** in some direction	**akármerre** **bármerre** in any direction	**mindenfelé** in every direction
meddig how far how long	**eddig** until now/here **addig** until now/there	**semeddig** for no length of time or distance	**valameddig** for some length of time or distance	**akármeddig** **bármeddig** for any length of time or distance	**mindeddig** so far, up until now
mikor when	**ekkor** at this time **akkor** at that time	**semmikor** at no time **soha** **sohasem** **sosem** never	**valaha** once, sometime **valamikor** at some time	**akármikor** **bármikor** whenever	**mindig** **mindenkor** always
hogy(an) how	**így** in this way **úgy** in that way	**sehogy(an)** in no way	**valahogy(an)** in some way	**akárhogy(an)** **bárhogy(an)** in any way	**mindenképpen** **mindenhogy(an)** anyway, in any case

| 11.6.1 | *Interrogative* |

Mikor született Bartók? When was Bartók born?

Hova akarsz menni ma este? Where do you want to go
tonight?

Honnan jön a lárma? Where is the noise coming from?

| 11.6.2 | *Relative* |

The relative adverbials are formed by prefixing **a-** to the interrogative.
An exception is **amíg** 'while', which often replaces **ameddig** 'as long as'.

Odaraktam a kabátomat, ahol a többi kabát van.
I put my coat where the other coats are.

Amióta találkoztam vele, másra nem is tudok gondolni.
Since I met him I can't think of anything else.

**Amíg veszekedtek a nappaliban, leégett a vacsora a
konyhában.**
While they were arguing in the living room, the dinner burned in
the kitchen.

| 11.6.3 | *Demonstrative* |

Erre gyere, erre!
Come here, this way!

**Úgy kell vágni a hajamat, hogy ne lássák, hogy kopa-
szodom.**
You have to cut my hair so that you can't see that I'm going
bald.

All demonstrative pronouns may be prefixed with **ugyan-** to denote 'same'.

Szólt a telefon és ugyanakkor csengettek.
The phone rang and at the same time the doorbell did too.

Most már ugyanúgy teniszezel, mint a tanárod.
You play tennis the same way now as your teacher.

11.6.4	Cataphoric use of demonstrative adverbials

As with other demonstrative pronouns, the demonstrative adverbials may be used to refer ahead to a forthcoming clause or back to an earlier statement. The back vowel demonstratives refer ahead; front vowel demonstratives refer back.

Úgy beszél franciául az a német lány, mintha Párizsban született volna.
That German girl speaks French as if she were born in Paris.

Bárcsak így tudnék franciául én is.
If only I knew French like that.

Arra megyek, amerre viszel.
I'll go where you take me.

Addig üsd a vasat, amíg meleg!
Strike while the iron is hot!

Ott akarok lakni, ahol csend van.
I want to live where it is quiet.

11.6.5	Negative

The verb must always be negated when using negative adverbials (double negation); the exceptions are **sohasem, sosem** 'never' where the negative particle is already built into the word.

Sohasem/sosem voltunk Kuala Lumpurban.
We have never been to Kuala Lumpur.

Sehova sem megyek késő este.
I never go anywhere late at night.

11.6.6	Indefinite

As is found in the nouns and adjectives, there are several indefinite pronouns. The **vala-** prefix denotes 'some (undefined)' and the **akár-** and **bár-** prefixes denote 'any, ~ever'

Valamikor szeptemberben ismerkedtek meg.
They became acquainted sometime in September.

Akármikor telefonálok, elfoglalt.
Whenever I call she's busy.

Bármikor jöhetsz, csak gyere!
You may come any time, just come!

11.6.7 | Universal

Mindenképpen keress fel, ha Budapesten vagy.
No matter what, look me up if you are in Budapest.

Mindenhol koszos volt.
It was dirty everywhere.

Imre mindig csak enni akar.
Imre always wants to eat.

Chapter 12

Word formation

Word formation (also called derivation) is perhaps the richest area of Hungarian grammar. Suffixes can be added singly or in combination to change one part of speech into another or otherwise qualify the root. The verb **megszentségtelenít** 'defile', 'profane' is an illustration of how several suffixes and a prefix combine with a single root.

szent holy; saint

szentség holiness, sanctity (addition of the noun-forming suffix **-ség** '-ness')

szentségtelen impious, sacrilegious (addition of the adjective-forming suffix -**telen** 'un-')

megszentségtelenít defile, profane (addition of verb-forming suffix -**ít** and coverb **meg**)

Some of the suffixes are extremely productive, others are more limited in their use. This chapter lists the most important derivational suffixes.

12.1   Noun-forming suffixes

12.1.1 *Nouns formed from verbs*

12.1.1.1 *-ás/-és*

This suffix is added to verb stems; it usually attaches to the same stems as the present participle. It is 100 percent productive (may be used with all verbs) and denotes the (abstract) action. It is translated by the gerund in English.

dohányzik	smoke	dohányzás	act of smoking
énekel	sing	éneklés	act of singing
ír	write	írás	act of writing
olvas	read	olvasás	act of reading

Abbahagyta az olvasást.   He stopped reading.

Nem tetszett neki az éneklés.   He didn't like the singing.

The -ás/-és suffix may also denote the result of an action.

főz	cook	főzés	cooking, cuisine
ír	write	írás	writing (sample)
kér	ask for	kérés	request
mond	say	mondás	saying

Nagyon találó az a közmondás.   That proverb is quite apt.

Lenne egy pár kérésem.   I have a few requests.

12.1.1.2   -at/-et

This suffix is added to verb stems to denote a result of the verb.

épül	build	épület	building
felad	assign	feladat	assignment
felel	answer	felelet	answer, response
ír	write	irat	document
mond	say	mondat	sentence

12.1.1.3   -alom/-elem, -(a)dalom/-(e)delem

This suffix is attached to verbs to form collective or abstract nouns

forr	boil	forradalom	revolution
hat	have an effect	hatalom	power
ír	write	irodalom	literature
jön	come	jövedelem	income

késik	be late	**késedelem**	delay
történik	happen	**történelem**	history

12.1.1.4   *-(o)mány/-(e)mény*

This suffix is added to verbs to denote a result of the action.

ad	give	**adomány**	grant
fest	paint	**festmény**	painting
gyűjt	collect	**gyűjtemény**	collection
kezd	begin	**kezdemény**	initiative
költ	compose, invent	**költemény**	poetry, poem
olvas	read	**olvasmány**	a piece/selection of reading
süt	bake	**sütemény**	pastry
tud	know	**tudomány**	knowledge, science

12.1.1.5   *-vány/-vény*

This suffix is added to verbs to denote a result or product of an action.

áll	stand	**állvány**	stand, scaffolding
igazol	justify	**igazolvány**	certificate
jön	come	**jövevény**	newcomer
kér	ask for	**kérvény**	questionnaire
kiad	publish	**kiadvány**	publication
köt	tie	**kötvény**	bond, security
mutat	show	**mutatvány**	specimen; spectacle

12.1.2   *Nouns formed from noun, adjective or verb stems*

12.1.2.1   -ász/-ész

This suffix is added to stems (of nouns, adjectives or verbs) to form occupations.

213

bánya	mine	bányász	miner
építy	build	építész	architect
erdő	forest	erdész	forester
gyógy-[1]	cure	gyógyász	doctor
hal	fish	halász	fisherman
mű	opus	művész	artist
nyelv	language	nyelvész	linguist
szín	scene	színész	actor
szobor	statue	szobrász	sculptor
szül	give birth	szülész	obstetrician

| 12.1.2.2 | -ászat/-észet |

This suffix (formed by adding -at/-et to the previous suffix) is added to stems to denote the field of work associated with the aforementioned occupations.

épít	build	építészet	architecture
gyógy-[2]	cure	gyógyászat	medicine
mű	opus	művészet	art
nyelv	language	nyelvészet	linguistics
szobor	statue	szobrászat	sculpture
szül	give birth	szülészet	obstetrics

| 12.1.2.3 | -ista |

Similar to the English suffix '-ist', this suffix is added to roots to denote one belonging to the general activity or school of the root.

| alkohol | alcohol | alkoholista | alcoholic |
| egyetem | university | egyetemista | university student |

---

[1] The hyphen indicates that this form is found only as a stem, or combinatory form. i.e., it does not occur as a self-standing word.
[2] See n. 1 above.

| gimnázium | high school | gimnázista | high school student |
| zongora | piano | zongorista | pianist |

This suffix is found in many cognates with English.

buddhista	Buddhist	nacionalista	nationalist
germanista	Germanist	optimista	optimist
imperialista	imperialist	pesszimista	pessimist
kapitalista	capitalist	szocialista	socialist

12.1.2.4 -s

This is perhaps the most widely used derivational suffix. In addition to making nouns, its most common use is in forming adjectives (see section **12.2.2**).

The suffix -s requires a linking vowel when attaching to stems ending in a consonant. In most cases, the choice of linking vowel is the same as in forming the plural. When adding the suffix -s to words ending in **a** or **e**, the vowel is lengthened to **á**, **é**, respectively; with stems ending in other vowels, there is no change in the stem.

The suffix -s makes nouns from other nouns to denote the person who operates or works at or with that noun.

asztal	table	asztalos	carpenter
ének	song	énekes	singer
könyvtár	library	könyvtáros	librarian
óra	watch	órás	watchmaker
tánc	dance	táncos	dancer
taxi	taxi	taxis	taxi driver
telefon	telephone	telefonos	telephone operator
zöldség	vegetable	zöldséges	greengrocer

| 12.1.2.5 | -ság/-ség[3] |

Another widely used suffix, -ság/-ség makes nouns out of adjectives and other nouns. Its general meaning is similar to the English suffixes '-ness' or '-hood', but it has a collective function as well.

anya	mother	**anyaság**	motherhood
barát	friend	**barátság**	friendship
boldog	happy	**boldogság**	happiness
buta	stupid	**butaság**	stupidity
egész	whole	**egészség**	health
hegy	mountain	**hegység**	mountain range
képtelen	incapable	**képtelenség**	inability
lehető	possible	**lehetőség**	possibility

| 12.1.2.6 | -né |

This suffix is added to a name or noun to mean 'Mrs.' or the person's wife.

Kövér Csaba	Csaba Kövér
Kövér Csabané	Mrs. Csaba Kövér
Kövérné	Mrs. Kövér

| **pék** | baker | **pékné** | baker's wife |
| **pap** | minister | **papné** | minister's wife |

| 12.1.2.7 | -ék |

This suffix is added to a name or noun to denote the family, or usual entourage, of the person.

| **Kovács** | **a Kovácsék** | the Kovács family |
| **Gyula** | **a Gyuláék** | Gyula and his family and/or friends |

---

[3] This suffix never lengthens a final a or e when attaching.

a barátom my friend   **a barátomék**   my friend and his family
and/or friends

12.2   Adjective-forming suffixes

12.2.1   *-i*

This suffix forms adjectives from nouns, adverbs and postpositions.[4]

12.2.1.1

It is often added to expressions of place or time and can be translated by 'of' or a possessive construction in English.

fent	above	**fenti lakás**	upstairs apartment
közel	nearby	**közeli bolt**	nearby store
ma	today	**mai újság**	today's newspaper
tavaly	last year	**tavalyi idő**	last year's weather
utóbb	later	**utóbbi évek**	recent years

12.2.1.2

It is added to nouns to give them an attributive function.

hegy	mountain	**hegyi tó**	mountain lake
hely	place	**helyi idő**	local time
nő	woman	**női ruha**	women's clothing
tavasz	spring	**tavaszi zápor**	spring shower

12.2.1.3

The suffix -i may be added to postpositions to turn the entire postpositional phrase into an attribute.

a ház előtt	in front of the house
a ház előtti kert	the garden in front of the house

---

[4] See n. 3 above.

az asztal fölött	above the table
az asztal fölötti festmény	the painting over the table
a háború után	after the war
a háború utáni évek	the post-war years

12.2.1.4

The suffix -i is 100 percent productive when added to place names to denote a person or other entity from that place. Note that although the place name is written with a capital letter, the adjectival form is not. Although the resulting forms always decline as adjectives, they may be used as nouns as well.

Budapest	budapesti	(a person/thing) from Budapest
London	londoni	(a person/thing) from London
Madrid	madridi	(a person/thing) from Madrid
Szeged	szegedi	(a person/thing) from Szeged

A budapestiek büszkék lehetnek a városukra.
People from Budapest can be proud of their city.

Külföldön a szegedi paprika a leghíresebb.
Paprika from Szeged is the most famous abroad.

12.2.2 -s

This suffix is added to nouns, adjectives and numerals to make new adjectives.

12.2.2.1

It has the meaning 'endowed with', 'qualified as having'. This suffix also makes nouns (see section 12.1.2.4).

vaj	butter	vajas kenyér	bread and butter (lit., buttery bread)
erdő	forest	erdős terület	wooded area

12.2.2.2

Concrete characteristics of a person or thing can be expressed with the use of -s.

név	name	**neves professzor**	famous professor
ötlet	idea	**ötletes gyerek**	clever or ingenious child
család	family	**családos férfi**	man with a family (children)
kalap	hat	**kalapos hölgy**	lady with a hat
kert	garden	**kertes ház**	house with a garden
szemüveg	glasses	**szemüveges bácsi**	man (uncle) with glasses

12.2.2.3

The suffix -s can be attached to time expressions to indicate duration. Note that the time expression is consequently written as one word.

tíz perc	ten minutes	**tízperces szünet**	ten-minute break
egy év	one year	**egyéves tanfolyam**	one-year course
két hét	two weeks	**kéthetes szabadság**	two-week vacation
egy óra	one hour	**egyórás előadás**	one-hour lecture

12.2.2.4

Attached to an adjective -s can modify the meaning of the adjective.

barna	brown	**barnás**	brownish
beteg	sick	**beteges**	sickly, ailing
fiatal	young	**fiatalos**	youngish
magyar	Hungarian	**magyaros**	in a Hungarian style
zöld	green	**zöldeskék**	greenish-blue

12.2.2.5

It can be attached to numerals to yield both adjectives and nouns.

hat	six	**hatos villamos**	number six tram
hét	seven	**a hetes szám**	the number seven
tíz	ten	**tizes szoba**	room number ten
száz	hundred	**százas**	one-hundred (forint) banknote

| **12.2.3** | -tlan/-tlen, -atlan/-etlen, -talan/-telen |

This suffix is attached to nouns, adjectives, and verbs and denotes 'without', or 'qualified as not having'.

arány	proportion	**aránytalan**	disproportionate
rend	order	**rendetlen**	messy
ismer	know	**ismeretlen**	unknown

The suffix has three variants. Although there are many exceptions, the following are the tendencies in forming words with this suffix.

1   -tlan, -tlen is added to stems ending in a vowel; word-final vowel **a** or **e** is lengthened to **á** or **é**, respectively.

béke	peace	**békétlen**	restless, turbulent, quarrelsome
erő	force	**erőtlen**	weak, feeble, powerless
hiba	mistake	**hibátlan**	faultless
só	salt	**sótlan**	unsalted

2   -talan, -telen is added to stems ending in a single consonant:

bátor	brave	**bátortalan**	cowardly
érték	value	**értéktelen**	worthless
haszon	use	**haszontalan**	useless

3   -atlan, -etlen is added to all verb stems.

ismer	know	**ismeretlen**	unknown
kér	ask for	**kéretlen**	unrequested, unsolicited
vár	expect, wait	**váratlan**	unexpected

| 12.2.3.1 | Grammatical features of the *-tlan/-tlen* suffix

| *12.2.3.1.1* |

This suffix is commonly found with verbs formed with the potential suffix -hat/-het and forms the antonym of the potential present participle.

eszik	eat	**ehető**	edible
		ehetetlen	inedible
hisz	believe	**hihető**	believable
		hihetetlen	unbelievable
lát	see	**látható**	visible
		láthatatlan	invisible
megváltoztat	change	**megváltoztatható**	changeable
		megváltoztathatatlan	immutable, irrevocable

| *12.2.3.1.2* |

Sometimes more than one variant can be attached to the same root, yielding two different meanings.

íz	taste, flavor	**ízetlen**	tasteless (abstract, as of decoration)
		íztelen	tasteless (concrete, as of food)
gond	worry, care	**gondatlan**	careless
		gondtalan	carefree
lélek	soul, spirit	**lelketlen**	heartless
		lélektelen	lacking in spirit or enthusiasm
tárgy	object, theme	**tárgyatlan**	(of sentences or verbs) having no object, intransitive
		tárgytalan	(a matter) not worth discussion, invalid, unnecessary

12.2.3.1.3

Unlike most adjectives, those formed with -tlan/-tlen and their variants form their adverbs with -ul/-ül.

hibátlan	faultless	**hibátlanul**	faultlessly
váratlan	unexpected	**váratlanul**	unexpectedly

12.2.3.1.4

The suffixes -s and -tlan/-tlen (and its variants) often form antonyms.

arányos	proportionate	**aránytalan**	disproportionate
egészséges	healthy	**egészségtelen**	unhealthy
figyelmes	considerate	**figyelmetlen**	inconsiderate
hasznos	useful	**haszontalan**	useless
nős	married man	**nőtlen**	bachelor
rendes	tidy	**rendetlen**	disorderly
rendszeres	systematic	**rendszertelen**	unsystematic
sós	salty	**sótlan**	saltless
udvarias	polite	**udvariatlan**	impolite
ügyes	clever, agile	**ügyetlen**	awkward, inept

12.2.4 -ú/-ű (-jú/-jű)

This suffix has a similar meaning to the suffix -s.

12.2.4.1

It makes adjectives out of nouns and is used when it is in turn modified by another adjective.

fekete haj	black hair	**fekete hajú lány**	a girl with black hair
kék szem	blue eyes	**kék szemű kisfiú**	blue-eyed boy
jó étvágy	good appetite	**jó étvágyú beteg**	a patient with a good appetite

| érdekes | interesting | érdekes témájú | book with an |
| téma | theme | könyv | interesting theme |

12.2.4.2

Adjectives derived by -ú/-ű may have a stronger (more permanent, inalienable) connection to the noun they are modifying. Adjectives derived by -s (may) have a looser (more temporary) connection to the noun.

hosszú ruhás lány a girl with a long dress

hosszú hajú lány a girl with long hair

12.2.4.3

The variants -jú and -jű are attached to stems ending in a vowel; if the final vowel is a or e it is lengthened to á or é, respectively.

| erő | force | nagy erejű | having great power |
| téma | theme | tabu témájú | having a taboo theme |

12.2.5 -ékeny/-ékony

This suffix forms adjectives from verb stems. It denotes an inclination to the activity expressed in the next stem.

érez	feel	érzékeny	sensitive
félt	fear for; be jealous of	féltékeny	jealous
folyik	flow	folyékony	fluent
hajlik	bend, lean	hajlékony	flexible, pliable
tör	break	törékeny	fragile

12.2.6 -nyi

This suffix is added to nouns to form adjectives of measure or size.

| méter | meter | méternyi | (one) meter long |
| pillanat | moment | pillanatnyi | (lasting) a moment |

tenyér	palm	tenyérnyi	palm-sized
ujj	finger	ujjnyi	width of a finger

12.3 Verb-forming suffixes

12.3.1 -z(ik)[5]

This suffix yields perhaps the most common way of making verbs out of nouns. When added to stems ending in a consonant it requires a linking vowel – usually the same vowel as is required for forming the plural; when added to stems ending in a or e, the vowel is lengthened to á or é, respectively. These verbs may or may not take the -ik ending. The -z(ik) suffix has many uses; only a few are mentioned here.

12.3.1.1

This suffix is commonly added to stems to denote using the stem in playing sports or music or otherwise spending time at an activity.

foci	soccer	focizik	play soccer
fuvola	flute	fuvolázik	play the flute
kosárlabda	basketball	kosárlabdázik	play basketball
levél	letter	levelezik	correspond
tenisz	tennis	teniszezik	play tennis
zongora	piano	zongorázik	play the piano

12.3.1.2

It can be used with foods or meals.

kávé	coffee	kávézik	drink coffee
reggeli	breakfast	reggelizik	eat breakfast

---

[5] If the stem is a low-vowel noun that loses length when forming the plural, it will usually lose length when suffixing -z(ik) and -l as well: út 'trip', utazik 'travel'; nyár 'summer', nyaral 'spend summer vacation'.

sör	beer	sörözik	drink beer
tea	tea	teázik	drink tea
vacsora	dinner	vacsorázik	eat dinner

12.3.1.3

To use an instrument or tool.

csavar	screw	csavaroz	fasten with a screw
gereblye	rake	gereblyézik	use a rake
kocsi	car	kocsizik	go by car, drive

12.3.1.4

To supply/furnish with an object.

fal	wall	falaz	put up a wall
fegyver	weapon	felfegyverezik	arm

12.3.2 -l[6]

This suffix is also widely used to form verbs from nouns. When added
to stems ending in a consonant, it requires a linking vowel (usually the
same one as required when forming the plural of the stem). When added
to stems ending in a or e, the vowel is lengthened to á or é, respectively.

ebéd	lunch	ebédel	eat lunch
ének	song	énekel	sing
kéz	hand	kezel	handle, treat
lapát	shovel	lapátol	dig with a shovel
nyár	summer	nyaral	spend the summer (vacation)
vásár	market	vásárol	shop

---

[6] See n. 5 above.

Note that the same stem may take both verb-forming suffixes and result in two different meanings:

rend	order	**rendez**	organize	**rendel**	place an order
vizsga	test	**vizsgázik**	take a test	**vizsgál**	examine

12.3.3 -ít

This suffix makes transitive verbs. It is added to stems ending in a consonant; if the stem ends in a vowel, the vowel is dropped before suffixing. Verbs ending in -ít are often the transitive counterpart of the intransitive verbs ending in -ul/-ül; see section 12.3.5.

12.3.3.1

This suffix is commonly added to adjectives.

csúnya	ugly	**csúnyít**	make ugly
éles	sharp	**élesít**	sharpen
fekete	black	**feketít**	blacken
kész	ready	**készít**	prepare
nagyobb	bigger	**nagyobbít**	enlarge
széles	wide	**szélesít**	widen
szép	beautiful	**szépít**	beautify

12.3.3.2

It may be added to nouns and other roots.

alak	form	**alakít**	shape (something)
alap	base	**alapít**	establish
gyógy-[7]	cure	**gyógyít**	heal
tan	study	**tanít**	teach

---

[7] See n. 1 above.

12.3.4   -esz/-aszt

This suffix is found on transitive verbs. It is not nearly as productive as
the transitive suffix -ít. It is often attached to stems that occur only
as roots of derivations. These verbs often have intransitive counterparts
ending in -ad/-ed; see section 12.3.6.

ébreszt	wake someone up	**halaszt**	postpone
fáraszt	tire (someone)	**ijeszt**	frighten, startle
fejleszt	develop	**riaszt**	alarmed

12.3.5   -ul/-ül

This suffix forms intransitive verbs and often is the counterpart to the
transitive verbs formed with -ít. It is added to stems ending in a consonant;
should the stem end in a vowel, the vowel is dropped.

12.3.5.1

The suffix -ul/-ül is often added to adjectives.

ép	intact	**épül**	be built
kész	ready	**készül**	become prepared, ready
sárga	yellow	**sárgul**	turn yellow
szép	beautiful	**szépül**	become beautiful

12.3.5.2

This suffix may be added to non-adjective stems as well.

alak	form	**alakul**	take shape
alap	base	**alapul**	be founded
gyógy-[8]	cure	**gyógyul**	be cured
tan	learn	**tanul**	learn

---

[8] See n. 1 above.

12.3.6 -ad-/-ed

This suffix makes intransitive verbs. Verbs with this suffix often find their transitive counterparts in verbs ending in -szt (see above, section 12.3.4).

ébred	wake up	**ijed**	become frightened
fárad	become tired	**riad**	become alarmed
halad	progress, advance	**szárad**	become dry

12.3.7 -kodik/-kedik/-ködik, kozik/-kezik/-közik

This suffix makes intransitive verbs. There is no way to predict whether the suffix will contain a **d** (-kodik) or a **z** (-kozik). This suffix has many uses; only a few are listed here.

12.3.7.1

Often the meaning is reflexive, i.e., to do the activity to oneself. (The reflexive pronouns are never used with these verbs.)

fésül	use a comb	**fésülködik**	comb one's hair
mos	wash	**mosakodik**	wash oneself
öltöz	dress (trans.)	**öltözködik**	get dressed
töröl	wipe	**törölközik**	dry oneself with a towel

12.3.7.2

It may be used to identify occupations.

lektor	lector	**lektorkodik**	work as a lector
pincér	waiter	**pincérkedik**	work as a waiter

12.3.7.3

This suffix may describe a way of behaving.

szemtelen	impertinent	**szemtelenkedik**	misbehave
szerelmes	in love	**szerelmeskedik**	act lovey-dovey
szomorú	sad	**szomorkodik**	act sad

12.3.7.4

It may be added to other roots to express mutual behavior.

barát	friend	**barátkozik**	make friends
szeret	love	**szeretkezik**	make love

12.3.8	**-skodik/-skedik/-sködik**

This suffix makes intransitive verbs. After stems ending in a consonant it requires the linking vowel o/e/ö; stems ending in a or e lengthen to á or é, respectively. It denotes behaving as the noun or adjective of its root.

cimbora	pal	**cimboráskodik**	fraternize
hülye	idiot(ic)	**hülyéskedik**	act stupidly
nagylelkű	generous	**nagylelkűsködik**	act generously
tanú	witness	**tanuskodik**	bear witness

12.3.9	**-odik/-edik/-ödik**

This suffix makes intransitive verbs. It is most often attached to adjectives, but is found with other roots as well. Verbs formed with this suffix usually find their transitive counterparts with verbs ending in -ít.

halvány	obscure, dim	**halványodik**	become obscure, fade
kanyar	curve	**kanyarodik**	bend, curve (as in a road or river)
keskeny	narrow	**keskenyedik**	become narrow

12.3.10	**-ódik/-ődik**

This suffix makes intransitive verbs. It is often attached to transitive verb stems.

befejez	finish	**befejeződik**	come to an end, become finished
csuk	close, shut	**csukódik**	close, shut (by itself)

229

elvégez	finish	elvégződik	come to an end
kezd	begin	kezdődik	start (intrans.)
zár	close, lock	záródik	close, lock (by itself)

Mikor kezdték az előadást?	When did they start the lecture?
Mikor kezdődött az előadás?	When did the lecture start?
Becsukta az ajtót.	She closed the door.
Becsukódik az ajtó.	The door is closing.

12.3.11 -ll(ik)

This suffix is added to adjectives and expressions of quantity; the verb denotes that something appears to have the quality of the root – sometimes in excess. Stems ending in a consonant require the linking vowel (and other stem alternations) found in forming the adverb. Word-final a and e are lengthened to á and é, respectively.

sok	much	sokall	consider something too much
kevés	few	kevesell	consider something too little, not enough
fekete	black	feketéllik	show, appear black

Kevesellte a fizetést.   He thought the pay was too low.

12.3.12 -ászik/-észik

This suffix forms verbs denoting a trade or hobby.

vad	wild	vadászik	hunt
madár	bird	madarászik	hunt birds
sólyom	hawk	sólymászik	hunt hawks

12.4 Diminutives

Diminutives are suffixes added to names, nouns, and sometimes adjectives and denote the smallness of, or fondness toward, a person or object. They are very common in Hungarian; parents almost always use them with the names of their children, and depending on the idiosyncracies of the speaker, they can find their way into many sentences.

Diminutives take several shapes. The most common are given here.

12.4.1 -cska/-cske

This diminutive can be attached to most nouns and some adjectives. After nouns ending in a consonant, it requires the linking vowel used to form the plural; any other stem changes required in the plural are also required when attaching this suffix. Word-final vowels **a** or **e** are lengthened to **á** or **é**, respectively.

girl	**lány**	**lányocska**	face	**arc**	**arcocska**
cloud	**felhő**	**felhőcske**	hand	**kéz**	**kezecske**
milk	**tej**	**tejecske**	house	**ház**	**házacska**
fork	**villa**	**villácska**	horse	**ló**	**lovacska**
big	**nagy**	**nagyocska**	bird	**madár**	**madaracska**

12.4.2 -ka/-ke

This diminutive is usually attached to polysyllabic words not ending in -k or -g. It attaches directly to the stem and does not require the linking vowel or the stem changes found when forming the plural.

poor	**szegény**	**szegényke**	piece	**darab**	**darabka**
cow	**tehén**	**tehénke**	bird	**madár**	**madárka**
person	**ember**	**emberke**	table	**asztal**	**asztalka**
small	**kicsi**	**kicsike**	short	**rövid**	**rövidke**

12.4.3 -i

This suffix is used with stems that have already been shortened.

cigarette	**cigaretta**	**cigi**
chocolate	**csokoládé**	**csoki**
thank you	**köszönöm**	**köszi**

12.4.4

Perhaps the most common use of diminutives is with people's names. Often the names are shortened and several different diminutives may be attached. A name with front-vowel assonance may change to a nickname with back-vowel assonance and vice versa. The -ka/-ke suffix is the most common with names and the first person singular possessive suffix is often attached. Several common variations with names are given here.

John	**János: Jani, Janika, Jánoska, Jancsi, Jancsika, Jancsó, Jancsóka**
Charles	**Károly: Károlyka, Karcsi, Karesz**
George	**György: Gyuri, Gyurika**
Stephen	**István: Isti, Istvánka, Pista, Pisti, Pistike, Pityu**
Elizabeth	**Erzsébet: Erzsi, Erzsike, Erzsó, Erzsóka, Zsóka, Bözsi, Bözsike, Böske, Örzse, Örzsi, Örzsike**
Mary	**Mária: Mari, Marika, Maris, Mariska, Marcsi**

The first person singular possessive suffix is often attached to diminutives when addressing the person directly.

Erzsikém, gyere ide!   Come here, Erzsi!

Úgy szeretlek, Jánoskám.   I love you so much, János.

Children (and people speaking with them) commonly use the following diminutives:

father	**apa**	**apu, apuka, apus, apuska, api, apika, apuci, papus**
mother	**anya**	**anyu, anyuka, anyus, anyuska, anyuci**

rabbit	**nyúl**	**nyuszi, nyuszika, nyulacska, nyuszóka**
dog	**kutya**	**kutyu, kutyus, kutyuska**
cat	**macska**	**cica, cica-mica, cicus**

Chapter 13

Conjunctions

13.1   Coordinating conjunctions

Coordinating conjunctions join clauses, phrases or words. A comma is usually used before conjunctions joining clauses. The following are the most important coordinating conjunctions in Hungarian.

13.1.1   *Connecting conjunctions*

These may be single words or pairs of words:

és 'and'

Imre és János most vacsorázik.	Imre and János are eating dinner now.
Esik az eső és fúj a szél.	It's raining and the wind is blowing.

s 'and' (pronounced as one with the following syllable):

Megjött a levél, s rögtön elolvasta.	The letter arrived and he read it immediately.
Zsófia s én együtt dolgozunk.	Zsófia and I work together.

meg 'and' (when joining clauses, **meg** is usually in the second position of the clause):

Péter moziba megy, én meg színházba megyek.
Péter is going to the movies and I am going to the theater.

Kettő meg kettő, az négy.
Two and two are four.

is 'too', 'also' (this word always follows the phrase to which it refers):

Nekünk van kutyánk, macskánk is.
We have a dog and a cat (too).

se, sem 'neither', 'nor'

Nekem nem ízlett a bor, (s) Jánosnak sem.
I didn't like the wine, and neither did János.

sőt 'moreover', 'indeed', 'even'

Nagyon tetszik a húgod, sőt, meghívtam vacsorára.
I really like your sister, I even invited her to dinner.

is ... is 'both ... and'

Apám is, anyám is Budapesten lakik.
Both my father and mother live in Budapest.

mind ... mind 'both ... and'

Mind a gyerekek, mind a felnőttek szerették azt a játékot.
Both the children and the adults loved that game.

sem ... sem, se ... se 'neither ... nor'

Sem kalapot, sem kesztyűt nem hord télen.
He wears neither a hat nor gloves in the winter.

Mi történt veled? Se nem írsz, se nem telefonálsz.
What is up with you? You neither write nor call me.

nemcsak ... hanem ... is 'not just ... but ... too'

Nemcsak főz a férjem, hanem porszívóz is!
My husband doesn't just cook, he vacuums too!

| 13.1.2 | *Contrasting conjunctions* |

de 'but'

Meghívtam a bátyámat, de nem tud eljönni.
I invited my brother, but he is unable to come.

hanem 'but', 'rather' (Always preceded by a nem-clause.)

Nem Prágába akar menni, hanem Bécsbe.
She doesn't want to go to Prague, rather to Vienna.

mégis '(but) still', 'even so'

Az előadás unalmas volt, mégis tanultam valamit belőle.
The lecture was boring, but I still learned something from it.

mégsem '(but) still . . . not'

Rengeteget eszik, mégsem hízik.
He eats so much, but still he doesn't put on weight.

azonban 'however', 'but' (This word is usually in the second position of the clause.)

Hazavittem a számítógépemet, a könyveimet azonban az irodában hagytam.
I brought my computer home, but I left my books in the office.

ellenben 'on the other hand'

A bátyám nagyon gazdag, ellenben az öcsém elég szegény.
My older brother is very rich, my younger brother on the other hand is rather poor.

viszont 'but, on the other hand'

Imádom a nyarat, viszont a telet egyáltalán nem bírom.
I love summer, but I can't stand winter at all.

| 13.1.3 | *Conjunctions of choice* |

vagy 'or'

Eljössz velem, vagy itthon maradsz?
Are you coming with me or staying home?

vagy . . . vagy 'either . . . or' (Used when the choice between two options results in two different outcomes.)

Ma este vagy moziba megyünk, vagy színházba.
We are either going to the movies or to the theater tonight.

akár. ... .akár 'whether ... or' (Used when the choice between two options results in the same outcome.)

Akár hiszed, akár nem, a hatéves fiam már tud síelni.
Whether you believe it or not, my six-year-old son already knows how to ski.

13.1.5 | Explanatory conjunctions

These conjunctions are used to explain or account for the assertion in the preceding clause.

ugyanis 'for', 'since', 'because'

A felesége jól beszél magyarul, ugyanis egy évig Budapesten élt.
His wife speaks Hungarian well, for she lived in Budapest for a year.

hiszen 'for', 'since', 'because'

Nagyon berúgott, hiszen egymaga megivott egy egész üveg bort.
He got very drunk, for he drank a whole bottle of wine by himself.

tudniillik 'because', 'since'

Nem tudom olvasni az újságot, tudniillik nem találom a szemüvegemet.
I can't read the newspaper, because I can't find my glasses.

The explanatory conjunctions **azaz** and **vagyis** provide a more detailed explanation of the preceding phrase or assertion.

azaz 'that is to say'

A pincér szorgalmasan dolgozott, azaz nem csak álldogált a konyhában.
The waiter worked hard, that is to say, he did not just hang about the kitchen.

vagyis 'in other words'

A betegnek ágyban kell maradnia, vagyis nem szabad sokat mozognia.
The patient must stay in bed, in other words, he must not move around much.

13.1.6 | Concluding conjunctions

These conjunctions suggest the consequence of the preceding phrase.

ezért 'for this reason', 'this is why'

Későn érkeztem haza, ezért nem hívtalak fel.
I came home late, that's why I didn't call you.

tehát 'therefore', 'thus'

Gondolkodom, tehát vagyok.
I think, therefore I am.

ennélfogva 'consequently', 'thus'

Egész nap csak énekelt, ennélfogva tönkretette a hangját.
She sang the whole day, consequently she ruined her voice.

13.2 Subordinating conjunctions

hogy 'that' (used to introduce an imbedded sentence)

Tudod, hogy holnaptól megyek szabadságra?
Do you know that my vacation begins tomorrow?

Érted, hogy mit mondok?
Do you understand what I am saying?

mint 'as' (used in clauses of comparison)

A szeme olyan zöld, mint a smaragd.
His eyes are as green as emeralds.

Úgy fut, mint a nyúl.
She runs like a rabbit.

ha 'if', 'when'

Ha Budapesten vagy, mindenképpen keress fel!
When you are in Budapest, by all means look me up.

Ha több időm lenne, zongorázni tanulnék.
If I had more time I would learn to play the piano.

mintha 'as if', 'as though' (usually followed by the conditional form of the verb)

Úgy tesz, mintha boldog lenne.
She acts as though she is happy.

hacsak 'if only'

Hacsak tehetem, ott leszek a bulin.
I'll be at the party if I possibly can.

(a)mikor 'when'

Éppen leültünk, mikor megszólalt a telefon.
We had just sat down when the phone rang.

miután 'after'

**Miután megfürdetem a lányomat, egyszerre leteszem
aludni.**
After I bathe my daughter, I'll put her to bed.

mielőtt 'before'

Mielőtt hazamentek, megisztok egy kávét?
Will you have a cup of coffee before you go home?

(a)mióta 'since'

Amióta megnősült, sokkal vidámabb.
He is a lot more cheerful since he got married.

bár 'although'

Nem írtam a barátaimnak, bár gyakran gondoltam rájuk.
I didn't write my friends, though I thought of them often.

mert 'because'

Nem mentek el kirándulni, mert esni kezdett az eső.
They didn't go on the outing because it started to rain.

mivel 'because', 'since'

A lépcsőn kellett felmenniük, mivel rossz a lift.
Since the elevator is not working, they had to take the stairs.

| 13.2.1 | -e 'whether'

The particle -e is placed on the verb of the subordinate ('whether') clause
(if the sentence contains no verb the particle is placed on the nominal

predicate). In Hungarian, the 'whether' and 'if' clauses are not inter-changeable: if, in the English sentence, 'whether' can substitute for 'if', use only the 'whether' construction in Hungarian.

Nem tudjuk, hogy Pál eljön-e.
We don't know whether (if) Pál is coming.

Kíváncsi vagyok, hogy drága-e az étterem.
I wonder whether (if) the restaurant is expensive.

| 13.2.2 | Relative pronouns |

Subordinate clauses may be introduced by relative pronouns. These are formed in Hungarian simply by prefixing a- to an interrogative pronoun.

Ismered a lányt, aki a másik asztalnál ül?
Do you know the girl who is sitting at the other table?

Nem értem az elméletet, amiről beszélnek.
I don't understand the theory they are talking about.

Úgy készíti a rétest, ahogy a nagyanyám.
She makes strudel just as my grandmother does.

Chapter 14

Numerals

14.1   Cardinal and ordinal numbers

	Cardinal	Ordinal
0	nulla	nulladik
1	egy	első
2	kettő (két)	második
3	három	harmadik
4	négy	negyedik
5	öt	ötödik
6	hat	hatodik
7	hét	hetedik
8	nyolc	nyolcadik
9	kilenc	kilencedik
10	tíz	tizedik
11	tizenegy	tizenegyedik
12	tizenkettő	tizenkettedik
13, etc.	tizenhárom	tizenharmadik
20	húsz	huszadik
21, etc.	huszonegy	huszonegyedik
30	harminc	harmincadik
31, etc.	harmincegy	harmincegyedik

40	negyven	negyvenedik
41, etc.	negyvenegy	negyvenegyedik
50	ötven	ötvenedik
51, etc.	ötvenegy	ötvenegyedik
60	hatvan	hatvanadik
61, etc.	hatvanegy	hatvanegyedik
70	hetven	hetvenedik
71, etc.	hetvenegy	hetvenegyedik
80	nyolcvan	nyolvanadik
81, etc.	nyolvanegy	nyolcvanegyedik
90	kilencven	kilencvenedik
91, etc.	kilencvenegy	kilencvenegyedik
100	száz	századik
101	százegy	százegyedik
200	kétszáz	kétszázadik
1,000	ezer	ezredik
1,100	ezeregyszáz	ezeregyszázadik
2,000	kétezer	kétezredik
10,000	tízezer	tízezredik
100,000	százezer	százezredik
1,000,000	(egy)millió	(egy)milliomodik

14.1.1

Hungarian uses the singular after all numbers or expressions of quantity:

Két bátyám van.
I have two brothers.

Körülbelül háromezer diák tanul ezen az egyetemen.
Approximately three thousand students are at this university.

14.1.2

The number *two* – or any number ending in *two* – **kettő** uses the shorter form **két** when preceding nouns.

Két kocsi van a ház előtt.   Two cars are in front of the house.

Hány kocsi? Kettő.   How many cars? Two.

The long form may also be used before nouns to avoid a possible misunderstanding with the word **hét**.

Kettőszáz forintba kerül.   It costs *two* hundred forints.

14.2 Declension of numerals

14.2.1

The accusative of cardinal numbers is irregular (the plural is rare, but formed along the same pattern):

egyet	**négyet**	**hetet**	**tizet**
negyvenet	**hetvenet**	**százat**	
kettőt	**ötöt**	**nyolcat**	**húszat**
ötvenet	**nyolcvanat**	**ezret**	
hármat	**hatot**	**kilencvenet**	**harmincat**
hatvanat	**kilencvenet**	**milliót**	

Csak egyet kérünk.   We would like just one (of them).

Ezret láttam.   I saw a thousand (of them).

Ezreket láttam.   I saw thousands (of them).

14.2.2

The accusative of the ordinal numbers requires the low linking vowel a/e before the -t:[1]

harmadikat   **negyediket**

---

[1] Except **első**: (acc.) **elsőt**; (third person poss.) **elseje**.

| 14.2.3 |

The rest of the declension is regular.[2]

| 14.2.4 |

The possessive third person singular possessive suffix (used in dates) is formed with a/e:[3]

február huszonkettedike   February 22

május tizenhatodika   May 16

Hányadika van ma?   What is today's date?

14.3 Adverbial use of expressions of quantity

If the subject of a sentence is *a number of people*, the adverbial form of the number or other expression of quantity is often used. The verb must be in the plural and the word **ember** is omitted. Often it is only the verb conjugation that indicates the subject.

ketten	**hatan**	**tízen**	**negyvenen**	**kevesen**
hárman	**heten**	**tizenegyen**	**százan**	**hányan**
négyen	**nyolcan**	**húszan**	**ezren**	**többen**
öten	**kilencen**	**harmincan**	**sokan**	**ezreken**

Ketten mentünk moziba.   The two of us went to the movies.

Többen jöttek, mint múltkor. More people came than last time.

Hányan maradtok itt?   How many of you are staying here?

Sokan voltunk az előadáson. Many of us were at the lecture.

Tízen vártak a sorban.   Ten people were waiting in line.

---

[2] The word **három** 'three' declines as a fleeting vowel sound.
[3] See n. 1 above.

14.4 Fractions

14.4.1

Fractions are easily formed from the ordinal numbers by removing the last letters -ik. The word **fél** (or **egyketted**) 'half' is an exception.

⅓	**egyharmad**	⅔	**kéthatod**	⅘	**négykilenced**
¼	**egynegyed**	2/7	**kétheted**		
⅕	**egyötöd**	⅜	**kétnyolcad**		

14.4.2

The accusative is formed by adding the vowel o/e/ö before -t (**fél** 'half' loses vowel length: **felet**).

Csak egyötödöt kérek szépen.   I would like only one fifth,
please.

14.4.3

The third person singular possessive is formed with or without the **j** (unless used in dates, when it is always formed without the **j**):

harmada ~ harmadja   one third (of it)

negyede ~ negyedje   one fourth (of it)

14.4.4

Also in use:

másfél   1½

14.5 Decimals

Decimals are marked with a comma in Hungarian; the presence of a decimal may be articulated by the word **egész** 'whole'.

36.7	36,7	harminchat egész hét ~ harminchat egész héttized
20.07	20,07	húsz egész nulla hét ~ húsz egész hétszázad

14.6 Nouns and adjectives derived from numbers

Numbers are used to indicate tram, bus, metro or lines, addresses, banknotes, etc. When referring to something by its number, use the derivational ending -s. With the exception of **kettő** 'two' the numbers add this derivational ending exactly as though adding an accusative ending:

egyes	kettes	hármas
négyes	ötös	hatos
hetes	nyolcas	kilences
tizes	tizenegyes	huszas
harmincas	negyvenes	százas
ezres	hányas	

Fel kell szállnom a *négyes* villamosra.
I have to board the number 4 tram.

Tudsz adni egy *százast*?
Can you give me a 100 forint/dollar note?

Zsuzsa az 512-es (*ötszáztizenkettes*) szobában dolgozik.
Zsuzsa works in room 512.

***Hányas* a cipőd?**
What size (lit. number) are your shoes?

14.7 Multiplicative -szor/-szer/-ször

14.7.1

This suffix is added to numbers, fractions and other expressions of quantity to mean 'time(s)'.

Csak egyszer voltam Londonban.
I've only been to London once.

Most már ötödször olvasom ezt a könyvet.
I'm reading this book for the fifth time.

Hányszor láttad már a kedvenc filmedet?
How many times have you seen your favorite movie?

Milliószor csókollak.
I kiss you a million times.

| 14.7.2 |

This suffix is used to multiply numbers.

Háromszor négy az tizenkettő.   Three times four is twelve.

Kétszer kettő az négy.   Two times two is four.

Chapter 15

Interjections

Interjections are isolated words or phrases outside the rules of grammar. They may express joy, fear, frustration, pain, etc. The following are some common interjections in Hungarian:

Csitt!	Sshhh!
Ejnye, ejnye!	Tsk, tsk!
Ejnye-bejnye!	Tsk, tsk!
Ez az.	That's it.
Hát ...	Well ...
Hurrá!	Hurray!
Hű-ha!	Uh-oh.
Íme	Behold, voilà!
Isten őrizz!	God forbid!
Így van.	Right, that's the way it is.
Ja?	Really/Is that so?
Jaj, istenem!	Oh my God!
Jaj-jaj	Oh, no!/Oh, dear.
Jézus, Mária	Jesus and Mary!
Kár.	It's a shame.
Lám.	There we go.
Na!	Well!
Naná.	You see? (I told you so.)

Nini!	Look! (children's word)	Interjections
Nos ...	Well ...	
Nosza ...	Well ...	
Pfuj!	Yuck!	
Tyű!	Wow!	

PART III

Sentence structure

Chapter 16

Sentence elements and word order

Word order in Hungarian is quite different from English in a number of ways. In English, it is the word order of sentences that tells us what the subject and object are. For example in the sentence, 'The dog chased the postman', we know the subject is 'the dog'. In 'The postman chased the dog' we know the subject is 'the postman'. Though both sentences contain the same words, because of the difference in word order, the meanings of the two are entirely different – particularly from the postman's point of view!

Before examining the differences from English in Hungarian word order, the similiarities should be clear. The subject–verb–object word order found in English is very common in Hungarian too, especially when the object is preceded by an article:

Mária szereti az anyját.　　Mária loves her mother.
　　　　　　　　　　　　　　(subject–verb–object)

Lajos ír egy levelet.　　　　Lajos is writing a letter.
　　　　　　　　　　　　　　(subject–verb–object)

The above Hungarian sentences, however, may be written in a variety of word orders and would have English equivalents requiring either a change in intonation or a different expression altogether. The following Hungarian sentences have the possible English equivalents given (among others).

Szereti Mária az anyját.　　Mária *loves* her mother.

Mária az anyját szereti.　　Mária loves her *mother*.

In Hungarian, the extensive case system clearly marks the grammatical function, i.e., part of speech, of nouns or noun-phrases. Because subjects and objects are easily distinguished by their case markings, Hungarian need not rely on word order to determine grammatical function. Therefore, Hungarian allows a freedom of word order unknown in English. This, however, does not mean that Hungarian word order is free; word order is used instead as a means of backgrounding and/or highlighting information.

'Topic-comment structure' is the term generally applied to Hungarian word order. By this it is meant that topics, i.e., previously known or background information, begin the sentence; the 'comment' (or new information) follows. In this way topics set the communicative stage for the essential points of discourse. In Hungarian, the topic typically includes subjects, general time expressions or reference to previously mentioned material.

Two main sentence types are pertinent for Hungarian in the discussion of word order; although both retain the topic-comment structure, word order restrictions are different for each type. The first type is the 'neutral sentence', the second is traditionally referred to as the 'focus' type. Both require an understanding of sentence positions; their characteristics are outlined below.

16.1   Sentence positions

To see how Hungarian word order works in neutral or focussed sentences, it is helpful to establish the following sentence positions:

Topic —— || Neutral Preverb || —— Verb —— X

|| ~Focus Preverb ||

16.1.1 Topic

The topic position is in the beginning of the sentence and is usually filled with subject(s), general time expressions, previously referred to expressions (i.e., known information) and/or any other information which serves to set the background for more essential information to come. It may contain several constituents or remain empty.

16.1.2 Preverb

The preverb occupies the position immediately before the conjugated verb. The preverb is the crux of the sentence for it is primarily here that the grammaticality of a sentence is determined. It is filled by different elements of speech depending on whether the sentence is neutral or focussed. Although the preverb position may be empty, it is rarely filled by more than one constituent.

16.1.2.1 Neutral preverb

In neutral sentences the preverb position is filled by

(a) a coverb (**be, ki, le, fel, el, meg,** etc.),
(b) an adverb or adverbial phrase (**jól, itt, a házban,** etc.) or
(c) a verbal complement. See section 16.2 for a full description of verbal complements.

16.1.2.2 Focus preverb

Focus is a category in Hungarian that consists of

(a) question words or phrases,
(b) answers to questions,
(c) negation or negated phrases,
(d) stressed words or phrases.

When a focussed element is introduced in a sentence it *must* occupy the **focus preverb** position. As a consequence of this, any element which would occupy the preverb position in a neutral sentence is removed to a position immediately behind the conjugated verb. Thus it may be helpful to think of the focussed element as 'kicking out' the neutral preverb element. The topic position is unaffected by focus; it remains the communicative backdrop of the sentence.

16.1.3 Verb

This is the position for the conjugated verb; other verbal forms (infinitives, participles, etc.) are found elsewhere in the sentence. In neutral sentences, if the verb is prefixed with a coverb, the coverb occupies the preverb position.

16.1.4 | X

This position is filled by any part of speech (except the conjugated verb);
it may contain several constituents; it may be empty. For the most part,
the constituents may occur in the X position in any order without a
difference in meaning. In sentences with focus, however, it is usual that
the first element of X is the element that was removed from the neutral
preverb position. (The initial position of X is identical with the position
immediately following the verb.)

16.1.5 | A note on grammaticality

Broadly speaking, the well-formedness of a sentence depends on how the
position immediately preceding the conjugated verb is filled; the sentence
is ungrammatical if the **preverb** position is incorrectly filled. The **topic**
and X positions have less to do with grammaticality and more to do with
the logical flow or presentation of information; thus they exhibit a greater
freedom of word order. The word order of the **preverb** and **verb** positions
is fixed.

16.2   Verbal complements

Verbal complements may be any part of speech, but they are character-
istically what might be considered a 'natural' complement to the verb.

16.2.1

The verbal complement may be the predicate nominative or predicate
adjective.

Én *mérnök* vagyok. I am an engineer.

***Magasak* vagytok.**   You (pl.) are tall.

16.2.2

In there is/there are constructions, the verbal complement is the subject.

Sok szék van a teremben.	There are many chairs in the room.	Verbal complements
Víz van a pohárban.	There is water in the glass.	

16.2.3

In 'have' constructions, the verbal complement is what one has (the grammatical subject):

Nekem *két testvérem* van.	I have two siblings.
Lacinak *kevés ideje* van.	Laci has little time.

16.2.4

The verbal complement is often the direct object:

Dénes *könyvet* olvas.	Dénes is reading a book.

This sentence has the more literal, though clumsy, English translation 'Dénes is book-reading'. The complement of the verb is the direct object **könyvet** 'book'. This is a common sentence type in Hungarian which conveys the idea that a generic activity is taking place with no reference to specifics, i.e., in this case no individual book is mentioned. In Hungarian this sentence structure can be applied to many activities, as long as the verbal complement is not individuated. In English only a limited number of idiomatic constructions of this type occur (some examples would include babysitting, apartment-hunting, people-watching).

More examples of direct object verbal complements include:

Apám *újságot* vesz.	My father is buying a newspaper.
Tévét nézek.	I am watching television.
János *tollat* keres.	János is looking for a pen.

16.2.5

Verbal complements may also be adverbials:

Moziba megyünk.	We are going to the movies.
Színházba mennek.	They are going to the theater.

Erzsi *egyetemre* jár. Erzsi attends college.

A Kovácsék *vidéken* laknak. The Kovácses live in the
countryside.

Whatever part of speech occupies the preverb position – whether it is a
subject, object or adverbial – it is typically not preceded by an article –
definite or indefinite.[1]

16.3 Neutral sentence structure

Neutral sentences have a level intonation pattern; they are further characterized by *not* containing elements with heavy stress or emphasis,
interrogatives, answers or negation.

With the sentence positions established as above, we may consider the
word order of the following sentences:

1 **Attila itt van.**
   Attila is here.
2 **Klára szépen énekel.**
   Klára sings beautifully.
3 **Az orvos megvizsgálja a beteget.**
   The doctor will examine the patient.
4 **Megvizsgálja az orvos a beteget.**
   The doctor will examine the patient.
5 **Múlt évben a szülei Budapesten laktak.**
   Last year his parents lived in Budapest.
6 **Múlt évben Budapesten laktak a szülei.**
   Last year his parents lived in Budapest.
7 **Dénes könyvet olvas a nappaliban.**
   Dénes is reading a book in the living room.
8 **Reggel a gyerekek a kertben játszanak.**
   In the morning the children play in the yard.
9 **Reggel a kertben játszanak a gyerekek.**
   In the morning the children play in the yard.

---

[1] The indefinite article, however, may be used and the same word order maintained
(in this case, the verbal complement not a generic, but an individuated one):

Apám egy újságot vesz. My father is buying a newspaper.
János egy tollat keres. János is looking for a pen.

10 **Zsuzsa el akar utazni Prágába.**[2]
Zsuzsa wants to travel to Prague.

11 **Amerikaiak vagyunk.**
We are American.

12 **Péter jól megtanulta a leckét.**
Péter learned the lesson well.

The above sentences are categorized according to sentence position in the following table. Topic position is filled by subjects and/or time expressions or remains empty. The preverb position is filled with adverbs or adverbials of place (sentences 1, 5, 6, 8, 9), adverbs of manner (sentences 2, 12), verbal complements (sentences 7, 11, 12) or coverbs (sentences 3, 4, 10). Sentence 12 illustrates the word order for the preverb position containing two elements. The coverb is usually not separated from the verb in these instances. (But see focus structure below.)

	Topic	Neutral preverb	Verb	X
1	**Attila**	**itt**	**van.**	
2	**Klára**	**szépen**	**énekel.**	
3	**Az orvos**	**meg-**	**vizsgálja**	**a beteget.**
4		**Meg-**	**vizsgálja**	**az orvos a beteget.**
5	**Múlt évben a szülei**	**Budapesten**	**laktak.**	
6	**Múlt évben**	**Budapesten**	**laktak**	**a szülei.**
7	**Dénes**	**könyvet**	**olvas**	**a nappaliban.**
8	**Reggel a gyerekek**	**a kertben**	**játszanak.**	
9	**Reggel**	**a kertben**	**játszanak**	**a gyerekek.**
10	**Zsuzsa**	**el**	**akar**	**utazni Prágába.**
11		**Amerikaiak**	**vagyunk.**	
12	**Péter**	**jól meg-**	**tanulta**	**a leckét.**

---

[2] See section 16.4 for more on this sentence type.

16.4 Sentence structure with focus elements

Focussed sentences have an intonation pattern containing the main (often heavy) stress on the focussed element. Focus affects the word order of neutral sentences by usurping the preverb position for itself and removing the neutral preverb element to a position immediately behind the verb. The topic position remains unaffected.

Focussed sentences contain interrogatives, answers, negation or emphasis (stressed words or phrases).

Consider the following sentences with focus elements. These are all permutations of the neutral sentence (5) **Dénes könyvet olvas.** Dénes is reading a book.

13 **Ki olvas könyvet?**   (Contains a question word)
    Who is reading a book?

14 **Dénes olvas könyvet.**   (As answer to the previous sentence,
    Dénes is reading a book.   **Dénes** is the answer,
                                    the focussed element)[3]

15 **Dénes nem olvas könyvet.**   (Contains negation)
    Dénes is not reading a book.

16 **Csak Dénes olvas könyvet.**   (Contains a stressed element –
    Only Dénes is reading a book.   the **csak**-phrase.)

Sentence	Topic	Focus preverb	Verb	X
13		**Ki**	olvas	**könyvet?**
14		**Dénes**	olvas	**könyvet.**
15	**Dénes**	nem	olvas	**könyvet.**
16		**Csak Dénes**	olvas	**könyvet.**

The table illustrates the permutations of word order for focussed elements in a sentence. In sentence (13), although **Ki** 'who' is the sentence subject,

---

[3] The answer **Dénes** need not begin the sentence, but it must be in the focus preverb position.

it is found in focus position because it is a question word. In sentence (14), **Dénes**, though it is the subject, is the answer to the question **Ki?** of the previous sentence, and therefore is found in the focus position. Negation occupies the focus position in sentence (15). Emphatic or stressed phrases (as illustrated here by the phrase beginning with **csak** 'only') are found in focus position. In all four sentences the focus position has usurped the preverb position of neutral sentences. The word **könyvet** 'book, *acc.*', which had occupied the preverb position in the neutral sentence (5), has consequently been removed to a position immediately behind the verb.

To further examine the possibilities of word order, consider again sentence (8):

Reggel a gyerekek a kertben játszanak.
In the morning the children play in the yard.

We may rephrase the sentence as a question 'Where do the children play in the morning?' In Hungarian it is most common to begin questions with the interrogative, but there is nonetheless a flexibility of word order which depends on how the speaker wishes to frame the question. The only firm requirement is that the interrogative **hol** 'where' be immediately before the conjugated verb. The topic position may be filled or empty.

'Where do the children play in the morning?			
Topic	Focus	Verb	X
	Hol	játszanak	**reggel a gyerekek?**
	Hol	játszanak	**a gyerekek reggel?**
Reggel	**hol**	játszanak	**a gyerekek?**
A gyerekek	**hol**	játszanak	**reggel?**
Reggel a gyerekek	**hol**	**játszanak?**	
A gyerekek reggel	**hol**	**játszanak?**	

Similarly, other sentences with focussed elements relative to sentence (8) include questions such as 'who?, when? what do the children do in the morning?' Naturally, answers can be offered as well. The sentence – or certain elements of the sentence – can be negated (i.e., it is *not the children who* play in the yard ...). Finally, any part of the sentence can be stressed for communicative need. (It is easiest for our purposes here to demonstrate stress by creating a **csak**-phrase – always inherently stressed in Hungarian.) The following table illustrates the word order possibilities for such focussed sentences. Note the free variation of word order in the Topic and X positions and the fixed word order of the focus and verb positions.

17 **Reggel kik játszanak a kertben?**
   Who plays in the garden in the morning?
18 **Reggel a gyerekek játszanak a kertben.** (answer to (1))
   The children play in the garden in the morning.
19a **A gyerekek mikor játszanak a kertben?**
19b **Mikor játszanak a kertben a gyerekek?**
   When do the children play in the garden?
20 **A gyerekek reggel játszanak a kertben.** (answer to (19a, b))
   The children play in the garden in the morning.
21 **A gyerekek sohasem játszanak a kertben reggel.**
   The children never play in the garden in the morning.
22 **A gyerekek nem reggel játszanak a kertben, hanem délután.**
   The children don't play in the garden in the morning, rather in the afternoon.
23 **A gyerekek csak reggel játszanak a kertben, este soha.**
   It is only in the morning that the children play in the garden, never in the evening.
24 **Reggel a gyerekek csak a kertben játszanak, a házban soha.**
   The children play only in the garden, never in the house.

	Type of focus	Topic	Focus	Verb	X
17	*Question*	**Reggel**	**kik**	**játszanak**	**a kertben?**
18	*Answer*	**Reggel**	**a gyerekek**	**játszanak**	**a kertben.**
19a	*Question*	**A gyerekek**	**mikor**	**játszanak**	**a kertben?**
19b	*Question*		**Mikor**	**játszanak**	**a kertben a gyerekek?**
20	*Answer*	**A gyerekek**	**reggel**	**játszanak**	**a kertben.**

	Type of focus	Topic	Focus	Verb	X
21	*Negation*	**A gyerekek**	**sohasem**	**játszanak**	**a kertben reggel.**
22	*Negation*	**A gyerekek**	**nem reggel**	**játszanak**	**a kertben, hanem délután.**
23	*Stress*	**A gyerekek**	**csak reggel**	**játszanak**	**a kertben, este soha.**
24	*Stress*	**Reggel a gyerekek**	**csak a kertben**	**játszanak,**	**a házban soha.**

In the above sentences the neutral preverb position of (8) **a kertben** has been 'kicked out' to a position immediately behind the verb by each element of focus – a position which coincides with the beginning of X. Note that this is not an exhaustive list of possible permutations. The topic position is filled according to context and previously mentioned material; often in natural dialogue, only one-word answers are given and questions usually begin with the question word.

16.4.1 | More on focus

16.4.1.1 | Questions

Yes–no questions are characterized by not having a question word in them. In this instance the word or phrase being questioned is in the focus position. This may be any part of speech. If it is the verb, the coverb is in the focus position. It is often difficult for English speakers to determine what is specifically being questioned. See section 2.7.3 for intonation patterns of yes–no questions.

	Topic	Focus	Verb	X
Were they *nice*?			**Kedvesek**	**voltak?**
Did the people wait			**Sokáig**	**vártak az emberek?**
a long time?	**Az emberek**	**sokáig**	**vártak?**	
Will you *wait* for me?		**Meg**	**vársz**	**engem?**
		Meg	**fogsz**	**várni engem?**
Are you waiting for *me*?		**Engem**	**vársz?**	
Are you looking for *Ildikó*?		**Ildikót**	**keresed?**	

16.4.1.2	Questions and negation

If a sentence contains both a question word and negation, they both occur
in the focus preverb position; the question word precedes the negation.

	Topic	Focus	Verb	X
Who doesn't want coffee?		**Ki nem**	**kér**	**kávét?**
Why doesn't Péter want to dance?	**Péter**	**miért nem**	**akar**	**táncolni?**
Whom didn't you invite to the party?		**Kit nem**	**hívtál**	**meg a bulira?**

16.4.1.3	Imperatives

An imperative sentence usually begins with the conjugated imperative verb
followed by the coverb.

Vedd meg azt az inget!   Buy that shirt!

Gyertek ide!   Come here!

If the imperative is negated, the negation fills the focus position.

Ne menjetek el nélkülem! Don't go without me!

Ne csukd be az ajtót!   Don't close the door!

See the Subjunctive section 4.3.6 for further discussion on possible word orders.

16.5   Word order of the quasi-auxiliary[4] verbs: *kell, akar, tud, lehet, szokott, tetszik, fog*

The verbs **kell** 'be necessary', **akar** 'want', **tud** 'know how, can, be able', **lehet** 'be possible', **szokott** 'used to, usually', **tetszik** 'be pleasing', **fog** 'will (future)' often occur in constructions with a second verb in the infinitive. When they do, they require that the preverb position be filled. In such sentences, the quasi-auxiliary is the conjugated verb (accordingly it occupies the verb position) and the preverb position is filled with the verbal complement or modifier of the *infinitive* – not of the conjugated verb (16.5.1–2). If the infinitive has no verbal complement/modifier, then it fills the preverb position itself (16.5.3).

16.5.1

Although the quasi-auxiliary verbs do not have coverbs, the coverb of the infinitive with which they occur fills the preverb position, thus separating itself from the infinitive.

Le tetszik szállni az autóbuszról?   (< **leszáll**)
Are you getting off the bus?

Be tudod fejezni a munkát?   (< **befejez**)
Can you finish the work?

Fel fog hívni holnap.   (< **felhív**)
He will call me tomorrow.

Fel kell mennem Pestre.   (< **felmegy**)
I have to go up to Budapest.

El szokott aludni a vonaton.   (< **elalszik**)
He usually falls asleep on the train.

---

[4] In addition to their use as auxiliary verbs, these verbs may also stand alone – hence, the term 'quasi-auxiliary'.

16.5.2

If the infinitive of the verb does not have a coverb, its modifying adverb, adverbial or verbal complement fills the preverb position of the quasi-auxiliary verb.

A diákoknak sokat kell olvasniuk.   (< **sokat olvas**)
The students must read a lot.

Anita levelet akar írni.   (< **levelet ír**)
Anita wants to write a letter.

Gyula Pécsen fog lakni.   (< **Pécsen lakik**)
Gyula will live in Pécs.

16.5.3

If the infinitive has neither a coverb, modifying adverb, adverbial or verbal complement, the infinitive itself occupies the preverb position.

Márta aludni akar.   Márta wants to sleep.

Reggel mosni szokott.   In the morning he usually does the laundry.

Nekünk tanulnunk kell.   We have to study.

Este zongorázni lehet.   At night you (one) may play the piano.

16.5.4

In non-neutral sentences, the focus element must occupy the focus position immediately before the conjugated verb; in this case the modifier of the infinitive (coverb, adverb, etc.) precedes the infinitive.

Neutral: **Le tetszik szállni az autóbuszról?**
Are you getting off the bus?
Focus: **Nem tetszik leszállni az autóbuszról?**
Aren't you getting off the bus?

Neutral:	**Fel fog hívni holnap.**
	He will call me tomorrow.
Focus:	**Mikor fog felhívni?**
	When will he call me?
Focus:	*Holnap* **fog felhívni.** (answer to question)
	He will call me *tomorrow.*

Neutral:	**A diákoknak sokat kell olvasniuk.**
	The students must read a lot.
Focus:	**Kinek kell sokat olvasnia?**
	Who has to read a lot?
Focus:	**Miért kell sokat olvasniuk?**
	Why do they have to read a lot?

Neutral:	**Gyula Pécsett fog lakni.**
	Gyula will live in Pécs.
Focus:	***Gyula* fog Pécsett lakni, nem a húga.**
	Gyula is going to live in Pécs, not his sister.
Focus:	**Gyula nem fog Pécsett lakni.**
	Gyula is not going to live in Pécs.

Neutral:	**Márta aludni akar.**
	Márta wants to sleep.
Focus:	**Ki akar aludni?**
	Who wants to sleep?
Focus:	***Márta* akar aludni.** (answer to question)
	Márta wants to sleep.

16.5.5

More verbs that often follow the word order patterns of quasi-auxiliaries:

bír	can, manage to	**próbál**	try
kezd	begin	**szándékozik**	wish
kíván	wish	**szeretne**	would like
mer	dare	**talál**	happen to
óhajt	desire		

Chapter 17

Special constructions

17.1 Usage of *van* 'be'

17.1.1 Present tense

In the present tense **van** 'be' is used in the third person (singular and plural) only in sentences containing existential (i.e., there is/there are) constructions or adverbial complements. Otherwise predicate nouns and adjectives do not occur with the verb **van/vannak**. Compare the following:

Attila itt van./Attila jól van.   (adverbial complement)
Attila is here./Attila is well.

Attila gazdag/tanár.   (predicate adjective/noun)
Attila is rich/a teacher.

Van Isten?   (existential construction)
Is there a God?

Régi könyvek vannak a szekrényben.   (existential construction)
There are old books in the closet.

A könyvek régiek.   (predicate adjective)
The books are old.

The first and second persons (singular and plural) always use the verb **van** 'be' (in its correctly conjugated form, of course).

Angol tanár/vidám vagyok.   (predicate adjective/noun)
I am an English teacher/cheerful.

Jól vagyok, köszönöm.   (adverbial complement)
I'm well, thank you.

Magyarok vagyunk.	(predicate adjective/noun)
We are Hungarian(s).	

Egy gyönyörű kertben vagyunk.	(adverbial complement)
We are in a beautiful garden.	

Szép vagy.	(predicate adjective/noun)
You are beautiful.	

Rosszul vagy?	(adverbial complement)
Are you ill?	

17.1.2 | *Past tense*

Usage in the past tense is regular: the verb is used in all persons whether it is an adverbial construction or not. The past tense stem of **van** is **volt**. The verb **lesz** 'will be, become' has the stem **lett** in the past tense and means 'became'.

Attila tanár volt, de most fogorvos.
Attila was a teacher, but now he is a dentist.

Meleg lett./Meleg volt.
It got hot. /It was hot.

17.1.3 | *Subjunctive/imperative*

The subjunctive/imperative is formed from the **lesz** 'will be, become' variant and is used in all persons.

Legyél pontos!	Be on time.
Apám akarja, hogy mérnök legyek.	My father wants me to be an engineer.

17.1.4 | *Conditional*

The conditional may be formed from either the **volna-** or **lenne-** stem; the latter is somewhat more common.

Bárcsak itt lenne!	If only she were here.
Bárcsak itt volna!	If only she were here.

Future

The verb **lesz** 'will be' is the future form of **van** 'be'. It is used in place of the future **fog** construction. It is not used as an auxiliary verb.

Mikor lesz már jó idő?　　　When will there be some good
　　　　　　　　　　　　　　weather?

Remélem, hogy boldog leszel.　I hope you will be happy.

17.2　Negation and *van* 'be'

The negation of **van** is **nincs/nincsen**; the negation of **vannak** is **nincsenek**.

Attila nincs itt./Attila nincs jól./Attila nincs a házban.
Attila is not here./Attila is not well./Attila is not in the house.

Nincsenek régi könyvek a szekrényben.
There are no old books in the closet.

In all other cases the negation of verbs (or nominal and adjectival predicates) is **nem**.

Attila nem gazdag./Attila nem tanár.
Attila is not rich./Attila is not a teacher.

A könyvek nem régiek.
The books are not old.

Nem vagyok otthon./Nem vagyunk otthon.
I am not at home./We are not at home.

Péter nem rajzol jól.
Péter does not draw well.

Nem may be used to negate a phrase other than the verb, in which case it may occur in sentences containing **van/vannak**; a negated phrase usually requires a **hanem** 'rather', 'but' phrase later in the sentence:

Attila nem a házban van, hanem a kertben.
Attila is not in the house, but in the garden.

Nem Attila van a házban, hanem Tamás.
It is not Attila who is in the house, rather Tamás.

17.3 Existential constructions

17.3.1

Existential constructions, i.e., 'there is/there are' constructions, use the verb **van** in Hungarian. The verbal complement is 'what' there is/are and therefore fills the preverb position in neutral sentences.

Sok gyerek van a parkban.	There are many children in the park.
Víz van az asztalon.	There is water on the table.
Nincs igazság a Földön.	There is no justice in the world.

17.3.2

Hungarian also uses the existential constructions in many expressions of time and weather.

Hétfő van.	It is Monday.
Szeptember 22-e van.	It is September 22.
Két óra van.	It is two o'clock.
Szép idő van.	The weather is beautiful.
Hűvös/meleg/hideg van.	It is chilly/hot/cold.
Vihar/szél/van.	There is a storm/wind.

17.3.3

It is helpful to consider the 'have' construction an existential construction (see section 17.4 for more discussion).

Zsuzsának három gyereke van.	Zsuzsa has three children.
(Nekünk) sok munkánk van.	We have a lot of work.

17.4 'Have' construction

Hungarian does not have a verb with the meaning 'to have'; instead it uses a compound construction using **van** 'be'. The following are the components of the 'have' construction:

(a) The possessor is in the dative case; should this be a pronoun, it may be omitted.
(b) The possessed item is marked with a possessive ending which agrees with the possessor. In the 'have' construction, the definite article is never used before the possessed item.[1]
(c) The verb **van** is in the third person and agrees in number with the possessed item(s) (which, in fact, is the grammatical subject).
(d) In neutral sentences the possessor is in the topic position, the possessed item is in preverb position (but see below for other word orders).

17.4.1 | *Possessed item is singular*

(Nekem) szép kutyám van.
I have a beautiful dog.

(Neked) szép kutyád van.
You (sg.) have a beautiful dog.

(Neki), Gábornak, Magának szép kutyája van.
S/he/Gábor/You (*polite sg.*) have a beautiful dog.

(Nekünk) szép kutyánk van.
We have a beautiful dog.

(Nektek) szép kutyátok van.
You (pl.) have a beautiful dog.

(Nekik), a lányoknak, Maguknak szép kutyájuk van.
They/The girls/You (*polite pl.*) have a beautiful dog.

---

[1] Compare with the possessive construction where the definite article is almost always used.

| **17.4.2** | *Possessed item is plural* |

(Nekem) kedves testvéreim vannak.
I have nice siblings.

(Neked) kedves testvéreid vannak.
You (sg.) have nice siblings.

(Neki), Zsuzsának kedves testvérei vannak.
S/he/Zsuzsa/has nice siblings.

(Nekünk) kedves testvéreink vannak.
We have nice siblings.

(Nektek) kedves testvéreitek vannak.
You (pl.) have nice siblings

(Nekik) A barátaimnak kedves testvéreik vannak.
They/My friends have nice siblings.

| **17.4.3** | *egy and the 'have' construction* |

It is common to use an indefinite article before a (singular) possessed item. At such times, it usually follows the verb:

(Nekem) van egy jó ötletem!
I have a good idea.

(Nekünk) van egy régi szótárunk.
We have an old dictionary.

| **17.4.4** | *Moods and tenses of the 'have' construction* |

The verb **van** may occur in all its forms yielding past and future tenses, subjunctive, conditional, and potential moods of the 'have' construction:

(Nekem) jó tanáraim voltak az egyetemen.
I had good teachers in college.

(Neked) jó állásod lesz, ha idejössz dolgozni.
You will have a good job if you come here to work.

Évának több pénze lenne, ha többet dolgozna.
Éva would have more money if she would work more.

273

Magának sok baja lehet vele.
You (formal, sg.) must have a lot of problems with him/her/it.

| 17.4.5 | *Negation and the 'have' construction* |

Negation of the 'have' construction is consistent with the regular rules of negation and focus word order: the negation of **van, vannak** is **nincs(en)**, **nincsenek**, respectively; otherwise use the regular patterns of negation. Negation occupies the focus position; the possessed item is consequently removed to a position immediately behind the verb.

(Nekem) nincs tollam.
I don't have a pen.

(Neked) nincsenek rokonaid Budapesten?
Don't you have (any) relatives in Budapest?

Erzsinek soha nem volt saját kocsija.
Erzsi never had her own car.

(Nekünk) nem lesz elég időnk.
We will not have enough time.

(Nektek) ne legyen már rossz kedvetek!
Don't be in a bad mood!

| 17.4.6 | *Common expressions with the 'have' construction* |

(valakinek)	kedve van	(someone)	is in a mood (to do something)
"	ideje van	"	has time
"	melege van	"	is (too) warm, hot
"	igaza van	"	is right
"	köze van (valamihez)	(something)	is somebody's business
"	fogalma sincs	(someone)	has no idea

Nincs kedvünk dolgozni ma.	We don't feel like working today.	Comparison of possessive and 'have' constructions
Lesz időd holnap?	Will you have some time tomorrow?	
Melegem van.	I'm hot.	
Anyámnak mindig igaza van.	My mother is always right.	
Semmi közöd hozzá!	It's none of your business!	
Fogalmam sincs!	I have no idea!	

17.5   Comparison of possessive and 'have' constructions

Because of the subtle differences between the two, it is helpful to compare the possessive paradigm with the 'have' construction. Note that in the possessive paradigm for nominal possessors the plurality of the possessor is marked on the possessor and *not* on the possessed. This difference in marking does not occur in the 'have' construction.

Possessive paradigm

Pronominal possessors:
Singular possessed: *Plural possessed:*

---

az én szobám	my room	**az én szobáim**	my rooms
a te szobád	your (sg.) room	**a te szobáid**	your (sg.) rooms
az ő szobája	his/her room	**az ő szobái**	his/her rooms
a mi szobánk	our room	**a mi szobáink**	our rooms
a ti szobátok	your (pl.) room	**a ti szobáitok**	your (pl.) rooms
az ő szobájuk	their room	**az ő szobáik**	their rooms

Nominal possessors:

a nő szobája	~ **a nőnek a szobája**	the woman's room (one woman, one room)
a nő szobái	~ **a nőnek a szobái**	the woman's rooms (one woman, several rooms)
a nők szobája	~ **a nőknek a szobája**	the women's room (several women, one room)
a nők szobái	~ **a nőknek a szobái**	the women's rooms (several women, several rooms)

The 'have' construction

Singular possessed:	Plural possessed:
(Nekem) szép szobám van.	**(Nekem) szép szobáim vannak.**
I have a nice room.	I have nice rooms.
(Neked) szép szobád van.	**(Neked) szép szobáid vannak.**
You have a nice room.	You have nice rooms.
(Neki) szép szobája van.	**(Neki) szép szobái vannak.**
She/He has a nice room.	She/He has nice rooms.
A nőnek szép szobája van.	**A nőnek szép szobái vannak.**
The woman has a nice room.	The woman has nice rooms.
(Nekünk) szép szobánk van.	**(Nekünk) szép szobáink vannak.**
We have a nice room.	We have nice rooms.
(Nektek) szép szobátok van.	**(Nektek) szép szobáitok vannak.**
You have a nice room.	You have nice rooms.
(Nekik) szép szobájuk van.	**(Nekik) szép szobáik vannak.**
They have a nice room.	They have nice rooms.
A nőknek szép szobájuk van.	**A nőknek szép szobáik vannak.**
The women have a nice room.	The women have nice rooms.

17.6   Differences in 'have' constructions

The verb 'have' in English may be translated into Hungarian in a variety of ways depending on the circumstances of ownership and possession.

(a) **Sok pénze van.**   She has a lot of money. (She's rich.)

(b) **Sok pénz van nála.**   She has a lot of money with her.

(c) **Megvan a pénze.**   She's got her money (for the train ticket, etc.).

The 'have' construction in (a) is used when someone possesses or owns something or has an inalienable relation to it.

Gábornak háza/két húga/sok munkája/hosszú lába/van.
Gábor has a house/two younger sisters/a lot of work/long legs.

The construction with the adessive -nál/-nél case is used when a person is carrying something along with him or her.

Nincs nála az olvasószemüvege.
She doesn't have her reading glasses with her.

Kinél van a kulcs?
Who has the key?

Nem volt nála szótár, tehát nem tudta lefordítani a reklámot.
He didn't have a dictionary with him, so he couldn't translate the ad.

The construction with **megvan** in (c) is used when a person has an expected item with him/her, it is not lost, and/or it is ready for use. Unlike the 'have' construction in (a) where a definite article is never used, sentences with **megvan** always use the definite article.

Megvan a házi feladatod?
Have you got your homework?/Is your homework ready?

Megvan a repülőjegyem, az útlevelem, kész vagyok az utazásra.
I've got my plane ticket and my passport, I'm ready to travel.

Ha nincs meg a kulcs, hogy tudunk bemenni?
If we don't have the key, how will we get in?

This is also the construction used to express having something that belongs to someone else.

Megvan a telefonszámom, ugye?
You've got my telephone number, haven't you?

17.7 Impersonal constructions

Impersonal constructions are characterized by having no personal pronoun in subject position. In Hungarian, impersonal constructions consist of the following:

(a) a dative-marked 'subject' (i.e., what would correspond to the subject in English). If this is a pronoun it may be omitted.
(b) a third person verb or predicate adjective
(c) an infinitive declined to agree with the person of the dative-marked 'subject'

(Nekem) tanulnom kell.	I must study.
(Neked) tanulnod kell.	You (sg.) must study.
(Neki)/Tamásnak tanulnia kell.	She/he/Tamás must study.
(Nekünk) tanulnunk kell.	We must study.
(Nektek) tanulnotok kell.	You (pl.) must study.
(Nekik)/A fiúknak tanulniuk kell.	They/The boys must study.

17.7.1 *Verbs occurring in impersonal constructions*

fáj	hurt	**lehet**	may
illik	be suitable, fitting	**muszáj**	must
kell	must	**sikerül**	succeed, manage

Jenőnek várnia kell.
Jenő has to wait.

Sikerült (neked) elérned a főnököt?
Did you manage to reach the boss?

17.7.2 *Adjectives occurring in impersonal constructions*

érdemes	be worth(while)	**szabad**	be allowed
hasznos	be useful	**szükséges**	be necessary
jó	be good	**szükségtelen**	be unnecessary
könnyű	be easy	**rossz**	be bad
nehéz	be difficult	**tilos**	be forbidden

Nem érdemes megnéznem a filmet.
It is not worth it for me to see the film.

Neked nem szabad tejet innod.
You are not allowed to drink milk.

(Neki) könnyű volt válaszolnia.
It was easy for him/her to answer.

Nehéz dolgoznunk, mikor szép idő van kint.
It is hard for us to work when the weather is nice outside.

| **17.7.3** | *Impersonal constructions without declined infinitives* |

It is very common to use the infinitive without the possessive endings in the impersonal constructions. Thus, the following three sentences have the same meaning:

(Nekem) dolgozonom kell.   I have to work.

Nekem dolgozni kell.   "

Dolgozni kell.   "

Conversely, the impersonal construction without a dative complement or declined infinitive may refer to any person at all:

Dolgozni kell. I, you, we, they, people, etc. have to work.

The verb **lehet** is only used without declined infinitives; when the person must be specified, the potential suffix **-hat/-het** is used on the substantive verb (see section 4.5.2). Compare the following:

Itt lehet szép cipőt kapni. One can get nice shoes here.

Itt kaphatunk szép cipőt. We can get nice shoes here.

| **17.7.4** | *Impersonal 'you', 'one'* |

Any construction may be made impersonal by using the impersonal **az ember** 'one'; it may be any part of speech and may translate into English in a variety of ways.

Az embernek szórakoznia is kell néha.
People have to/You have to/One has to have fun sometimes, too.

Sajnos az ember nem tud pénz nélkül élni.
Unfortunately, we/you/people can't live without money.

17.8 Agent-less sentences (passive)

Modern Hungarian does not have a passive inflection, but the use of the
third person plural conjugation with no subject or subject pronoun can
be translated as a passive in English.

Óránként közlik a híreket.
They broadcast the news every hour./The news is broadcast
every hour.

Ritkán fordítják jól Kosztolányit.
Kosztolányi is rarely translated well.

17.9 Adverbial participle with *van*

In the spoken language it is common to form constructions with the
adverbial participle (-va/-ve)[2] of a substantive verb and use the verb **van**
as an auxiliary. This construction usually results in describing the state
or condition of the subject and is often translated into the passive voice
in English.

In these constructions **van** is the conjugated verb and can occur in any
mood or tense; in neutral sentences the preverb position is filled by the
coverb of the substantive verb.

A kenyér meg van sütve.	The bread is baked.
Meg vagyok fázva.	I have a cold.
Meg lesztek híva.	You (pl.) will be invited.
A munka be lett fejezve.	The work got done.

In the absence of a coverb, the substantive verb marked with the adverbial
participle is in the preverb position.

Az ajtó nyitva van.	The door is open.
Az üzlet zárva van.	The shop is closed.

---

[2] See section 4.4.3 on how to form the adverbial participle.

When these constructions are negated (or other focussed elements occur), the negation occupies the focus preverb position and the coverb is not separated from its verb.[3]

A kenyér nincs megsütve.	The bread is not baked.
Az ajtó nincs nyitva.	The door is not open.
Az üzlet nincs bezárva.	The shop is not closed.
Nem vagyok megfázva.	I do not have a cold.
Nem lesztek meghíva.	You will not be invited.
A munka nem lett befejezve.	The work did not get finished.

17.10   Answering questions

17.10.1 | *Answering questions in the affirmative*

Yes–no questions may be answered affirmatively in several ways.

17.10.1.1

They may always be answered by **igen** 'yes'.

Eljössz moziba ma este?	Will you come to the movies tonight?
Igen.	Yes.
Lajos orvos?	Is Lajos a doctor?
Igen.	Yes.

---

[3] It may be helpful to realize that the coverb has been removed from the neutral preverb position to a position immediately behind the conjugated verb – thereby re-prefixing to its verb. This is consistent with rules of word order and focus outlined in chapter 15.

17.10.1.2

If the question refers to the verb, the verb may be used to answer in the
affirmative (it may need to be reconjugated to fit the sense of the answer).
If the verb has a coverb, repetition of the coverb alone is sufficient.

Eljössz moziba ma este?	Will you come to the movies tonight?
El.	Yes.
Eljövök.	
Tanulsz?	Are you studying?
Tanulok.	Yes.
Kell a toll?	Do you need the pen?
Kell.	Yes.

17.10.1.3

If the question pertains to a particular word other than the verb, the
affirmative answer may be a repetition of that word.

Lajos orvos?	Is Lajos a *doctor*?
Orvos.	Yes.
Lajos orvos?	Is *Lajos* a doctor?
Lajos.	Yes.

17.10.1.4

The affirmative answer may be a combination of the above.

Tanulsz?	Are you studying?
Igen, tanulok.	Yes, I am.
Eljössz moziba ma este?	Will you come to the movies tonight?
Igen, el(jövök).	Yes, I will.

| **Lajos orvos?** | Is Lajos a doctor? |
| **Igen, orvos.** | Yes, he is. |

17.10.1.5

In sentences with predicate nouns or adjectives, the affirmative answer may take yet another shape:

Lauri finn?	Is Lauri Finnish/a Finn?
Igen, az.	Yes, he is (that).
Az.	Yes.

Toll ez?	Is this a pen?
Toll.	Yes.
Igen.	"
Az.	"
Igen, toll.	"
Igen, az.	"
Igen, ez az.	"

17.10.1.6

Emphatic affirmative answers are **persze, hogyne** 'of course'.

| **Kifizetted a számlát?** | Did you pay the bill? |
| **Persze.** | Of course. |

| **Tetszett a szálloda?** | Did you like the hotel? |
| **Hogyne.** | Of course. |

17.10.1.7

When contradicting a question asked in the negative, use **de** or **de, igen** 'but', 'yes'. The verb may or may not be repeated.

| **Nem kérsz már kávét?** | You don't want any more coffee? |
| **De, igen, kérek.** | Yes I *do*. |

De, kérek.   "

De, igen.   "

De.   "

17.10.1.8

To emphatically contradict a question asked in the negative use **dehogy-nem, dehogyisnem** 'but, of course'.

Nem akarod megkóstolni ezt a vörösbort?
Don't you want to have a taste of this red wine?

Dehogynem (akarom). ~ Dehogyisnem.
Of course, I do.

17.10.2 | *Answering questions in the negative*

17.10.2.1

Yes–no questions are usually answered with **nem** 'no' in the negative.

Elolvastad a verset?   Did you read the poem?

Nem.   No.

17.10.2.2 | Emphatic negative answers use **dehogy, dehogyis** 'of course not'.

Befejezted a munkát?   Did you finish the work?

Dehogy!   Of course not.

Dehogyis!   "

Appendix 1
Some irregular verbs

lesz become, will be

	present	*past*	*subjunctive*	*conditional*
én	**leszek**	**lettem**	**legyek**	**lénnék**
te	**leszel**	**lettél**	**légy/legyél**	**lennél**
ő	**lesz**	**lett**	**legyen**	**lenne**
mi	**leszünk**	**lettünk**	**legyünk**	**lennénk**
ti	**lesztek**	**lettetek**	**legyetek**	**lennétek**
ők	**lesznek**	**lettek**	**legyenek**	**lennének**

infinitive: **lenni**

present participle: **való, levő/lévő**

past participle: **volt, lett**

future participle: **leendő**

adverbial participle: **léve, lévén**

potential: **lehet**

---

[1] The verb **tesz** is conjugated exactly as **vesz**.

vesz¹ take; buy

	present		*past*	
	indef.	*def.*	*indef.*	*def.*
én	veszek	veszem	vettem	vettem
te	veszel	veszed	vettél	vetted

	present		*past*	
	indef.	*def.*	*indef.*	*def.*
ő	vesz	veszi	vett	vette
mi	veszünk	vesszük	vettünk	vettük
ti	vesztek	veszitek	vettetek	vettétek
ők	vesznek	veszik	vettek	vették
én (téged/benneteket/titeket)	veszlek			vettelek

	subjunctive		*conditional*	
	indef.	*def.*	*indef.*	*def.*
én	vegyek	vegyem	vennék	venném
te	végy/vegyél	vegyed/vedd	vennél	vennéd
ő	vegyen	vegye	venne	venné
mi	vegyünk	vegyük	vennénk	vennénk
ti	vegyetek	vegyétek	vennétek	vennétek
ők	vegyenek	vegyék	vennének	vennék
én (téged/benneteket/titeket)	vegyelek			vennélek

infinitive: **venni**

present participle: **vevő**

past participle: **vett**

future participle: **veendő**

adverbial participle: **véve**

potential: **vehet**

visz take, carry

	present		past	
	indef.	*def.*	*indef.*	*def.*
én	viszek	viszem	vittem	vittem
te	viszel	viszed	vittél	vitted
ő	visz	viszi	vitt	vitte
mi	viszünk	visszük	vittünk	vittük
ti	visztek	viszitek	vittetek	vittétek
ők	visznek	viszik	vittek	vitték
én (téged/benneteket/ titeket)	viszlek			vittelek

	subjunctive		conditional	
	indef.	*def.*	*indef.*	*def.*
én	vigyek	vigyem	vinnék	vinném
te	vigyél	vigyed/vidd	vinnél	vinnéd
ő	vigyen	vigye	vinne	vinné
mi	vigyünk	vigyük	vinnénk	vinnénk
ti	vigyetek	vigyétek	vinnétek	vinnétek
ők	vigyenek	vigyék	vinnének	vinnék
én (téged/benneteket/ titeket)	vigyelek			vinnélek

infinitive: **vinni**

present participle: **vivő**

past participle: **vitt**

future participle: **viendő**

adverbial participle: **vive**

potential: **vihet**

*his*z **believe**

	present		past	
	indef.	*def.*	*indef.*	*def.*
én	hiszek	hiszem	hittem	hittem
te	hiszel	hiszed	hittél	hitted
ő	hisz	hiszi	hitt	hitte
mi	hiszünk	hisszük	hittünk	hittük
ti	hisztek	hiszitek	hittetek	hittétek
ők	hisznek	hiszik	hittek	hitték
én (téged/benneteket/ titeket)	hiszlek			hittelek

	subjunctive		conditional	
	indef.	*def.*	*indef.*	*def.*
én	higgyek	higgyem	hinnék	hinném
te	higgy/higgyél	higgyed/hidd	hinnél	hinnéd
ő	higgyen	higgye	hinne	hinné
mi	higgyünk	higgyük	hinnénk	hinnénk
ti	higgyetek	higgyétek	hinnétek	hinnétek
ők	higgyenek	higgyék	hinnének	hinnék
én (téged/benneteket/ titeket)	higgyelek			hinnélek

infinitive: hinni

present participle: hívő

past participle: hitt

adverbial participle: híve

potential: hihet

eszik eat

	present indef.	def.	past indef.	def.
én	eszek ~ eszem	eszem	ettem	ettem
te	eszel	eszed	ettél	etted
ő	eszik	eszi	evett	ette
mi	eszünk	esszük	ettünk	ettük
ti	esztek	eszitek	ettetek	ettétek
ők	esznek	eszik	ettek	ették
én (téged/ benneteket/ titeket)	(meg)eszlek		(meg)ettelek	

	subjunctive indef.	def.	conditional indef.	def.
én	egyek ~ egye	egyem	ennék ~ enném	enném
te	egyél	egyed/edd	ennél	ennéd
ő	egyen ~ egyék	egye	enne ~ ennék	enné
mi	együnk	együk	ennénk	ennénk
ti	egyetek	egyétek	ennétek	ennétek
ők	egyenek	egyék	ennének	ennék
én (téged/ benneteket/ titeket)	(meg)egyelek		(meg)ennélek	

infinitive: enni

present participle: evő

past participle: evett

potential: ehet

iszik **drink**

	present indef.	def.	past indef.	def.
én	iszok ~ iszom	iszom	ittam	ittam
te	iszol	iszod	ittál	ittad
ő	iszik	issza	ivott	itta
mi	iszunk	isszuk	ittunk	ittuk
ti	isztok	isszátok	ittatok	ittátok
ők	isznak	isszák	ittak	itták
én (téged/ benneteket/ titeket)	(meg)iszlak			(meg)ittalak

	subjunctive indef.	def.	conditional indef.	def.
én	igyak ~ igyam	igyam	innék ~ innám	innám
te	igyál	igyad ~ idd	innál	innád
ő	igyon ~ igyék	igya	inna~innék	inná
mi	igyunk	igyuk	innánk	innánk
ti	igyatok	igyátok	innátok	innátok
ők	igyanak	igyák	innának	innák
én (téged/ benneteket/ titeket)	(meg)igyalak			(meg)innálak

infinitive: **inni**

present participle: **ivó**

past participle: **ivott**

potential: **ihat**

megy come

	present	past	subjunctive	conditional
én	megyek	mentem	menjek	mennék
te	mész ~ mégy	mentél	menj ~ menjél	mennél
ő	megy	ment	menjen	menne
mi	megyünk	mentünk	menjünk	mennénk
ti	mentek	mentetek	menjetek	mennétek
ők	mennek	mentek	menjenek	mennének

infinitive: **menni**

present participle: **menő**

past participle: **ment**

adverbial participle: **menve**

potential: **mehet**

jön go

	present	past	subjunctive	conditional
én	jövök	jöttem	jöjjek	jönnék
te	jössz	jöttél	jöjjél ~ gyere	jönnél
ő	jön	jött	jöjjön	jönne
mi	jövünk	jöttünk	jöjjünk ~ gyerünk	jönnénk
ti	jöttök	jöttetek	jöjjetek ~ gyertek	jönnétek
ők	jönnek	jöttek	jöjjenek	jönnének

infinitive: **jönni**

present participle: **jövő**

past participle: **jött**

adverbial participle: **jöve**

potential: **jöhet**

In the imperative the forms **gyere, gyertek, gyerünk** are more common; the forms **jöjjél, jöjjetek, jöjjünk** are more common in the subjunctive use of this verb.

Gyere ide!   Come here!

Ne gyertek be a házba!   Don't come into the house!

Azt üzente, hogy hazajöjjél.   He sent word that you should come home.

Nem akarja, hogy kijöjjünk a vízből.   He doesn't want us to come out of the water.

The verb *van* 'be'

	present	past	subjunctive	conditional	
én	vagyok	voltam	legyek	volnék	~ lennék
te	vagy	voltál	légy~legyél	volnál	~ lennél
ő	(van)	volt	legyen	volna	~ lenne
mi	vagyunk	voltunk	legyünk	volnánk	~ lennénk
ti	vagytok	voltatok	legyetek	volnátok	~ lennétek
ők	(vannak)	voltak	legyenek	volnának	~ lennének

infinitive: **lenni**

present participle: **való ~ levő/lévő**

past participle: **volt**

future participle: **leendő**

potential: **lehet**

Sample inflectional/derivational paradigm (for first person singular)

I('ll) iron my shirt.	**Kivasalom az ingemet.**
I ironed my shirt.	**Kivasaltam az ingemet.**
Should I iron my shirt?	**Kivasaljam az ingemet?**
Iron my shirt!	**Vasald ki az ingemet!**
I would iron my shirt.	**Kivasalnám az ingemet.**
I would have ironed my shirt.	**Kivasaltam volna az ingemet.**
I may/can iron my shirt.	**Kivasalhatom az ingemet.**
I could iron my shirt.	**Kivasalhatnám az ingemet.**
I could have ironed my shirt.	**Kivasalhattam volna az ingemet.**
I must iron my shirt.	**Ki kell vasalnom az ingemet.**
I had to iron my shirt.	**Ki kellett vasalnom az ingemet.**
I should iron my shirt.	**Ki kellene vasalnom az ingemet.**
I should have ironed my shirt.	**Ki kellett volna vasalnom az ingemet.**
Lest I should have to iron my shirt.	**Nehogy ki kelljen vasalnom az ingemet.**
I'll have you iron my shirt.	**Kivasaltatom veled az ingemet.**
I had you iron my shirt.	**Kivasaltattam veled az ingemet.**
Should I have you iron my shirt?	**Kivasaltassam veled az ingemet?**
I would have you iron my shirt.	**Kivasaltatnám veled az ingemet.**

I would have had you iron my shirt.	**Kivasaltattam volna veled az ingemet.**
I can/may have you iron my shirt.	**Kivasaltathatom veled az ingemet.**
I could have you iron my shirt.	**Kivasaltathatnám veled az ingemet.**
I could have had you iron my shirt.	**Kivasaltathattam volna veled az ingemet.**
I must have you iron my shirt.	**Ki kell vasaltatnom veled az ingemet.**
I had to have you iron my shirt.	**Ki kellett vasaltatnom veled az ingemet.**
I should have you iron my shirt.	**Ki kellene vasaltatnom veled az ingemet.**
I should have had you iron my shirt.	**Ki kellett volna vasaltatnom veled az ingemet.**
My shirt is ironed.	**Az ingem ki van vasalva.**
My shirt was ironed.	**Az ingem ki volt vasalva.**
My shirt will be ironed.	**Az ingem ki lesz vasalva.**
Let my shirt be ironed!	**Legyen kivasalva az ingem!**
My shirt would be ironed.	**Az ingem ki lenne/volna vasalva.**
My shirt would have been ironed.	**Az ingem ki lett volna vasalva.**
My shirt may/might be ironed.	**Az ingem ki lehet vasalva.**
My shirt could be ironed.	**Az ingem ki lehetne vasalva.**
My shirt may have been ironed.	**Az ingem ki lehetett volna vasalva.**
I *will* iron my shirt.	**Ki fogom vasalni az ingemet.**

And I ironed it too.

I didn't even iron it.

I was doing a little ironing.

Ki is vasaltam.

Ki sem vasaltam.

Vasalgattam egy kicsit.

Appendix 2
Sample noun declensions

Low vowel, no loss of length

	back vowel		front vowel	
	singular	*plural*	*singular*	*plural*
	'house'	'houses'	'book'	'books'
nominative	ház	házak	könyv	könyvek
accusative	házat	házakat	könyvet	könyveket
illative	házba	házakba	könyvbe	könyvekbe
inessive	házban	házakban	könyvben	könyvekben
elative	házból	házakból	könyvből	könyvekből
sublative	házra	házakra	könyvre	könyvekre
superessive	házon	házakon	könyvön	könyveken
delative	házról	házakról	könyvről	könyvekről
allative	házhoz	házakhoz	könyvhöz	könyvekhez
adessive	háznál	házaknál	könyvnél	könyveknél
ablative	háztól	házaktól	könyvtől	könyvektől
dative	háznak	házaknak	könyvnek	könyveknek
instrumental	házzal	házakkal	könyvvel	könyvekkel
translative	házzá	házakká	könyvvé	könyvekké
causal-final	házért	házakért	könyvért	könyvekért
essive-formal	házként	házakként	könyvként	könyvekként
terminative	házig	házakig	könyvig	könyvekig
distributive	házanként	——	könyvenként	——
sociative	házastul	——	könyvestül	——

Low vowel, loses length

	back vowel singular 'glass'	plural 'glass'	front vowel singular 'hand'	plural 'hands'
nominative	pohár	poharak	kéz	kezek
accusative	poharat	poharakat	kezet	kezeket
illative	pohárba	poharakba	kézbe	kezekbe
inessive	pohárban	poharakban	kézben	kezekben
elative	pohárból	poharakból	kézből	kezekből
sublative	pohárra	poharakra	kézre	kezekre
superessive	poháron	poharakon	kézen	kezeken
delative	pohárról	poharakról	kézről	kezekről
allative	pohárhoz	poharakhoz	kézhez	kezekhez
adessive	pohárnál	poharaknál	kéznél	kezeknél
ablative	pohártól	poharaktól	kéztől	kezektől
dative	pohárnak	poharaknak	kéznek	kezeknek
instrumental	pohárral	poharakkal	kézzel	kezekkel
translative	pohárrá	poharakká	kézzé	kezekké
causal-final	pohárért	poharakért	kézért	kezekért
essive-formal	pohárként	poharakként	kézként	kezekként
terminative	pohárig	poharakig	kézig	kezekig
distributive	poharanként	——	kezenként	——
sociative	poharastul	——	kezestül	——

Regular noun, ending in vowel

	back vowel		front vowel	
	singular 'bag'	*plural* 'bags'	*singular* 'melon'	*plural* 'melons'
nominative	táska	táskák	dinnye	dinnyék
accusative	táskát	táskákat	dinnyét	dinnyéket
illative	táskába	táskákba	dinnyébe	dinnyékbe
inessive	táskában	táskákban	dinnyében	dinnyékben
elative	táskából	táskákból	dinnyéből	dinnyékből
sublative	táskára	táskákra	dinnyére	dinnyékre
superessive	táskán	táskákon	dinnyén	dinnyéken
delative	táskáról	táskákról	dinnyéről	dinnyékről
allative	táskához	táskákhoz	dinnyéhez	dinnyékhez
adessive	táskánál	táskáknál	dinnyénél	dinnyéknél
ablative	táskától	táskáktól	dinnyétől	dinnyéktől
dative	táskának	táskáknak	dinnyének	dinnyéknek
instrumental	táskával	táskákkal	dinnyével	dinnyékkel
translative	táskává	táskákká	dinnyévé	dinnyékké
causal-final	táskáért	táskákért	dinnyéért	dinnyékért
essive-formal	táskaként	táskákként	dinnyeként	dinnyékként
terminative	táskáig	táskákig	dinnyéig	dinnyékig
distributive	táskánként	——	dinnyénként	——
sociative	táskástul	——	dinnyéstül	——

Regular noun, ending in consonant

	back vowel singular 'girl'	plural 'girls'	front, unrounded vowel singular 'chair'	plural 'chairs'	front, rounded vowel singular 'guard'	plural 'guards'
nom.	lány	lányok	szék	székek	őr	őrök
acc.	lányt	lányokat	széket	székeket	őrt	őröket
ill.	lányba	lányokba	székbe	székekbe	őrbe	őrökbe
iness.	lányban	lányokban	székben	székekben	őrben	őrökben
elat.	lányból	lányokból	székből	székekből	őrből	őrökből
sublat.	lányra	lányokra	székre	székekre	őrre	őrökre
sup.	lányon	lányokon	széken	székeken	őrön	őrökön
delat.	lányról	lányokról	székről	székekről	őrről	őrökről
allat.	lányhoz	lányokhoz	székhez	székekhez	őrhöz	őrökhöz
adess.	lánynál	lányoknál	széknél	székeknél	őrnél	őröknél
abl.	lánytól	lányoktól	széktől	székektől	őrtől	őröktől
dat.	lánynak	lányoknak	széknek	székeknek	őrnek	őröknek
instr.	lánnyal	lányokkal	székkel	székekkel	őrrel	őrökkel
transl.	lánnyá	lányokká	székké	székekké	őrré	őrökké
caus.-fin.	lányért	lányokért	székért	székekért	őrért	őrökért
ess.-for.	lányként	lányokként	székként	székekként	őrként	őrökként
term.	lányig	lányokig	székig	székekig	őrig	őrökig
distr.	lányonként	——	székenként	——	őrönként	——
sociat.	lányastul	——	székestül	——	őrestül	——

Fleeting vowel

	back vowel singular 'bush'	plural 'bushes'	front, unrounded vowel singular 'twin'	plural 'twins'	front, rounded vowel singular 'mirror'	plural 'mirrors'
nom.	bokor	bokrok	iker	ikrek	tükör	tükrök
acc.	bokrot	bokrokat	ikret	ikreket	tükröt	tükröket
ill.	bokorba	bokrokba	ikerbe	ikrekbe	tükörbe	tükrökbe
iness.	bokorban	bokrokban	ikerben	ikrekben	tükörben	tükrökben
elat.	bokorból	bokrokból	ikerből	ikrekből	tükörből	tükrökből
sublat.	bokorra	bokrokra	ikerre	ikrekre	tükörre	tükrökre
sup.	bokron	bokrokon	ikren	ikreken	tükrön	tükrökön
delat.	bokorról	bokrokról	ikerről	ikrekről	tükörről	tükrökről
allat.	bokorhoz	bokrokhoz	ikerhez	ikrekhez	tükörhöz	tükrökhöz
adess.	bokornál	bokroknál	ikernél	ikreknél	tükörnél	tükröknél
abl.	bokortól	bokroktól	ikertől	ikrektől	tükörtől	tükröktől
dat.	bokornak	bokroknak	ikernek	ikreknek	tükörnek	tükröknek
instr.	bokorral	bokrokkal	ikerrel	ikrekkel	tükörrel	tükrökkel
transl.	bokorrá	bokrokká	ikerré	ikrekké	tükörré	tükrökké
caus.-fin.	bokorért	bokrokért	ikerért	ikrekért	tükörért	tükrökért
ess.-for.	bokorként	bokrokként	ikerként	ikrekként	tükörként	tükrökként
term.	bokorig	bokrokig	ikerig	ikrekig	tükörig	tükrökig
distr.	bokronként	——	ikrenként	——	tükrönként	——
sociat.	bokrostul	——	ikrestül	——	tükröstül	——

V-stems

	singular 'lake'	plural 'lakes'	singular 'stone'	plural 'stones'	singular 'word'	plural 'words'
nom.	tó	tavak	kő	kövek	szó	szavak ~ szók
acc.	tavat	tavakat	követ	köveket	szót	szavakat
ill.	tóba	tavakba	kőbe	kövekbe	szóba	szavakba
iness.	tóban	tavakban	kőben	kövekben	szóban	szavakban
elat.	tóból	tavakból	kőből	kövekből	szóból	szavakból
sublat.	tóra	tavakra	kőre	kövekre	szóra	szavakra
sup.	tavon	tavakon	kövön	köveken	szavon	szavakon
delat.	tóról	tavakról	kőről	kövekről	szóról	szavakról
allat.	tóhoz	tavakhoz	kőhöz	kövekhez	szóhoz	szavakhoz
adess.	tónál	tavaknál	kőnél	köveknél	szónál	szavaknál
abl.	tótól	tavaktól	kőtől	kövektől	szótól	szavaktól
dat.	tónak	tavaknak	kőnek	köveknek	szónak	szavaknak
instr.	tóval	tavakkal	kővel	kövekkel	szóval	szavakkal
transl.	tóvá	tavakká	kővé	kövekké	szóvá	szavakká
caus.-fin.	tóért	tavakért	kőért	kövekért	szóért	szavakért
ess.-for.	tóként	tavakként	kőként	kövekként	szóként	szavakként
term.	tóig	tavakig	kőig	kövekig	szóig	szavakig
distr.	tavanként	——	kövenként	——	szavanként	——
sociat.	tavastul	——	kövestül	——	szavastul	——

Possessive declension

| | Low vowel (no loss of length) **ház** house | | Low vowel (loss of length) **levél** letter | | V-stem **ló** horse | |
	singular 'my house'	plural 'my houses'	singular 'your letter'	plural 'your letters'	singular 'his/her horse'	plural 'his/her horses'
nom.	házam	házaim	leveled	leveleid	lova	lovai
acc.	házamat	házaimat	leveledet	leveleidet	lovát	lovait
ill.	házamba	házaimba	leveledbe	leveleidbe	lovába	lovaiba
iness.	házamban	házaimban	leveledben	leveleidben	lovában	lovaiban
elat.	házamból	házaimból	leveledből	leveleidből	lovából	lovaiból
sublat.	házamra	házaimra	leveledre	leveleidre	lovára	lovaira
sup.	házamon	házaimon	leveleden	leveleiden	lován	lovain
delat.	házamról	házaimról	leveledről	leveleidről	lováról	lovairól
allat.	házamhoz	házaimhoz	leveledhez	leveleidhez	lovához	lovaihoz
adess.	házamnál	házaimnál	levelednél	leveleidnél	lovánál	lovainál
abl.	házamtól	házaimtól	leveledtől	leveleidtől	lovától	lovaitól
dat.	házamnak	házaimnak	levelednek	leveleidnek	lovának	lovainak
instr.	házammal	házaimmal	leveleddel	leveleiddel	lovával	lovaival
transl.	házammá	házaimmá	leveleddé	leveleiddé	lovává	lovaivá
caus.-fin.	házamért	házaimért	leveledért	leveleidért	lováért	lovaiért
ess.-for.	házamként	——	leveledként	——	lovaként	lovaiként
term.	házamig	házaimig	leveledig	leveleidig	lováig	lovaiig

	-alom **jutalom** reward		fleeting vowel **álom** dream		regular noun **kép** picture	
	singular 'our reward'	*plural* 'our rewards'	*singular* 'your dream'	*plural* 'your dreams'	*singular* 'their picture'	*plural* 'their pictures'
nom.	jutalmunk	jutalmaink	álmotok	álmaitok	képük	képeik
acc.	jutalmunkat	jutalmainkat	álmotokat	álmaitokat	képüket	képeiket
ill.	jutalmunkba	jutalmainkba	álmotokba	álmaitokba	képükbe	képeikbe
iness.	jutalmunkban	jutalmainkban	álmotokban	álmaitokban	képükben	képeikben
elat.	jutalmunkból	jutalmainkból	álmotokból	álmaitokból	képükből	képeikből
sublat.	jutalmunkra	jutalmainkra	álmotokra	álmaitokra	képükre	képeikre
sup.	jutalmunkon	jutalmainkon	álmotokon	álmaitokon	képükön	képeiken
delat.	jutalmunkról	jutalmainkról	álmotokról	álmaitokról	képükről	képeikről
allat.	jutalmunkhoz	jutalmainkhoz	álmotokhoz	álmaitokhoz	képükhöz	képeikhez
adess.	jutalmunknál	jutalmainknál	álmotoknál	álmaitoknál	képüknél	képeiknél
abl.	jutalmunktól	jutalmainktól	álmotoktól	álmaitoktól	képüktől	képeiktől
dat.	jutalmunknak	jutalmainknak	álmotoknak	álmaitoknak	képüknek	képeiknek
instr.	jutalmunkkal	jutalmainkkal	álmotokkal	álmaitokkal	képükkel	képeikkel
transl.	jutalmunkká	jutalmainkká	álmotokká	álmaitokká	képükké	képeikké
caus.-fin.	jutalmunkért	jutalmainkért	álmotokért	álmaitokért	képükért	képeikért
ess.-for.	jutalmunkként	——	álmotokként	——	képükként	——
term.	jutalmunkig	jutalmainkig	álmotokig	álmaitokig	képükig	képeikig

Appendix 3 Noun types and exceptions

Low vowel nouns

(Deviations from regular declension of these noun types are in parentheses. Regular declensions are found in appendix 2.)

Monosyllabic (no loss of length)

láb leg, foot
kád tub (sg3px[1]: kádja)
nád reed (sg3px: nádja)
vád accusation (sg3px: vádja)
had army, troops
hold moon
föld land (sg3px: földje)
térd knee
ág branch
fog tooth
szög nail
agy brain

ágy bed
vágy desire
háj fat
máj liver
nyáj flock
száj mouth
táj landscape
héj peel
íj bow
díj prize, fee
szíj strap
nyak neck
lyuk hole
hal fish
fal wall
nyál saliva

ín tendon (acc.: ínt)
meny daughter-in-law
árny shade
szörny monster
szárny wing
talp heel
ár price
ár awl (sg3px: árja)
gyár factory
nyár poplar
szár stalk
tár repository (acc. tár(a)t)
vár fortress
has belly

---

[1] sg3px = 'third person singular possessive suffix'.

hölgy lady
tölgy oak
völgy valley
tőgy udder
tárgy object
ügy matter
rügy bud
szügy breast (zool.)
báj charm (acc.:
   bájt)

szál stick, piece
tál bowl
áll chin
váll shoulder
jel sign
mell breast
toll pen, feather
ól sty (acc.:
       ólat~ólt; sg3px: olja)
fül ear
hely place

vas iron
hárs linden
nyárs spit, skewer
társ mate
hát back
ív arch
ház house
váz vase
íz taste
őz deer
törzs trunk, tribe

Monosyllabic loses length

híd bridge
  (sg3px: hídja)
lúd goose
  (sg3px: lúdja)
rúd rod, pole
  (sg3px: rúdja)
ég sky
jég ice
légy fly
bél intestine
dél south, noon
fél half

nyél handle
szél edge
tél winter
nyíl arrow
nyúl rabbit
szén coal
nyár summer
sár mud
ér vein
dér white frost
tér space, plaza
úr sir, gentleman

ész mind
mész lime
hét seven, week
út road
  (sg3px: útja)
kút fountain,
  (sg3px: kútja)
kéz hand
réz copper
szűz virgin
tűz fire
víz water

Bisyllabic (no loss of length)

oldal side (acc.: oldalt)
fonal yarn, thread
vonal line
arany gold

Bisyllabic loses length

veréb sparrow	cserép tile	mozsár mortar
elég enough	közép center	egér mouse
fenék bottom	mocsár swamp	szekér cart
kerék wheel	madár bird	gyökér root
kanál spoon	agár greyhound	kenyér bread
fonál yarn, thread	bogár bug	tenyér palm
fedél roof	sugár ray, beam	szemét garbage
kötél rope	pohár glass	nehéz difficult
levél letter	szamár donkey	darázs wasp
tehén cow	kosár basket	parázs glowing embers

V-stems

Nominative singular and plural and singular accusative forms:

	nom. sg.	nom. pl.	acc. sg.
snow	hó	havak	havat
good	jó	jók	jót
horse	ló	lovak	lovat
word	szó	szavak	szót
lake	tó	tavak	tavat
pipe	cső	csövek	csövet
stone	kő	kövek	követ
stem	tő	tövek	tövet
grass	fű	füvek	füvet
opus	mű	művek	művet
maggot	nyű	nyüvek	nyüvet

Other sometime *v*-stems:

	nom. (sg.)	nom. (pl.)	acc. (sg.)	sg3px.	adjective
louse	tetű	tetvek	tetűt	tetűje ~ tetve	tetves
village	falu	faluk ~ falvak	falut ~ falvat	faluja ~ falva	
ash	hamu	hamuk ~ hamvak	hamut ~ hamvat	hamuja	hamvas
crane	daru	daruk ~ darvak	darut	daruja	
hollow	odú	odúk ~ odvak	odút ~ odvat	odúja ~ odva	odvas

Metathesis

Consonant switching takes place in the following nouns when suffixing endings requiring a linking vowel:

	nom. sg.	nom. pl.	acc. sg.
load	**teher**	**terhek** (pl.)	**terhet** (acc.)
flake	**pehely**	**pelyhek** (pl.)	**pelyhet** (acc.)
chalice	**kehely**	**kelyhek** (pl.)	**kelyhet** (acc.)

Fleeting vowel words requiring the linking vowel *a*

In the following words, the last vowel is omitted and the required linking vowel is **a** when suffixing endings requiring a linking vowel:

	nom. sg.	nom. pl.	acc. sg.	sg3px.
lip	**ajak**	**ajkak**	**ajkat**	**ajka**
haystack	**kazal**	**kazlak**	**kazlat**	**kazla**
manger	**jászol**	**jászlak**	**jászlat**	**jászla**
veil	**fátyol**	**fátylak**	**fátylat ~ fátyolt**	**fátyla**
canvas	**vászon**		**vásznat**	**vászna**
tent	**sátor**	**sátrak**	**sátrat ~ sátort**	**sátra**

Words with variation in accusative

The accusative singular may take either form with the following nouns. (There may be some nuanced change in meaning.)

	nominative	accusative		
greyhound	**agár**	**agarat**	~	**agárt**
tusk	**agyar**	**agyarat**	~	**agyart**
owl	**bagoly**	**baglyot**	~	**bagolyt**
veil	**fátyol**	**fátylat**	~	**fátyolt**
place	**hely**	**helyet**	~	**helyt**

twin	**iker**	**ikret**	~	**ikert**
manger	**jászol**	**jászlat**	~	**jászolt**
sign	**jel**	**jelet**	~	**jelt**
bosom	**kebel**	**keblet**	~	**kebelt**
chalice	**kehely**	**kelyhet**	~	**kehelyt**
shroud	**lepel**	**leplet**	~	**lepelt**
glaze	**máz**	**mázat**	~	**mázt**
oil	**olaj**	**olajat**	~	**olajt**
bay/gulf	**öböl**	**öblöt**	~	**öbölt**
flake	**pehely**	**pelyhet**	~	**pehelyt**
Renaissance	**reneszánsz**	**reneszánszot**	~	**reneszánszt**
rye	**rozs**	**rozsot**	~	**rozst**
tent	**sátor**	**sátrat**	~	**sátort**
bag	**szatyor**	**szatyrot**	~	**szatyort**
store	**tár**	**tárat**	~	**tárt**
line	**vonal**	**vonalat**	~	**vonalt**

and nouns ending in -ns (the single -t accusative is always correct):

graduate student	**aspiráns**	**aspiránsot**	**aspiránst**
patient	**páciens**	**pácienset**	**pácienst**

Index